TESTIMONY TO THE TRUTH

The Teachings of Pope Pius XII

Edited by MICHAEL CHINIGO

CLUNY
Providence, Rhode Island

CLUNY EDITION, 2024

This Cluny edition is a republication of *The Pope Speaks*,
originally published in 1957 by Pantheon Books.

For more information regarding this title
or any other Cluny Media publication,
please write to info@clunymedia.com, or to
Cluny Media, P.O. Box 1664, Providence, RI 02901

VISIT US ONLINE AT WWW.CLUNYMEDIA.COM

ISBN: 978-1685953348

IMPRIMATUR: Francis Cardinal Spellman, *Archbishop of New York*
MARCH 21, 1957

Cover design by Clarke & Clarke
Cover image: El Greco, *Saint James the Less* (detail),
between c. 1610 and c. 1614, oil on canvas
Courtesy of Wikimedia Commons

CONTENTS

PART TWO: EDUCATION · THE SCIENCES · THE ARTS

Part Four: Society and Politics

EDITOR'S PREFACE

WHILE I was gathering material for a book on the Vatican, the necessity arose time and again to consult the Encyclicals, Apostolic Letters, and various Addresses of Pope Pius XII. Thus the idea of an anthology covering all the topics to which the Holy Father has dedicated attention was born.

In more than a year's work the Pontiff's Addresses, Encyclicals, and Apostolic Letters were sifted to select the material. Two basic criteria were applied to the selection: If one of several documents represented the most exhaustive treatment of a topic and the others were merely repetitive, then my choice fell on the principal pronouncement. In cases, however, where the Holy Father treated various aspects of a problem at different periods, I have taken the pertinent parts out of context and worked them into a harmonious whole in a single chapter, separating the excerpts by a line of space.

Many qualified advisers whose counsel I sought have made recommendations and helped me to realize this project. May I express the hope that this summary of the teachings of Pope Pius XII concerning the most crucial problems of our time will be useful to many.

These were the contents of an explanatory note which I sent with the manuscript to His Holiness Pope Pius XII. The manuscript was submitted to the Holy Father, who, in returning it, sent me through His Excellency Monsignor Angelo Dell'Acqua, Substitute of the Secretary of State, His Apostolic Blessing.

The English translations are my own, unless otherwise mentioned in the Acknowledgments. The religious and theological terms have been checked for accuracy by a qualified prelate. To him and to the Monsignori of the Vatican Secretary of State's Office, who helped me find him and otherwise encouraged me with this edition, go my heartfelt thanks. Grateful acknowledgment is made also to *Books On Trial* (Chicago, IL), for permission to use "The Duty and Responsibility of the Literary Critic," in the translation of Father Joseph M. O'Leary, C.P., and to the *Catholic Messenger* (Davenport, IA), for permission to use "The Boarding School—Its Effects and Its Purpose," in the translation of Dom Celestine Cullen, O.S.B.

Michael Chinigo

TESTIMONY TO THE TRUTH

The Teachings of Pope Pius XII

As Vicar of Him Who in a decisive hour pronounced before the highest earthly authority of that day, the great words: "For this was I born, and for this came I into the world; that I should give testimony to the truth. Every one that is of the truth, hearest My voice" (*John* 18:37)—*We feel We owe no greater debt to Our office and to Our time than to* **testify to the truth** *with Apostolic firmness:* **"to give testimony to the truth."** *This duty necessarily entails the exposition and confutation of errors and human faults; for these must be made known before it is possible to tend and to heal them. "You shall know the truth and the truth shall make you free"* (*John* 8:32).

Pope Pius XII,
in his first Encyclical Letter,
Summi Pontificatus

PART ONE

MAN

MAN

ON the day when God formed man and crowned his brow with the diadem of His image and likeness, making him king of all living animals in the seas, in the skies, and on the land, on that day the Lord, Omniscient God, made Himself man's master. He taught him agriculture, how to cultivate and care for the delightful garden in which He had placed him; led to him all the beasts of the fields and all the birds of the air so that man might name them. And he gave to each of them its true and fitting name. But, even among that multitude of beings subject to him, man felt sadly alone and looked in vain for a brow which resembled his own and had a ray of that divine image with which the eye of every son of Adam sparkles. From man only could another man issue forth who would call him father and progenitor; and the helpmate given by God to the first man also comes from him and is flesh of his flesh, fashioned into a mate for him, named from man because she was derived from him. On the topmost rung of the ladder of the living, God placed man, endowed with a spiritual soul, to be the prince and sovereign of the animal kingdom. Manifold research in the fields of paleontology, biology, and morphology on various problems regarding the origin of man has not yet yielded anything positively clear and certain. We must therefore leave it to the future to answer the question as to whether someday science, illuminated and guided by revelation, will be able to reach certain and definitive results in such a momentous matter.

True science neither lowers nor humiliates man in his origin. Rather, it elevates and exalts him because it perceives, recognizes, and admires in every member of the great human family greater or lesser traces of the divine image and likeness stamped upon him.

Man's Dominion over Nature

Man is great. The progress he makes in the physical, natural, mathematical, and industrial sciences, eager for ever better, wider, and surer advancement, what is it but the effect of the domination he still exercises—even if limited and strenuously gained—over inferior nature? And when has human ingenuity ever searched, scrutinized, penetrated nature as at present, in order to get to know its forces and forms so as to dominate them, bend them in its instruments, and make use of them as it pleases?

Man is great, and he was still greater when created. If he fell from his original greatness, rebelling against the Creator, and went, an exile and wanderer, out of the Garden of Eden, gathering in the sweat of his brow the bread which the earth gave him, amid tribulations and thorns; if the sky and the sun, the cold and the heat, if refuges and forests, if so much other wear and tear and travail, so many discomforts due to environment and conditions of life debased his face and figure; if the remnants of the command once given to him over the animal world are nothing more than a fading recollection of his former power and a tiny fragment of his throne, even in his ruin he looms great because of that divine image and likeness he carries in his spirit, and on account of which God was so pleased with the human creature, the last work of His creative hand, that He did not disarm or abandon him when he fell. Rather, in order to elevate man again, He made Himself like unto man, and in His condition was recognized as a man, suffering from our infirmities, similarly tempted in all, except sin (Hebrews 4:15).

Intellect and Will

Two gifts, which raise him very high between the world of celestial spirits and the world of bodies, make man great, even since his downfall: the intellect, whose view surveys the created universe and crosses the skies, yearning to contemplate God; and will, endowed with the power to choose freely, servant and master of the intellect, which makes us, in different degrees, masters of our own thoughts and of our actions before ourselves, before others, and before God.

The ingenuity, the will power, and the action of man with his machines and his tools, though they cannot upset the order of nature, may reveal it.

God is the sole commander and legislator of the universe. He is a sun that, in the infinite magnificence of its light, diffuses and multiplies its rays, resemblances of itself, in all the fields of creation; but no image can equal Him. Thus man too, when he does not find a word which alone can sufficiently express the concept of his mind, multiplies words in various ways. Similarly, in the multiplicity of creatures there is a diversity of natures and a different divine vestige, depending on how close they come to God in the resemblance of the being which is theirs.

God's Will Is the Primary Cause of All Nature

Does not the diversity of things demand that not all be equal but that a gradual order be resplendent there? In this order and in these gradations we see natures and forms differing in perfection and vigor, in action and object, in reaction and composition, in substance and quality, from which emerge different properties, operations, and agents with reciprocal impressions and diverse effects, which have their reason in the diversity impressed by the Creator in the nature of things, determined and directed to a particular end and action. In this natural necessity inherent in things, which is nothing but an impression produced by God, who guides everything to an end, just as an archer directs his arrow to the target, lies the law of the nature of bodies, a law which is one with their very nature. Just as a man by his commandment impresses upon another man subject to him an internal principle of operation, so God impresses in all nature the principles of its own actions, and in this manner the Supreme Maker of the universe, God and Master of all sciences, *praeceptum posuit et non praeteribit*—He has made a law for the whole, and it shall not pass away. Hence—as the great Doctor of Aquino masterfully teaches—when one asks the wherefore of a natural effect, we may explain it by some near cause, such as the natural property of things, provided we trace everything back to the will of God as the primary cause, the wise instructor of all nature. Thus, if someone, on being asked why fire heats, replies because God wishes it, he would be replying correctly, if he wanted to reduce the question to the first cause; wrongly, however, if he intended to exclude all other causes.

In us, too, who are God's creatures, the first cause impressed a law, which is a sublime instinct wholly peculiar to man, to seek knowledge of the Creator; a desire which is a spiritual movement, and never ceases—until it reaches enjoyment of the object of its love. If our flesh comes from dust and will return to dust, our spirit is immortal; it comes from God and yearns to return to God by this world's ladder of science, which, however, does not succeed in fully satisfying the immense thirst for truth which animates us. The school of God, Master of every science, is the world; if its figure passes, we remain alone before the Master. Let us bow before His wisdom, unfathomable in its mysteries and in His decision to give humanity as its dwelling this globe so full of wonders and surrounded by millions of wonders even more resplendent and immeasurable; wonders which, as the Creator contemplated His work on the day He accomplished it, were all seen by Him to be very good.†

Love

God is love, writes St. John, substantial and infinite love; He delights eternally, without desire and without satiety, in the contemplation of His infinite perfection; and, because He is the only absolute Being, beside whom there is nothing, if He wishes to call into existence other beings, He can draw them only out of His own wealth. Every creature, being a more or less remote derivation of infinite love, is therefore the fruit of love and does not move except through love.

In the chaotic nebula, one day a first force of attraction, that is to say, a first symbol of love, grouped together around a nucleus the cosmic elements, which formed a star; then the attraction of this first one called forth a second; and because another was attracted in its turn, the marvelous procession of worlds began its course around the firmament. But God's masterpiece is man,

† Allocution to Members of the Pontifical Academy of Sciences (November 30, 1941).

and to this masterpiece of love He has given a power to love unknown to irrational creatures. Man's love is personal, that is to say, conscious; free, that is to say, subject to the control of his responsible will.

In giving man body and soul, God had endowed him with the full powers of human nature. Beyond that man could not hope to reach; but God's intentions reached further. He gave to the human creature a new and superhuman gift: grace; grace, inscrutable prodigy of the love of God, a marvel the mystery of which human intelligence cannot penetrate, and which man has called "supernatural," thus humbly confessing that it surpasses his nature.

Even purely sensible love has such tender touching beauty that the Lord compares Himself to the eagle which trains his young to fly and hovers over them. But human love is incomparably nobler, because here the soul participates, animated by the impulse of the heart, that delicate witness and interpreter of the union between body and soul, which harmonizes the material impressions of the one with the superior feelings of the other. The charm exercised by human love has been for centuries the inspiring theme of admirable works of genius, in literature, in music, in the visual arts; a theme always old and always new, upon which the ages have embroidered, without ever exhausting it, the most elevated and poetic variations.

But what new and unutterable beauty is added to this love of two human hearts, when its song is harmonized with the hymn of two souls vibrating with supernatural life! Here, too, there is a mutual exchange of gifts; and then, through bodily tenderness and its healthy joys, through natural affection and its impulses, through a spiritual union and its delights, the two beings who love each other identify themselves in all that is most intimate in them, from the unshaken depths of their beliefs to the highest summit of their hopes.

Christian Matrimony

Such is Christian matrimony, modelled, according to the famous expression of St. Paul, on the union of Christ with His Church. In the one as in the other, the gift of self is total, exclusive, irrevocable; in the one and in the other the husband is head of the wife, who is subject to him as to the Lord; in the one and in the other the mutual gift becomes a principle of expansion and a source of life (Eph. 5).

Thus, married couples, in the providential mission assigned to them, are properly the collaborators of God and of Christ; something divine pertains to their achievements, so that they may call themselves *divinae consortes naturae*—partakers of the divine nature.

Is it surprising that these splendid privileges should entail grave duties? The nobility of the divine action obliges married Christians to considerable self-denial and to the performance of many acts of courage, so that matter may not hinder the spirit in its ascent toward truth and virtue and with its weight drag it down toward the abyss. But as God never commands what is impossible and with the order which He gives grants also the strength to fulfill it, matrimony, which is a great Sacrament, brings, together with its duties that may appear superhuman, help that shows itself to be supernatural.[†]

A mutual affection springing solely from the inclination which draws man toward woman, or from mere pleasure in the human gifts which one discovers with such satisfaction in one another; such an affection, however beautiful and deep it may prove to be, and however beautiful and deep may be its echo in the intimacy of the trusting conversations of the newly wed, would never be sufficient in itself. It could not even fully achieve the union of your souls in bringing you toward one another. Only supernatural charity, a bond of friendship between God and man, can tie knots strong enough to resist all the shocks, all the vicissitudes, all the inevitable trials of a long life spent together; only divine grace can make you rise superior to all the little daily miseries, all the nascent contrasts and disparities of tastes or of ideas, springing, like weeds, from the root of fallible human nature. And this charity and grace, is it not the strength and virtue which you went to ask of the great Sacrament you received? Divine charity, greater yet than faith and hope, is needed by the world, society, and the family!

Love, holy and sacred and divine: is it not—you will perhaps say—something too lofty for us? Will love so much above nature—you may even ask—still be that truly human love, which has been the beating of our hearts, which our hearts seek and in which they find peace, of which they have need and

† Address to Newlyweds (October 23, 1940).

which they are so happy to have found? Set your minds at rest: God with His love neither destroys nor changes nature, but perfects it; and St. Francis de Sales, who well knew the human heart, concluded his beautiful page on the sacred character of conjugal love with this twofold advice: "Keep, O husbands, a tender, constant, and cordial love for your wives... And you, wives, love tenderly, cordially, but with a love both respectful and full of deference, the husbands whom God has given you."

Cordiality and tenderness, then, from one side and from the other. "Love and faithfulness," he used to say, "always create intimacy and confidence; thus the saints were wont to give many demonstrations of affection in their marriages, demonstrations truly amorous, but chaste, tender, but sincere"; and he used to cite the example of the great king, St. Louis, no less stern toward himself than tender in his love for his wife, a man who knew how to bend his martial and brave spirit "to those littles duties necessary for the conservation of conjugal love," to those "little attestations of pure and frank friendship," which do so much to bring hearts together and make married life happy. What more and better than true Christian charity, devoted, humble, patient, which conquers and subdues nature, which is forgetful of itself and solicitous at all moments for the well-being and happiness of others, will know how to suggest and direct those thoughtful little attentions, those delicate signs of affection, and maintain them at the same time spontaneous, sincere, discreet, so that they may never seem irritating, but may always be welcomed with pleasure and appreciation? What better than grace, which is the fount and soul of that charity, will be your master and guide to make you choose almost by instinct the right moment for such human and divine tenderness?

Christian Love

However, you well understand that, if cordiality and tenderness have to be reciprocally exchanged by husband and wife and must adorn them both, they are nevertheless two flowers with a different beauty, springing as they do from a root somewhat different in man and woman. In man their root should be an uncompromising and inviolable faithfulness, which does not allow itself even the smallest deviation that would not be tolerated in his companion; as is fitting for him who is the head, it gives an open example of moral dignity and courageous frankness in never faltering from or shunning the full performance of his duty. In woman the root is wise, prudent, and watchful reserve, which removes and avoids even the shadow of anything that could soil the splendor of a spotless reputation or which could in any way endanger it.

From these two roots also springs that mutual trust which is the olive branch of perpetual peace in married life and in the flourishing of its love, for is it not true that without trust love faints, grows cold, freezes, dies, ferments, disrupts, tears and kills hearts? Therefore, observed St. Francis de Sales, "While I exhort you to grow always in that reciprocal love which you owe one another, take good care that it does not turn into a sort of jealousy; because it often happens that, as the worm is engendered in the most exquisite and ripest apple, so jealousy is born in the most ardent and devoted love, whose substance, however, it spoils and corrupts, provoking little by little disputes, dissensions, and divorces." No; jealousy, an exhalation and weakness of the heart, does not grow from a love that ripens and preserves the sap of true virtue, because "the perfection of friendship presupposes the certainty of that which is loved, while jealousy presupposes its uncertainty." Is not this the reason why jealousy, far from being a sign of the depth and true strength of a love, reveals instead its imperfect and base sides, which descend to suspicions that pierce innocent hearts and draw bitter tears? Is not jealousy, more often than not, perhaps a mitigated form of selfishness that alters the nature of affection; of selfishness bereft of that true gift, that self-forgetfulness, that faith unfraught with maligning thoughts, but trusting and benevolent, which, even here below, thus becomes the most profound and inexhaustible fount, no less than the safest guardian and preserver, of perfect love in a husband and wife?[†]

We detect true affection, without hardness as without weakness, true love, inspired and elevated by Christ, in those first families of Roman converts, such as the Flavii and the Acilii at the time of Domitian's persecution. We admire its splendor shining around a St. Paula and a St. Melania.

The secret of such a life? Always the same, that of all holy lives: Christ living and radiating with His sovereign grace in the soul, which meekly follows its inspirations and impulses. Our Lord alone was able to give birth in poor

† Address to Newlyweds (January 29, 1941).

human hearts, wounded and led astray by original sin, to a love which stays pure and strong without stiffening and hardening, a love sufficiently deeply spiritual to unchain itself from the brutal stimuli of the senses and to dominate them, while preserving its warmth intact and its gentle tenderness unaltered. He alone, through example and the inward action of His heart inflamed with love, was able to keep the promise already made to Israel: "*Auferam cor lapideum de carne vestra, et dabo vobis cor carneum*—I shall tear from your flesh your heart of stone, and I shall give you a heart of flesh." He alone knows how to stir up and keep alive in souls a true affection, tender and at the same time strong, because He alone can, through His grace, free them from that inborn selfishness which, more or less unconsciously, poisons purely human loves.[‡]

Conjugal Love, Its Meaning and Goal

"Personal values" and the need to respect them is a theme which for two decades has been treated more and more by writers. In many of their treatments also the specifically sexual act has a place assigned to it; it is presented as a means of personal completion of the married partners.

The proper and most profound meaning of the exercise of the conjugal rights would consist in this: that the union of bodies is the expression and realization of the personal affective union.

Articles, chapters, entire books, lectures, especially on the "technique of love," aim at propagating these ideas, at illustrating them with advice to the newly wed as a guide in marriage, in order that they may not forgo, through foolishness or misguided bashfulness, or through ungrounded scruples, that which God, who has also created natural inclinations, offers them. If from this complete reciprocal gift of the couple there springs a new life, it is a result which remains outside, or at most as if on the outskirts of, the "personal values"; a result which is not denied, but which is not wanted as the center of married relations.

‡ Address to Newlyweds (July 30, 1941).

Now, if this one-sided estimate merely stressed the personal value of the partners rather than that of the offspring, it would, strictly speaking, be possible indeed to leave that problem aside; but here it is a question of a serious inversion of the scale of values and of the ends ordained by the Creator Himself. We find ourselves faced with the spread of a body of ideas and feelings in direct opposition to the clarity, the depth, and the seriousness of Christian thought.

The truth is that marriage, as a natural institution, by virtue of the will of the Creator, has not as a primary and intimate end the personal perfecting of the couple but the procreation and education of a new life. The other ends, though also intended by nature, do not occupy the same place as the first, and still less are they superior to it; rather, they are essentially subordinate to it. This is the same for every marriage, even if without issue; as of every eye it can be said that it is intended and formed to see, even if, in abnormal cases, owing to special internal and external conditions, it will never be in a position to lead to visual perception.

It was precisely in order to put an end to all the uncertainties and deviations which threatened to spread errors concerning the scale of value of the ends of marriage and their reciprocal relations, that some years ago (March 10, 1944) We drew up a declaration regarding the order of those ends as it appears from the natural disposition, showing what has been handed down by Christian tradition, what the Supreme Pontiffs have repeatedly taught, and what was afterward formulated in the Code of Canon Law. And again, shortly after, in order to correct conflicting opinions, the Holy See, in a public decree, proclaimed as inadmissible the stand of some recent authors who deny that the primary end of marriage is the procreation and upbringing of children, or teach that the secondary ends are not essentially subordinate to the primary end, but of equal value and independent thereof.

Does this mean, perhaps, that We want to deny or diminish what is good and just in personal values resulting from marriage and its realization? Certainly not, because for the procreation of new life the Creator has appointed in marriage human beings made of flesh and blood, endowed with soul and heart, and these are called upon, as men and not as irrational animals, to be the authors of their descendants. It is to this end that the Lord wills the union of husbands and wives. The Holy Scriptures do in fact say of God that He made man in His image and made him male and female, and it was His wish—as is repeatedly affirmed in the Sacred Books—that "man leave his father and mother, and cleave to his wife, and that they form one flesh."

All this is therefore true and willed by God; but it must not be separated from the primary function of matrimony, that is, from service for a new life. Not only the mutually shared material achievements, but also such personal riches as intellectual and spiritual growth, yes, even all that which is most spiritual and deepest in conjugal love as such, have been placed, by the will of nature and of the Creator, at the service of posterity. By its very nature, perfect conjugal life also means the total devotion of parents to the wellbeing of the children, and conjugal love in its strength and tenderness is itself a postulate of the sincerest care of offspring and a guarantee of its actuation.

The Conjugal Act

To reduce the life in common of married people and the conjugal act to a purely organic function for the transmission of the seed would be to convert the home, sanctuary of the family, into nothing but a biological laboratory. Therefore, in Our address of September 29, 1949, to the International Congress of Catholic Physicians, We expressly barred artificial insemination in marriage. The conjugal act, in its natural structure, is a personal action, a simultaneous and immediate co-operation of husband and wife, which, owing to the very nature of the agents and the propriety of the act, is the expression of the reciprocal gift, which, according to the word of Scripture, effects the union "in one flesh."

That is much more than the union of two genes, which can be effected even artificially, that is to say, without the natural union of the couple. The conjugal act, ordained and willed by nature, is a personal co-operation, to which the couple, in contracting marriage, exchange the right.

When, therefore, this performance in its natural form is, from the beginning and permanently, impossible, the object of the matrimonial contract is vitiated in its essence. And this is what We said: "Do not forget: only the procreation of a new life according to the will and the design of the Creator brings with it, in a stupendous degree of perfection, the realization of the intended ends. At the same time it conforms to the corporal and spiritual nature and to the dignity of the couple, to the normal and happy development of the child."

The personal values of married life, whether they belong to the sphere of the body and the senses or to the spiritual sphere, are genuine in themselves, but have been placed by the Creator not in the first but in the second degree of the scale of values.

Here is another consideration which there is risk of forgetting. All these secondary values in the generative sphere and activity come within the scope of the specific duty of married couples, which is to be the authors and educators of a new life. A high and noble duty indeed. It does not, however, belong to the essence of a complete human being; if the natural generative tendency fails to come to its realization, this does not imply, in some way and in some degree, a diminution of the human person. The renunciation of this realization—especially if made for the noblest motives—is not a mutilation of personal and spiritual values. Of such free renunciation for love of the Kingdom of God the Lord said: *"Non omnes capiunt verbum istud, sed quibus datum est*—All do not understand this doctrine, but only those to whom it is given."

To exalt the generative function beyond measure, as is not seldom done today, even in the rightful and moral form of conjugal life, is therefore not only an error and an aberration; it also entails the danger of an intellectual and affective deviation, apt to prevent and stifle good and elevated feelings, especially in young people without experience and ignorant of the delusions of life. For what normal man, healthy in body and soul, would want to belong to the number of those who are deficient in character and spirit?

The Sexual Instinct

Our present explanation would be altogether incomplete if We did not add a few words concerning the defense of human dignity in the use of the generative instinct.

This same Creator, who in His goodness and wisdom desired the conservation and propagation of the human species to be served by the work of man and woman by uniting them in marriage, has also disposed that in this function the couple should experience pleasure and happiness in body and soul. The couple then, in seeking and enjoying this pleasure, do not do wrong. They accept what the Creator has destined for them.

Nevertheless, here too the couple must know how to keep themselves within the limits of just moderation. As in food and drink, so in sex they must not abandon themselves without restraint to the impulse of the senses. The golden rule is then this: The use of the natural generative instinct is morally licit only in marriage, in the service of and according to the order of the ultimate reason for marriage itself. From this it follows also that only in marriage, and by observing this rule, are the desire and the fruition of this pleasure and of this satisfaction licit. Because the pleasure is subordinate to the law of the action from which it derives, and not vice versa: the action is not subordinate to the law of pleasure. And this law, which is so reasonable, concerns not only the substance but also the circumstances of the action, so that, even when the substance of the act is not violated, it is possible to sin by the way it is performed.

The transgression of this norm is as ancient as original sin itself. But in our time there is a danger that people may lose sight of the fundamental principle itself. At present, in fact, it is usual to defend, in speeches and writings (and also by some Catholics), the necessary autonomy, the proper end, and the proper value of sensuality and its realization, independently of the scope of procreating a new life. There is a tendency to subject to a new examination and a new norm the very order established by God, to admit no other restraint to satisfying the instinct than observing the essence of the instinctive act itself. Thus for the moral obligation of dominating the passions one would substitute the license to serve blindly and without restraint the whims and impulses of nature; sooner or later this cannot but adversely affect morals, conscience, and human dignity.

If nature had aimed exclusively, or at least primarily, at a reciprocal gift and possession of couples in joy and delight, and if it had ordered this act only to make their personal experience happy in the highest possible degree, and not to stimulate them to the service of life, then the Creator would have adopted another design in the formation and constitution of the natural act. However, this is altogether subordinate to and ordered by that unique great law of the "*generatio et educatio prolis*" that is to say, for the fulfillment of the primary scope of marriage as the origin and source of life.

Unhappily, incessant waves of the pleasure principle are invading the world and threaten to submerge in the growing tide of its thoughts, desires, and acts the whole of married life, not without serious dangers and grave prejudice to the primary duty of married couples.

Too often this anti-Christian hedonism does not blush to make of itself a doctrine, propagating the intensification of pleasure in the preparation and in the realization of the conjugal union; as if in matrimonial relations the whole moral law were reduced to the regular fulfillment of the act itself, and as if all the rest, no matter how it is done, is to be justified by the warmth of reciprocal affection, sanctified by the Sacrament of Matrimony, worthy of praise and mercy before God and conscience. For the dignity of man and the dignity of the Christian, which put a check on the excesses of sensuality, one does not care at all.

To this one must say "No." The gravity and sanctity of the Christian moral law do not permit an unrestrained satisfaction of the sexual instinct, which tends only to pleasure and enjoyment; they do not allow rational man to let himself be dominated up to that point, as to either the substance or the circumstances of the act.

Some would allege that happiness in marriage is in direct proportion to the reciprocal enjoyment in conjugal relations. This is not so; happiness in marriage is instead in direct proportion to the reciprocal respect between husband and wife, even in their intimate relations; not that they simply judge immoral and refuse what nature offers and the Creator has given, but because this respect, with the mutual esteem which it generates, is one of the most efficacious elements of a pure and therefore all the more tender love.

This teaching of Ours has nothing to do with Manichaeism or Jansenism, as some would like to have one believe in order to justify themselves. It is only a defense of the honor of Christian marriage and of the personal dignity of the spouses.[†]

On Marriage

THE Sacrament of Marriage is a yoke of grace which, before the priest and the altar of Christ, unites two lives into one with an indissoluble bond.[‡]

† Address to Newlyweds (October 29, 1951).

‡ Address to Married Couples (March 18, 1942).

The conjugal bond is one. In the terrestrial paradise, the first image of the family paradise, the first bond was established by the Creator between man and woman, about which the Son of God incarnate will say one day: "*Quod Deus coniunxit, homo non separet*—What God has joined together, let no man put asunder"; because "*iam non sunt duo, sed una caro*—they are not two but one flesh." In that union of our progenitors in the garden of delights is the whole human species, all the future course of generations, which shall fill the earth and struggle to conquer it, and will dominate it in the sweat of their brows and make it yield them bread dampened by the bitterness of the original sin born from the stolen fruit of Eden. Why did God bring man and woman together in paradise? Not only that they might be custodians of that garden of happiness but also, in the words of the great Doctor of Aquino, because they were ordained for marriage to the end that they might generate and educate offspring, as well as for a common family life.

The seal of indissolubility is visibly stamped in the unity of the conjugal bond. Indeed, it is a bond to which nature tends, but one which is not necessarily caused by the principles of nature, being instead brought about by the exercise of free will. But the mere will of the contracting parties, though it can form the bond, cannot dissolve it. This holds not only for Christian nuptials but for every valid marriage contracted on earth through the mutual consent of the partners.

But if the will of the spouses, having contracted the matrimonial bond, cannot dissolve it, can the authority, which is above them and established by Christ for the religious life of man, do so? The bond of a Christian marriage is so strong that, if it has reached full stability by the use of conjugal rights, no power on earth, not even Our own, that is, that of the Vicar of Christ, is able to dissolve it. It is true that we may perceive and declare that a marriage, contracted as a valid one, was in reality void owing to some impediment, or an essential flaw in consent, or a substantial defect in the form. We can also in certain cases and for serious reasons dissolve marriages not having a sacramental character. We can even dissolve the bonds of a Christian marriage, rescind the "Yes" pronounced before the altar, if there is a just and proportionate cause, when it has been established that the marriage has not been brought to completion through realization of matrimonial cohabitation. But once that has taken place, no human agency may interfere with the bond. For has not

Christ led the matrimonial common life back to the fundamental dignity which the Creator had given it at the dawn of the human race in paradise, to the inviolable dignity of marriage, one and indissoluble?

Jesus Christ, the Redeemer of fallen humanity, did not come to take away, but to fulfill and restore the divine law; to bring about, as a lawmaker above Moses, as a sage above Solomon, as a prophet above the prophets, what had been predicted of Him; heralded like unto Moses, and awaited eagerly by the people of Israel; from whose lips the Lord would speak His word, while those who would not hear Him would be cast out of God's people. Therefore Christ, through His word which stands forever, elevated man in marriage and again raised up woman, who had been cast down by the ancients to the role of slave, and whom the most austere of the Roman censors had likened to "an unbridled nature and an unsubdued animal"; just as the Redeemer had exalted in Himself not only man but woman, taking human nature from a woman and sublimating His Mother, blessed among all women, to an immaculate mirror of virtue and grace for every Christian family throughout the centuries, crowned in Heaven Queen of the Angels and Saints.

Sanctification and Indissolubility

Through their presence, Jesus and Mary sanctified the wedding at Cana; it was there that the divine Son of the Virgin performed His first miracle, as if to show at the outset that He was beginning His mission in the world and the reign of God by the sanctification of the family and the conjugal union, which is the origin of life. It was there that began the elevation of marriage, which was to stand out in the supernatural world of symbols that produce sanctifying grace, to symbolize the union of Christ with the Church; an indissoluble and inseparable union fed by the absolute and endless love that flows from the heart of Christ. How could conjugal love represent and be called the symbol of such a union if it were deliberately limited, conditional, subject to dissolution, if it were a flame of love for a time only? No: having been elevated to the pure and sacred dignity of a Sacrament, imprinted and bound up in such close connection with the love of the Redeemer and the work of redemption, the marital union can only be indissoluble and perpetual.

In the face of this law of indissolubility, in all times human passions, curbed by it and repressed in the free satisfaction of their disordered appetites, have sought in every way to cast off its yoke, wanting to see in it only a hard tyranny arbitrarily weighing down conscience with an unbearable load, with a slavery repugnant to the sacred rights of the human being. It is true: a bond may sometimes constitute a burden, a coercion, like the chains which fetter a prisoner. But it may also be a powerful aid and a sure warranty, like the rope which binds the mountain climber to his companions in the ascent, or like the ligaments which unite the parts of the human body, making movement free and easy; and this is clearly the case with the indissoluble bond of marriage.

This law of indissolubility will appear and will be understood as a manifestation of vigilant motherly love, especially if viewed in the supernatural light in which it has been placed by Christ. In the midst of the difficulties, shocks, and covetous desires which life will perhaps sow in their path, two souls so inseparably linked will feel they are neither alone nor disarmed: the all-powerful grace of God, fruit of the Sacrament, will be with them constantly, to sustain their weaknesses at every step, to sweeten every sacrifice, to comfort and console them during even the hardest and longest trials. If, in obedience to the divine law, it may be necessary to refuse the promise of earthly joys glimpsed in the hour of temptation, to forgo "starting life anew," God's grace will still be there to put in full relief the teachings of faith: that the only true life, which must never be endangered, is life in Heaven, precisely the life which is assured by such renunciations, painful as they may be; these being, like all the events of our present life, something temporary, only meant to prepare the permanent state of the future life which will be the more happy and radiant as the inevitable afflictions met with along our way here below will have been accepted with greater courage and generosity.[†]

Marital Fidelity

As an indissoluble contract, marriage has the power to constitute and bind the wedded pair in a social and religious state having a legitimate and perpetual

† Address to Married Couples (April 22, 1942).

character, superior to all other contracts in this respect: that no power on earth—within the meaning and scope of Our previous declarations—is able to dissolve it. One of the parties would in vain attempt to free himself from it: the refuted contract, even if violated, disowned, torn up, does not loosen its grip; it continues to obligate with the same vigor as on the day when the consent of the contracting parties sealed it before God: not even the victim can be freed from the sacred tie which binds him or her to the one who has betrayed. That tie is not unknotted, or rather broken, except by death.

All this notwithstanding, fidelity says something still stronger, still deeper, but at the same time more tender and infinitely sweet. For, as the marriage contract unites the wedded couple in a community of social and religious life, it has to determine the precise limits within which it binds them, to refer to the possibility of external authority to which one of the parties may resort to force the other party to fulfill the duties which have been freely accepted. But, while these juridical particulars, which are, as it were, the material body of the contract, necessarily give it, so to speak, a cold, formal aspect, fidelity is like the heart and soul of the contract, its open proof, its clear witness.

Though it is more exacting, fidelity turns into sweetness the elements of rigor and austerity which juridical precision seemed to stamp on the contract. More exacting, yes; because fidelity considers faithless and a perjurer not only whoever makes an attempt through divorce—vain and ineffectual, anyhow—against the indissolubility of marriage, but also whoever, though not materially destroying the home he has founded and continuing the communion of conjugal life, yet takes the liberty of forming and maintaining another criminal relationship. He also is deemed unfaithful and a perjurer who, though not maintaining an illicit relationship for any length of time, makes use, be it once only, for someone else's pleasure or for his own selfish and sinful satisfaction, of a body to which—in the words of St. Paul—only the legitimate husband or wife has a right. True Christian fidelity, still more exacting and particular than strict natural fidelity, dominates and goes further; it rules and reigns, lovingly sovereign, over the whole expanse of the kingdom of love.

Indeed, what is fidelity if not religious respect for the gift that each mate has made to the other, of self, body, mind, and heart for the full course of life, with no other reserve save the sacred rights of God?

The freshness of youth in flower, modest elegance, the spontaneity and delicacy of her ways, the inner goodness of her soul, all these good and beautiful attractions which go to form the indefinable charm of a pure and innocent girl, have won the heart of a young man and have so drawn him toward her with the rapture of an ardent and chaste love that one would vainly seek elsewhere in nature for an image which could express so delightful an enchantment…

Love and Resignation

But the years, passing over handsomeness and beauty and the dreams of youth, take away some of love's freshness and give it in exchange a more thoughtful and austere dignity. The growing family adds to the burden which weighs on the father's shoulders. Maternity, with its cares, its sufferings, and its risks, calls for and exacts courage: the wife, in the field of honor of conjugal duty, must be no less heroic than her husband in the field of honor of civic duty, where he makes the gift of his life to his country. And if distance, absence, and forced separations, and other delicate circumstances, should intervene, obliging a husband and wife to live in continence, then the wedded couple, remembering that the body of each belongs to the other, will, without any hesitation, accept their duty, with all its claims and consequences, and will, with a generous heart and without weaknesses, maintain the stern discipline which virtue enjoins.

And when, with the advent of old age, there comes a multiplication of ailments and infirmities, and of the humiliating and painful consequences of bodily decay, a host of afflictions which, without love's strength and support, would make repugnant the body which had formerly been so attractive, the most tender cares will be lovingly lavished on that body. This is fidelity in the mutual gift of the bodies.

In their first meetings, during the time of their engagement, everything seemed enchanting: each gave to the other, with sincerity as much as innocent illusion, a tribute of admiration that aroused indulgent smiles in those who witnessed it… The expansion of joy and love gave to the conversations a candor, a vivacity, and a liveliness which lent sparkle to the minds and added a pleasing glitter to the treasure of knowledge each happened to possess; a very small treasure sometimes, but one which everything contributed to show off to the best advantage. This is attraction, enthusiasm; but it is not yet fidelity.

That season passes; failings are not slow in appearing, differences in character in coming forth and growing, and perhaps a limited intellect becomes more noticeable. The fireworks have died out, blind love opens its eyes, it suffers delusion. Then, for true and faithful love, begins the struggle, and at the same time the challenge. No longer blind, it becomes perfectly aware of these failings but accepts them with affectionate patience, conscious as it is of its own defects. And with the growth of discernment, it now goes on to discover and appreciate, under the rough surface, the qualities of judgment, good sense, and solid piety, rich treasures which, though hidden, are sound. While eager to bring to light and make the best of these spiritual gifts and virtues, love is no less clever and watchful in shielding from the eyes of others any gaps and blanks in intelligence or knowledge, as well as any eccentricities or asperities of character… Love is ready to perceive what brings together and unites, and not what divides; ready to rectify an error or dissipate an illusion, with so much good grace as never to irritate or offend. Far from showing off its own superiority, it tactfully asks advice of the partner, letting it appear that if it has something to give, it is also happy to receive. It is in this way, evidently, that a spiritual union is established in the wedded couple, an intellectual and practical co-operation which makes them both rise toward the truth in which there is unity, toward the supreme truth, toward God. What else is this but fidelity in the mutual gift of their minds?[†]

Rights Without Duties

Those times are gone when girls often approached marriage in a state of virtual ignorance; but unfortunately, the time still endures when there are newly-wed couples who believe they can allow themselves at first a period of moral license and enjoy their rights without any concern for their duties. This is a grave sin which provokes the divine wrath; a source of unhappiness, even here on

† Address to Married Couples (October 21, 1942).

earth, whose consequences should instill fear in everybody. The duty which is disavowed or scorned at the start will continue to be neglected for so long that it becomes at last almost forgotten, and with it the joys which come from its courageous observance. And when it returns to memory and there comes repentance, it is sometimes realized, with useless tears, that it is too late: the couple which has been unfaithful to its mission has nothing left but to wither without hope, in the desert of its sterile selfishness.[†]

Happiness in Married Life

An open heart is a source of happiness in the common life of a wedded couple, while a closed heart lessens its joy and peace. Do not make a mistake when you speak about the heart: it is a symbol and image of the will. As the physical heart is the principle of all bodily movement, so is the will the principle of all spiritual movements…

This mutual trust, this reciprocal opening of the heart, this mutual simplicity in sharing thoughts, aspirations, worries, joys, and sorrows, is a necessary condition, an element, indeed, an essential nourishment of happiness.

We do not wish to say that this reciprocal opening of the heart must be limitless. There are inviolable secrets which their nature, a promise, or their confidential communication cause to remain voiceless. A husband who is a doctor, a lawyer, an officer, a government official, an employee in some concern, will know or will come to know many things which professional secrecy does not allow him to divulge to anyone, not even to his wife, who, if she is wise and prudent, will show him her trust by respecting and admiring his silence, without doing or trying to do anything to pierce it.

Apart from these personal and sacred secrets of the inner and outer life, however, the souls of husband and wife should be put in common, as if to form of two souls one soul only.[‡]

In sanctity, through grace, the wedded pair are equally and immediately united with Christ.

---

† Address to Married Couples (July 24, 1940).

‡ Address to Married Couples (November 12, 1941).

Present-day living conditions tend to engender and practically introduce widespread levelling in male and female activities, so that not infrequently a husband and a wife come to find themselves in a situation which almost approaches equality.

And yet, the Christian conception of marriage which St. Paul taught his disciples at Ephesus, like those of Corinth, could not be clearer and more explicit: "Women shall be subject to their husbands as to the Lord, because man is the master of woman as Christ is the head of the Church... As the Church is subject to Christ, so are women subject to their husbands in everything. Men, love your wives as Christ loved the Church and gave Himself up for it... Let each man love his wife as himself, and let the wife respect her husband."[†]

Now—see what a strange thing it is—while nobody would ever think of suddenly becoming, without any preparation or training, a mechanic or engineer, or a doctor or lawyer, every day not a few young men and women marry and form a union without having thought for a moment about preparing themselves for the arduous tasks that await them in the education of their children.[‡]

Temptations

It is not necessary to have great knowledge and experience with regard to family life to know how frequent are the lamentable falls which overthrow and destroy a love that had originally been pure and sincere and, still less, to understand those weaknesses, fickle as passion but whose wounds leave a stinging scar deep down in two hearts, even after they have been forgiven and reparation has been made...

Consider, on the one hand, the husband who is not able to meet all the expenses of a life of luxury; and, on the other hand, the wife who, with her mind full of thoughts for her many children, and with limited economic means, cannot change her modest household, with a wave of a magic wand, into one of the castles described in fairytales; and then say whether it will not seem to

† Address to Married Couples (September 10, 1941).

‡ Address to Women of Catholic Action (October 26, 1941).

this married couple, whose days are monotonous and uneventful, that those days are paltry as compared with the romantic fantasies of novels and movies. Too bitter is the awakening for anyone who lives continually in a gilded daydream; too lively is the temptation to prolong and continue it in real life. How many tragedies of unfaithfulness have had no other origin than this! And if either of the partners, having remained faithful, weeps, uncomprehendingly, over the straying of the guilty one, still dear and loved, he or she is far from suspecting the personal share of responsibility in the slipping and final fall of the other. He or she does not know that conjugal love, as soon as it loses its healthy sereneness, its strong tenderness, its holy fecundity, and resembles selfish and profane love, is easily tempted to seek full enjoyment elsewhere.

Nor is the husband less imprudent who, in order to please his wife or to satisfy his own vanity, encourages her to abandon herself to all the whims and the most audacious extravagances of fashion in her dress and manner of living. Thoughtless young women do not perhaps even imagine the dangers to which they expose themselves and others...

Moderation

Virtue lies midway; as against excessive compliance, it is possible to fall into the opposite excess of too much austerity. This is undoubtedly a rare case, but not without its examples. Exaggerated strictness, which would transform the home into a place of sadness, with neither gaiety nor light, with no wholesome and Godly relaxations, without a wide scope for action, might lead to the same disorders as a too easy hand. Who does not foresee that the more rigorous the constraint, the more violent may perhaps be the reaction? The victim of this tyranny—the man or the woman, maybe even the oppressor himself—will be tempted at some time or other to put an end to married life. But if the ruinous consequences of frivolity frequently help to open people's eyes and lead them back to better counsels and more sobriety, the straying caused by an exasperating severity is, on the other hand, often ascribed to a lack of sufficient rigor, which leads to still greater harshness and provokes further harm.

Far from these two extremes—excessive indulgence and excessive severity—let there reign among you moderation, which simply means the virtuous sense of measure and of what is fitting. Let the husband wish to see, and enjoy seeing, his wife dressing and acting with becoming elegance according to his means and social standing, encouraging and cheering her occasionally by some thoughtful gift, by praise for her looks and charm. In turn, let the wife banish from her home all that is unfitting and offensive to the Christian eye and the sense of beauty, and likewise any severity that would wither the heart. Let both enjoy reading, maybe together, good, beautiful, useful books that can instruct them, broaden their knowledge of things and achievements and the horizons of their art or work, inform them of the course of events, and keep them firm and better indoctrinated in faith and in virtue. Let them freely, but moderately, indulge in healthy and decent amusements that bring relaxation and cheer the mind. Let each be happy to see the other excel in his or her professional or social activities, in making himself liked for his smiling pleasantness among their mutual friends; and let them never be envious of each other.

Jealousy

And lastly, a great stumbling block to be avoided is jealousy, which can spring from indulgence or be caused by too much severity; a most dangerous stumbling block to faithfulness. That incomparable psychologist, St. John Chrysostom, described it with masterly eloquence: "Everything that can be said of this evil can never sufficiently describe its gravity. Once a man begins to suspect the person he loves most in the world, the person he would gladly give his life for, in what may he then find comfort...? But if a husband is anxiously tossed by these evils, even when they have no foundation or reason, the poor, wretched wife is still more gravely tormented. He who should be her comforter in all her sufferings and her prop, is cruel to her and shows her only hostility... a soul thus prejudiced and struck by this disease is ready to believe everything, to accept all accusations, without discerning the true from the false, and more inclined to listen to one who confirms his suspicions than one who would dissipate them... Exits, entrances, words, glances, the smallest sighs, all is spied; the poor woman must bear everything in silence; chained, so to speak, to the conjugal bed, she cannot even allow herself a step, a word, or a sigh without having to give account thereof to the very servants." May not such a life become almost intolerable? And is there cause to wonder then if, when the light and support of true Christian virtue are lacking, an endeavor is made to break loose from that life and escape from it through the shipwreck of unfaithfulness?[†]

The Family

In the order of nature, among social institutions there is none that is dearer to the Church than the family. Christ elevated marriage, which is, as it were, its root, to the dignity of a Sacrament. The family has found and will always find in the Church defense, protection, and support, in all that concerns its inviolable rights, its freedom, the exercise of its lofty function.

We have often and on the most varied occasions spoken in favor of the Christian family, and in most cases to come, or to call others, to its help, to save it from the gravest perils. Above all, to succor it in the calamities of war. The damage wrought by the First World War was far from being completely repaired when the second and even more terrible conflagration came to fill the measure. Much time and effort will still be required, and also greater divine assistance, before the deep wounds that these two wars have inflicted on the family begin to heal properly. Another evil, also due in part to the devastation of war, but a consequence as well of overpopulation, is the housing crisis; all those, legislators, statesmen, members of social welfare institutions, who are seeking to find a remedy for this, are accomplishing, even if only indirectly, an apostolate of eminent value. The same is true of the struggle against the scourge of unemployment, for an adjustment in the matter of adequate family wages, so that a mother need not be obliged, as too often happens, to look for work outside the home, but may devote more of her time to her husband and children. To work for schools and religious education: that is another valuable contribution to the welfare of families, as is also to encourage in the family a healthy naturalness and simplicity of manners, to strengthen religious beliefs, fostering in the home an atmosphere of Christian purity, able to protect it

† Address to Married Couples (November 10, 1942).

from harmful outside influences and all the morbid excitement that arouses unregulated passions in an adolescent's mind...

Conjugal Morality

Another danger threatens the family, not by any means recent, but of long standing, which, though, growing visibly as it is at present, may become fatal to it, because it attacks it in its very root; We mean the disrupting of conjugal morality in all its extension.

In the course of the last few years, We have taken every opportunity of emphasizing one or other of the essential points of that morality, and more recently of expounding it as a whole, not only confuting the errors that corrupt it, but also showing positively its meaning, function, and importance, its value for the happiness of a married couple, their children, and the whole family, and for stability and greater social welfare, ranging from the home to the State and the Church itself.

At the center of this doctrine marriage appeared as an institution in the service of life. In close connection with this principle, We, in accordance with the constant teaching of the Church, expounded a thesis which is one of the essential foundations not only of conjugal morality but also of the morality of society at large: that is, that a direct attempt on innocent human life, as means to an end—in the present case the end being to save another life—is illicit.

Which Life Is More Precious?

Innocent human life, in whatever condition it may be, is, from the first instant of its existence, to be preserved from any direct voluntary attack. This is a fundamental right of the human person, of general value in the Christian conception of life; valid both for the life still hidden in the mother's womb and for the life that has already left it; equally so against the causing of abortion and the direct killing of the child before, during, or after birth. However justified the distinction may be between those different moments of the development of the life, already born or not yet born, for profane and ecclesiastical law and with respect to certain civil and penal consequences, according to the moral law all these are cases of a serious and illicit attempt on inviolable human life.

This principle holds good for the life of the child as for that of the mother. Never and in no case has the Church taught that the child's life must be preferred to that of the mother. It is a mistake to formulate the question with this alternative: either the child's life or the mother's. No; neither the mother's life nor the child's may be submitted to an act of direct suppression. For the one and for the other the requirement can be only this: to make every effort to save the life of both the mother and the child.

One of the finest and noblest aspirations of medicine is this constant seeking for new methods of safeguarding the lives of both. And if, in spite of all the progress of science, there still remain, and will still remain in future, cases in which the mother's death must be reckoned with, when she wants to carry to birth the life she bears within her and not to destroy it in violation of God's commandment: "Thou shalt not kill!" man, while endeavoring up to the last moment to help and to save, has no alternative but to bow in awe to the laws of nature, and the dispositions of divine Providence.

Preservation of the Mother's Life

But—it is objected—the mother's life, especially if she is the mother of a numerous family, is of far greater value than that of a child yet unborn. The application of the theory of the scale of values to the case with which we are here concerned has already found support in juridical discussions. The answer to this much debated objection is not difficult. The inviolability of the life of an innocent being does not depend on its greater or lesser value. More than ten years ago the Church formally condemned the killing of a life deemed "worthless"; and anyone who knows the pitiful antecedents that called forth this condemnation, anyone who can ponder the deadly consequences that would follow if the intangibility of an innocent life were to be measured by its value, can well appreciate the motives that led up to it.

Besides, who can judge with certainty which of the two lives is really more valuable? Who can tell what path that child will take and what heights of achievements and perfection it may reach? Here, two quantities are compared, about one of which nothing is known.

We have always used, in this connection, the expressions "direct attempt on the life of the innocent creature," "direct killing." For if, for example, the safeguarding of the life of the future mother, independently of her state of pregnancy, were to call for an urgent surgical intervention, or any other therapeutic application, which would have as an accessory consequence, in no way desired or intended but unavoidable, the death of the fetus, this could not be termed a direct attempt on innocent life. In these conditions the operation can be licit, like other similar medical interventions, provided the stake at issue is a high one, such as a life, and that it is not possible to postpone it until after the birth of the child or to have recourse to any other efficacious remedy.

Since, then, the primary function of marriage is to be at the service of life, Our special congratulations and Our paternal gratitude go to those generous married couples who, for love of God, and trusting in Him, courageously bring up a numerous family.

Legitimate Regulation of Progeny

On the other hand, the Church looks with sympathy and understanding at the real difficulties of matrimonial life in our days. We have, therefore, affirmed the legitimacy and at the same time the limits—which are indeed very wide—of a regulation of offspring, which, unlike what is termed "birth control," is compatible with the law of God. It may even be hoped (but in such a field the Church, of course, leaves judgment to medical science) that the latter will succeed in giving this legitimate method a sufficiently sure basis, and the most recent information seems to confirm such a hope.

However, to overcome the numerous trials of married life nothing is more efficacious than a lively faith and a frequent use of the Sacraments, from which spring the torrents of strength of which it is hardly possible for those living outside the Church to form a clear notion.[†]

† Address to the "Family Front" Congress (November 27, 1951).

To the Fathers

What else is fatherhood if not to communicate being; still more, to put into that being the mysterious ray of life? God is the Father of the Universe: "*Nobis unus est Deus, Pater, ex quo omnia*—for us there is only one God, the Father from whom are all things." God is the Father who creates the heavens, the sun, and the stars that shine in His presence and announce His glory; God is the Father who has created and shaped this world, who has planted its flowers and forests, who has multiplied and rendered prolific the airy nests of birds, the inaccessible haunts of fish, and the coral banks in the oceans, sheep- and cattle-folds, the lairs of wild beasts, the dens of roaring lions, alert and quick to fall upon their prey; all this multifarious, countless life is the child of God's love, directed, sustained, and enveloped in its growth and evolution by his Fatherly Providence…

But the boundless love of a God, which is charity, has superior and very lofty means of pouring out its light and its flame by communicating, as a Father, a life similar to His own.

Angel and man are the children of God and they reveal it by the image and resemblance which, in the natural order of simple creatures, they have received from Him; but God has a more sublime Fatherhood that begets children of adoption and of grace, in an order that stands above the human and angelic natures and that makes them partakers of, and sharers in, the divine nature itself, calling on them to share His own happiness in the vision of His essence, in that inaccessible light, wherein He reveals to the children of grace Himself and the innermost secret of His incomparable Fatherhood, together with the Son and the Holy Ghost. In that great light rules God, creator, sanctifier, and glorifier Who, out of predilection for the last of His intelligent creatures, man, regenerates him, from son of His wrath, because born from his guilty progenitor Adam, and causes him to be born again here on earth, with water and the Holy Ghost, as a child of grace, brother to Christ, a new spotless Adam, making him joint heir to His glory in Heaven. And He wished that man himself might be the parent of such glory and of supernatural life as well as natural life, by co-operating with God; that he might be a parent to its transmission and to its preservation and perfection. This is the incomparable mystery into the heart of which man is led by marriage.

A Life of Comfort and Pleasure?

How beautiful and worth recalling is the blessing that Rachel gives to young Tobias when she hears whose son he is: "*Benedictio sit tibi fili, quia boni et optimi viri filius es*—Blessed be thou, my son, because thou art the child of a good and honest man." Old Tobias was no longer rich in earthly possessions; the Lord had put him to the test through the ordeal of his exile and his blindness; but he was rich in something more valuable, that is, the admirable example of his virtue and the wise advice he gave to his son. We, too, are living in difficult times: perhaps it will not always be possible to give children the comfortable, pleasant life that one dreams of for them or to make them peaceful and satisfied through the goods one would like to secure for them, in addition to their daily bread, which we trust, with the help of divine Providence, they will not be lacking. But, more than any earthly goods, which cannot, even for the powerful and the feasters, ever transform this valley of tears into a heaven of delight, it is the parents who must give their children and heirs more valuable things, the bread and wealth of faith, the atmosphere of hope and charity, the incentive to a courageous and steadfast Christian life in which the sacred duties of fathers and mothers, conscious of the loftiness of the parenthood granted to them by Heaven, will make them grow up and improve before God and their fellow creatures.[†]

The Duties of Husband and Wife

The responsibility of man before his wife and children springs primarily from his obligations for their lives and involves his profession, his art, or his craft. With his professional labor he must procure for them a home, daily bread, the necessary means for a secure livelihood and sufficient clothing. His family must feel happy and safe under the protection he offers and gives with thoughtful foresight and the constructive activity of his hands.

† Address to Newlyweds (March 19, 1941).

The position of the man without a family is markedly different from that of a man with a wife and children for whom to provide. He is often confronted with hazardous undertakings, made attractive by the hope of large gains, but which too easily lead to ruin along unsuspected paths. Dreams of fortune often deceive the mind and unsettle calm judgment: moderation of the heart and its dreams is a virtue which never brings harm, because it is the daughter of prudence. Hence, the married man, even when there are no moral considerations involved, must not surpass the proper limits—limits imposed by his obligation to refrain, without grave reason, from exposing to danger the secure subsistence of his wife and children, those already born and those expected. It is another thing if the happiness of his family is jeopardized by circumstances beyond his control, as so often happens in times of great political and social upheaval which spreads throughout the world in millions of homes, carrying with it the malignant seeds of fear, misery, and death. However, in action or omission, undertaking or daring, he must always ask himself: May I assume this responsibility before my family?

In addition to being linked to his family by moral bonds, the married man is bound to society. These bonds are loyalty in the exercise of his profession, art, or craft; trustworthiness upon which his superiors may count unconditionally; correctness and integrity in conduct and action which earn him the trust of all those who deal with him; are not these bonds outstanding social virtues? And do not such splendid virtues constitute the outer defensive walls of domestic happiness and peaceful existence of the family, whose security, according to the law of God, is the first duty of the Christian father?

A Woman's Honor

We could add that since a woman's honor and social standing correspond to the public esteem of her husband, out of consideration for her, the man must strive to exceed his equals and rise above them in his own field of endeavor. Every woman as a rule wants to be proud of her life's companion. Is it not therefore praiseworthy that the husband, activated by noble feelings and affection for his wife, exert himself to furnish his best endeavor and, within the limits of his ability, reach for the highest aim?

For if by elevating himself creditably and honestly in society by means of his profession and labor the man confers esteem and security on his wife and children—since the pride of children is their father—the man must not forget how much he contributes to a happy domestic life if, in every circumstance, he shows, in his own heart as well as in his exterior behavior and speech, regard and respect for his wife, the mother of his children. The woman is not only the sun but also the sanctuary of the family; she is the little ones' refuge from tears; she guides the steps of the older ones, comforts their anxiety, resolves their doubts, and gives them faith in the future. Dispensing warmth and kindness, she is also mistress of the household. May it never happen, as is sometimes said, that married couples are distinguished from unmarried couples by the indifferent, less considerate, even rude behavior of the man toward his wife. No; the entire behavior of the husband toward his wife must never lack natural, noble, and dignified kindness and warmth, as is fitting in men of sound temperament and God-fearing soul; men who with their intellect perceive the inestimable value that mutually virtuous, kindly behavior between husband and wife has for the education of the children. The example of the father has a powerful effect: it is a vigorous, living stimulus which encourages the children to regard the mother—and the father—with respect, veneration, and love.

Marital Crises

But man's contribution to the happiness of the home must not stop at nor limit itself to kindness and consideration toward the consort of his life; it must advance to understand, appreciate, and recognize the work and effort of her who silently and assiduously dedicates herself to making the common home more comfortable, more pleasant, more gay. With what loving care, for example, a young woman has arranged everything to celebrate, as joyously as the circumstances permit, the anniversary of the day in which she was united before the altar with him who was to become the companion of her life and happiness, and who is now about to return from his office or workshop! But the man arrives, weary from the long hours of work, perhaps more exhausted than usual, nervous because of unforeseen vexations. He returns later than usual, somber and worried about other thoughts; the happy, affectionate words that greet him go unheeded and he remains silent; he appears unaware of the meal prepared with so much love: he only looks and notes that the dish which was selected especially to make him happy has been cooking too long, and he grumbles, without thinking that the reason was his own delay and the long wait. He eats hurriedly, since, he says, he must go out immediately after dinner. When the meal is over, the poor young woman, who had dreamed of the joy of a pleasant evening together with him, finds herself alone in the deserted room; she needs all her faith and courage to keep back her tears.

Such scenes are likely to occur in every life. A maxim laid down by the great philosopher Aristotle says that things appear to a man according to what he is in himself: in other words, things appear welcome to man or not according to his natural disposition or the passions which move him. And you see how even the most innocent concerns, such as business affairs and events, and their effects, change our thoughts and moods, cause us to forget the rules of propriety and courtesy, and to reject and disregard kindness and charm. Undoubtedly, the husband could give as his excuse the excessive fatigue of the day's work, aggravated by obstacles and worries. But does he believe that his wife neither feels nor experiences fatigue, nor encounters obstacles? True, deep love, in one or the other, must be stronger and show itself to be stronger than fatigue and boredom, stronger than the variations of personal humor or unforeseen misfortune... When, therefore, you find yourselves at home where conversation and repose restore your strength, do not be quick to search for the little defects inevitable in every human endeavor; be mindful, rather, of all that is good, be it much or little, which is offered to you as the fruit of toil, vigilant attention, affectionate feminine intuition, to make your home, no matter how modest it may be, a little paradise of happiness and joy. Do not be content to contemplate and love such goodness only in the recesses of your thoughts and heart; let your wife know it and feel it, since she has not spared herself in procuring it for you; for her the best and sweetest recompense is a loving smile, a gentle word, an appreciative glance, which makes her aware of your gratitude.[†]

† Address to Newlyweds (April 8, 1942).

A Happy Family Life

God has given woman the sacred, painful mission of maternity, which is also a fountain of pure joy, and the mother, above all others, has been entrusted with the early upbringing of the child in its first months and years.

Certainly a woman can do more than a man to contribute to the happiness of home life. The husband's first duty is to assure the subsistence and the future of the family and the home through decisions which bind him and his children for the future: woman must apply vigilant diligence to caring for those thousand particulars, those intangible daily attentions which create the elements of the internal family atmosphere. And according to whether her diligence is correctly applied, or misdirected, or lacking, the atmosphere is rendered salutary, fresh, and bracing, or oppressive, spoiled, unbreathable. The actions of the wife in the home should always be like the work of the valiant woman exalted in Holy Scriptures: a woman in whom the heart of her husband trusteth, a woman who will render him good and not evil for all the days of his life.

Is it not an ancient yet always new truth—a truth rooted in the physical condition of a woman's life, an inexorable truth proclaimed not only by the experience of remote centuries, but even more so in our own times—that the woman makes the home and cares for it, and that the man can never supplant her in this? Is it not the destiny which nature and her union with man have imposed on her for the good of society? Draw her away from her family with one of the many lures employed to win and bind her, and you will see the woman neglect her hearth; without this fire her home will become cold; in practice the hearth will cease to exist, and be changed into the precarious refuge of a few hours; the center of daily life will shift elsewhere for her husband, for her, and for her children.

Whether you like it or not, for whoever, man or woman, is married and firmly resolved to remain faithful to the duties of such a condition, the edifice of happiness can be raised only on the solid foundation of family life. But where can there be true family life without a hearth, without a visible center, a genuine meeting place, where the family may gather, collect, put down roots, maintain itself, deepen, unfold, and flower? Do not say that the hearth is created on the day in which the rings are placed on the two clasped hands and the newlyweds share a common room under the same roof, in their own apartment, their own residence, large or small, rich or poor. No, a material hearth is not enough for the spiritual structure of happiness. It is necessary to elevate matter to a spiritual realm and transform earthly fire into the living, life-giving flame of the new family. This is not the work of a day, especially if the new couple does not dwell in a home prepared by the preceding generations but rather—as is the case most frequently today, especially in the cities—in a temporary, rented domicile. Who, then, little by little, day by day, will create the true home, if not the woman who has become the "mistress of the house"? Whether the husband is a workman, farmer, professional worker, man of letters or science, artist, white-collar worker, or executive, it is inevitable that he spend the major part of his time away from his house, or, if he works at home, that he confine himself to the silence of his study away from the life of the family. The domestic hearth will become for him the place where at the end of the day's labor he will be restored physically and morally in repose, calm, and intimate joy. However, for the woman, this home will be her principal creation; through her labor it will develop into a refuge, no matter how poor, into a happy, tranquil residence adorned not by furniture and objects without personal touch, without individual expression, but rich in memories and objects that recall the events of a life lived together, the tastes, the thoughts, the joys, the shared suffering, from whose traces and signs, sometimes visible, at other times hardly perceptible, the material hearth in the course of time will take its soul. And the animating spirit of it all will be the feminine hand and heart which the wife employs to make every corner of the house attractive, if only through care, order, neatness, keeping everything ready to be used when needed and at the moment desired; making meals a comfort after work, and preparing the bed for repose. To woman more than man, the Lord has granted, with the sense of grace and harmony, the gift of lending attraction to the simplest things, precisely because she, made similar to man to help him establish the family, is born to spread gentleness and sweetness in the home of the family, and to ensure that their life together finds in the home its nucleus from which it grows, becomes fruitful, and flowers in its true unfolding.

Motherhood: A Life of Sacrifice

And when the Lord in His goodness has granted to the wife the dignity of motherhood beside a cradle, the cry of the newborn child will not lessen or destroy happiness in the home; rather, it will cause it to grow and infuse it with the sublimity of that divine halo which radiates around the angels in Heaven, and from which descends the ray of life, which conquers nature and transforms the sons of men into children of God. This is the sanctity of the nuptial bed. This is the loftiness of Christian motherhood. This is the salvation of the married woman. Because woman, according to the great Apostle Paul, shall be saved through her mission as a mother, as long as she remains in faith, and in charity, and in holiness with modesty. Now you will understand how "piety is useful for everything, since it contains the promise of life in the present and hereafter," and is, according to the teachings of St. Ambrose, the foundation of all virtues.

A cradle consecrates the mother of the family; and more cradles sanctify and glorify her before her husband and children, before Church and homeland. The mother who complains because a new child presses against her bosom seeking nourishment at her breast is foolish, ignorant of herself, and unhappy. The enemy of happiness in the home is complaint over the blessing of God, which fosters it and makes it grow. The heroism of motherhood is the exaltation and glory of the Christian bride: in the desolation of her home, if it is without the joy of an infant, her solitude becomes a prayer and invocation to Heaven; her tears flow with those of Anna, who supplicated the Lord at the gate of the temple for the gift of Samuel.[†]

O wives, this is your share of responsibility for the harmony of domestic happiness. If your husband's task is to procure and establish with his toil the life of the hearth, it is for you and your gifts to arrange for his well-being and to assure the peaceful serenity of your lives together. For you, this is not only a law of nature, but also a religious duty and an obligation of Christian virtue, through the strength of whose acts and merits you grow in love and the grace of God.

"But," some of you may say, "you are asking of us a lifetime of sacrifices!" Yes; yours is a life of sacrifice, but not of sacrifice only. Do you believe that

† Address to Women of Catholic Action, October 26, 1941.

here on earth you can enjoy true, solid happiness without winning it through some privation and renunciation, that some corner of this world contains the full, perfect beatitude of a terrestrial paradise? And do you think that your husband must not also make sacrifices, at times many and grave ones, in order to procure honored and secure bread for the family? It is these mutual sacrifices, brought together for common advantage, which give to marital love and family happiness their warmth and stability, their holy depth and that exquisite nobility which spells reciprocal respect of husband and wife and exalts them in the affection and gratitude of their children. If maternal sacrifice is more acute and painful, virtue from on high tempers it. It is through her sacrifice that woman learns pity for the afflictions of others. Love for the happiness of her home does not close her within herself; the love of God, which through her sacrifice raises her above herself, opens her heart to all piety and sanctifies her.

The Married Career Woman

"But," others may also object, "the modern social structure of labor, industry, and the professions demands that a large number of women, wives included, enter the fields of work and public life." We are not unaware of this. But it is doubtful that such a condition is the social ideal for the married woman. However, the fact must be kept in mind. Providence, which is constantly watchful in its government of humanity, has given to the spirit of the Christian family superior powers to mitigate and conquer such a social state and to avoid the perils which are doubtless hidden in it. Have you not observed how the sacrifice of a mother who, for special motives, must, beyond her domestic duties, also work to provide with hard daily toil for the upkeep of her family, not only conserves her children's love but makes it increase; and when religious sentiment and faith in God are the foundation of family life, their recognition of her difficulties and labor is even stronger. If such is the case in your marriage, in addition to faith in God, who always aids those who fear and serve Him, during the hours and days which you can dedicate entirely to your dear ones, add zealous attention to redoubled love, not only to assure the indispensable minimum for true family life, but also to transmit from yourself to the hearts of your husband and children those luminous rays of the sun which, even during the hours of exterior separation, comfort, foment, and nourish the spiritual framework of the hearth.†

The Modern Woman

In accordance with very ancient traditions, the woman's mode of life and the form given to her education used to be inspired by her natural instinct which made the family her field of endeavor, when she did not, for the love of Christ, prefer virginity. Kept away from public life and outside the public professions, a young woman, like a growing flower, tended and sheltered, was destined by her vocation to become a wife and mother. At her mother's side she learned womanly tasks and the care of the home and housework, and helped to look after her younger brothers and sisters, thus employing her strength and ingenuity and learning the art of governing the domestic hearth. The simple, natural forms which the lives of the people took, the homely and practical religious education which inspired all their activity until the late nineteenth century, the custom of marrying early, which was still possible under the economic and social conditions then existing, the pre-eminence of the family in the life of the people, all this and other circumstances, which have meanwhile radically changed, constituted the primary nourishment and support for that character and that kind of education of woman.

Today, by contrast, the old type of womanhood is rapidly changing. You now see women, especially the young women, leaving their retired position and entering nearly all the professions, hitherto fields of livelihood and action belonging exclusively to men. The first timid beginnings of this revolution had been manifest for a fairly long time, being due principally to the development of industry bound up with modern progress.

But for some years now, like a flood which, having overthrown its dams, breaks through every resistance, the march of women seems to have been

† Address to Newlyweds (February 25, 1944).

penetrating into the whole area of public life. And, if this current is not as yet spread equally everywhere, it is not unusual to encounter its course in even the remotest mountain villages; while, in the labyrinth of large cities, such as in workshops and factories, ancient customs and trends have been forced to surrender unconditionally to the modern movement.†

Woman's Dignity

Let Us make it clear at once that for Us the problem of women, both in its general aspect and in each one of its multiple details, consists entirely in the conservation and increase of the dignity woman has received from God. For Us, therefore, it is not a problem of a purely legal or economic, educational or biological, political or demographic order; but one which, in all its complexity, nevertheless always gravitates around the question: How to maintain and strengthen the dignity of woman, especially today, in the circumstances in which Providence has placed us? To look at the problem in any other way, to consider it unilaterally under any one of the above-mentioned aspects, would be the same as evading it, without benefit to anyone, least of all woman herself. To separate it from God, from the Creator's wise ordering, from His holy will, is to distort the essential point of the question, that is, the true dignity of woman, the dignity which she possesses only from God and in God.

It follows from this, that those systems which exclude God and His law from social life, and allow the precepts of religion a humble place, at most, in the private life of man, are not in a position justly to consider the problem of woman.

In what, then, does this dignity which woman has received from God consist? Ask it of human nature, as God formed, elevated, and redeemed it in Christ's blood.

In their personal dignity as children of God, man and woman are absolutely equal, also in regard to the ultimate end of human life, which is eternal union with God in the bliss of Heaven. It is an imperishable glory of the Church to have reinstated that truth and to have freed woman from a

† Address to Young Women of Catholic Action (April 24, 1943).

degrading bondage contrary to nature. But man and woman cannot maintain and perfect their equal dignity except by respecting and putting to use the peculiar qualities which nature has bestowed upon the one and the other, indestructible spiritual and physical qualities, whose order cannot be deranged without nature herself moving to re-establish it. These peculiar characteristics which distinguish the two sexes reveal themselves so clearly to the eyes of all, that only obstinate blindness or doctrinarianism, not less baneful than utopian, could, in a social organization, misunderstand or disregard its value.

The two sexes, through their peculiar qualities, themselves are co-ordinated in such a manner that their mutual co-ordination exercises its influence in all the multiple manifestations of human social life. We will be content here with recalling two of these because of their special importance: the state of matrimony and the state of voluntary celibacy according to the evangelical counsel.

Voluntary Renunciation of Married Life

In order to follow the counsel of Christ, for nearly twenty centuries now, in every generation, thousands and thousands of men and women among the best have been freely denying themselves a family and renouncing the holy duties and sacred rights of wedded life. Is the common good of peoples and of the Church perhaps exposed to danger on that account? On the contrary! Such generous spirits do indeed see that the association of the two sexes in matrimony is a great good. But when they leave the usual way, the beaten path, far from deserting humanity they devote themselves to its service through a complete detachment from self and from their own interests, in an incomparably wider, all-embracing, universal action. See them devoted to prayer and penitence; applying themselves to the instruction and education of youth and the ignorant; bending over the bedside of the sick and agonizing; with their hearts open to all afflictions and all weakness to rehabilitate them, comfort them, raise them up, sanctify them.

If one turns one's thoughts to the girls and women who voluntarily renounce matrimony in order to devote themselves to a higher life of contemplation, sacrifice, and charity, a luminous word comes to the lips immediately: Vocation! It is the only word that befits such an elevated sentiment. This vocation, this call of love, makes itself felt in the most diverse manners, as infinitely varied as are the modulations of the divine voice: irresistible invitations, affectionately soliciting inspirations, gentle impulses. But also the young Christian woman who has against her will remained unwedded, but firmly believes in the heavenly Father's Providence, recognizes the voice of the Master in the vicissitudes of life: *Magister adest et vocat te*—the Master is here and calls you! She responds; she renounces the fond dream of her adolescence and youth: to have a faithful companion in life, to form a family, and in the impossibility of marriage she espies her calling; then with a broken but submissive heart, she likewise gives her whole self to the works of charity.

In one state as in the other, the office of woman appears clearly traced by the features, by the inclinations, and by the faculties peculiar to her sex. She collaborates with man, but in accordance with her natural tendency. Now, the office of woman, her manner, her innate inclination, is motherhood. Every woman is destined to be a mother; mother in the physical sense of the word, or in a more spiritual and higher but no less real meaning.

The Creator has disposed to this end the entire being of woman, her organism, and even more her spirit, and above all her exquisite sensibility. So that a true woman cannot see and fully understand all the problems of human life otherwise than under the family aspect. For this reason, a sense of her own dignity makes her apprehensive whenever the social or political order threatens to be detrimental to her maternal mission and the good of the family.

Such are, unfortunately, the social and political conditions today; they might become even more unsettling for the sanctity of the domestic hearth and therefore the dignity of woman. Your hour has struck, Catholic women and girls; public life needs you: to each of you it can be said: *Tua res agitur*—Your interest is at stake.

The Working Mother

That for a long time now public trends have been developing in a manner not favorable to the true benefit of the family and of women is an undeniable fact.

Here is a woman who, in order to add to her husband's wages, also goes to work in a factory, leaving her home uncared for during her absence; and this home, perhaps squalid and small, becomes even more wretched because of lack of care; the various members of the family work each separately in the four corners of the city and at different hours; they are hardly ever together, either for meals or for a rest after the day's labor, much less for common prayers. What remains of family life? And what attraction can it have for the children?

To these painful consequences of the absence of the woman and mother from the home is added another even more deplorable; it concerns the education of the young girl especially, and her preparation for life.

Used to seeing her mother always absent and the home dismal in its abandonment, she will find no attraction in it, she will not feel the slightest inclination for domestic occupations, and she will be unable to understand their nobleness and beauty or desire to devote herself to them someday as a wife and mother.

This is true in all social strata, and in all conditions of life. The daughter of a woman of fashion, who sees the supervision of the home left to strangers and her mother engrossed in frivolous occupations and futile amusements, will follow her example, will want to emancipate herself as early as possible and, according to a truly sad expression, "live her own life." How could she conceive the desire to become someday a real "*domina*," that is, the mistress of the house, in a happy, prosperous, worthy family? As for the working classes, obliged to earn their daily bread, the woman, if she were to reflect properly, would probably realize that the extra earnings which she secures by working outside of her home are easily devoured by other expenses or even by waste, which is ruinous for the economy of the family.

In the face of theories and methods which, from different approaches, strip woman of her mission and, with the mirage of unbridled emancipation, or in the reality of a hopeless misery, divest her of her personal dignity, her woman's dignity, we have heard a cry of apprehension which invokes, as much as possible, her active presence at the domestic hearth.

In truth, woman is kept away from her home not only by her proclaimed emancipation, but often also by the necessities of life, by the goading thought of daily bread. Therefore, it serves no purpose to preach her return to the hearth, as long as the conditions which force her to remain away continue.

And thus becomes manifest the first aspect of your mission in social and political life, which opens up before you. Your entry into public life has come about suddenly, as an effect of the social events of which we are being spectators; that does not matter! You are called to take part in it; would you perhaps leave to others, to those who are the promoters and accomplices of the ruin of the domestic hearth, the monopoly of social organization, of which the family is the chief element in its economic, judicial, spiritual, and moral unity? The fortunes of the family, the fortunes of human coexistence, are at stake; they are in your hands, *tua res agitur!* Every woman, then, without exception, is strictly bound in conscience not to stand aloof but to come into action (in the forms and in the ways suited to the condition of each), in order to stem the currents which threaten the home and to fight the doctrines which undermine its foundations, to prepare, organize, and achieve its restoration.

To this impelling motive for the Catholic woman to enter the life which today opens up to her activity, yet another is added: her woman's dignity. She must compete with man for the good of civic life, in which she is, in dignity, equal to him. Each of the two sexes must take the part which belongs to it according to its nature, its characteristics, its physical, intellectual, and moral habits. Both have the right and the duty to co-operate for the total good of society and the nation, but it is clear that, if the man is by temperament more inclined to handle outside business and public affairs, the woman has, generally speaking, more perspicacity and greater tact to help her understand and solve the delicate problems of domestic and family life, which is the foundation of all social life; though this does not alter the fact that some women furnish an example of great skill in every field of public activity.

Woman's Role in Social Welfare

All this is not so much a question of distinct attributes as of the manner of judging and arriving at concrete, practical applications. Let us take the case of civil rights: at present they are the same for both. But with how much more discernment and efficacy will they be utilized, if man and woman come to each other's help. The sensibility and delicacy of feeling peculiar to woman, which might tempt her to be swayed by emotions and thus blur the clearness and breadth of her view and be detrimental to the calm consideration of future consequences, are, on the contrary, of valuable help in bringing to light needs, aspirations, and dangers in the domestic, welfare, and religious fields.

This effective collaboration in social and political life in no way alters the special character of the normal action of woman. Associating herself with man in his work in the area of civil institutions, she will apply herself principally to tasks which call for tact, delicate feelings, and maternal instinct, rather than administrative rigidity. Who, better than she, can understand what is required by the dignity of woman, the integrity and honor of girlhood, the protection and education of the child? And in all these questions how many problems require the attention and action of those who govern and legislate! Only woman will know, for example, how, without detriment to efficacy, to temper with kindness the repression of loose morals; only she will know how to preserve from humiliation and educate in decency and in the religious and civil virtues delinquent youth; only she will be able to render fruitful service in the rehabilitation of discharged prisoners and of delinquent girls.[†]

Fashion and Virtue

There is nothing wrong, intrinsically, in keeping up with fashion. It springs spontaneously from human sociability, from the impulse which tends to be in harmony with one's fellow men and the customs of the people among whom one lives.

God does not ask us to live outside our times, to ignore the dictates of fashion to the point of becoming ridiculous, dressing contrary to the tastes and habits common to our contemporaries, without ever worrying about their likes and dislikes. Hence, even the Angelic St. Thomas affirms that there is no vice in the outward things man uses, but that vice results when man makes immoderate use of them, either by making himself strangely different from the others, for his own sake and without regard for the customs of those with

† Address to Women of Catholic Action (October 21, 1945).

whom he lives, or by using these things—in harmony with or in excess of the use of others—with an inordinate attachment for an overabundance of clothes, for a luxury too frantically pursued, when humility and simplicity would have been sufficient to satisfy the requirements of dignity. And the same Holy Doctor goes so far as to say that feminine adornment may be a meritorious act of virtue, when it is in conformity with custom, with a woman's place in the world, and chosen with good intention, and when women wear ornaments in keeping with their station and dignity, and are moderate in adapting themselves to current fashion. Then even the act of adorning themselves will be the expression of that virtue of modesty which sets the style of walking, standing, dressing, and all the exterior movements.

In following fashion, too, virtue lies in the golden mean. What God asks is always to bear in mind that fashion is not, and cannot be, the supreme rule of conduct; that above fashion and its dictates there are higher and more imperious laws, superior and immutable principles, that can in no case be sacrificed to the whim of pleasure or caprice, and before which the idol of fashion must be ready to abdicate its fleeting omnipotence. These principles have been proclaimed by God, by the Church, by the Saints, by Christian reason and morals, as marking the borderline beyond which no lilies and roses can grow and blossom, where neither purity, modesty, decency, nor feminine honor can spread their radiance, but where there prevails and dominates an unhealthy atmosphere of superficiality, insincere talk, bold vanity, vainglory no less of the soul than of clothing. These are the principles which St. Thomas Aquinas points out for feminine adornment and which he recalls when he teaches what should be the order of our charity, or our affections: the good of the soul must precede that of our body, and to the advantage of our own body we must prefer the welfare of our neighbor's soul. Is it not, then, clear that there is a limit which no style of fashion can make us overstep, and beyond which fashion works the ruin of one's own soul and those of others?

Some young women may say perhaps that a certain style of clothing is more convenient, and also more healthful; but if it becomes a serious and imminent danger to the salvation of the soul, it is certainly not healthy for the spirit: it becomes a duty to renounce it...

If, for mere personal pleasure, one has not the right to endanger the physical health of others, is it not perhaps still less permissible to compromise the health, nay, the very life, of their souls? If, as some women claim, bold fashions do not have a pernicious influence on them, what do they know of the effect they may have on others? What assurance have they that they do not arouse evil incentives?...

If some Christian women suspected the temptations and the downfalls they cause in others by their dress and overfamiliarity, to which, in their levity, they give such scant importance, they would be horrified by their responsibility.[†]

Matrimonial Trials in Ecclesiastical Courts

The Sole Aim in the Handling of Matrimonial Cases

In principle it must be stated that the unity of human action results from the following elements: a single aim, a common course by all toward this single aim, a juridical-moral obligation to take and preserve such direction. You understand well that of these elements the single aim constitutes the formal beginning and end, from the objective standpoint as well as the subjective. For, as every movement receives its direction from the end to which it tends, so also every conscious human activity is conditioned by the goal at which it aims.

In a matrimonial trial the sole aim is to arrive at a decision which conforms to truth and law, concerning, in the procedure for annulment, the asserted inexistence of the conjugal bond, and in the informative procedure *de vinculo solvendo*, the existence or nonexistence of the necessary prerequisites for the dissolution of the bond. In other words, the aim is to ascertain authoritatively and to enforce the truth and the law corresponding to truth, relative to the existence or the continuation of a matrimonial bond.

† Address to the Delegation of Young Women of Catholic Action (May 22, 1941).

The personal direction is established by the will of the individuals who have a part in handling the case, since they direct and subordinate their every thought, wish, and action on the facts of the case to the achievement of that end. Therefore, if all the participants constantly follow this course, their unity of action or co-operation will come as a natural consequence.

Finally, the third element, that is the juridical-moral obligation to maintain such a course, in matrimonial cases, derives from divine law. The nuptial contract, by its very nature, and between baptized persons, by its elevation to the dignity of Sacrament, is ordered and determined not by the will of man, but by God. It suffices to recall the words of Christ: "That which God has joined together, let no man put asunder," and the teachings of St. Paul: "*Sacramentum hoc magnum est, ego autem dico in Christo et in Ecclesia*—This is a great mystery—I mean in reference to Christ and to the Church." The gravity of this obligation, originating in divine law as if from a supreme and inexhaustible fount, must be strongly affirmed and stressed in the service of truth at the matrimonial trial. May it never happen that in matrimonial cases before the ecclesiastical tribunals there should appear deceit, perjury, subornation, or fraud of any sort! Therefore, all those who have any part in the trial must keep vigilant watch over their conscience and, if need be, rouse it and revivify it, in order to remember that these cases are conducted not before the tribunal of men but before that of the omniscient Lord, and that, consequently, the relative decisions, should some fraud which concerns the substance falsify them, are not valid before God and in the field of conscience.

The Unity of Aim and Action of Individual Participants in Matrimonial Cases

Unity and collaboration in matrimonial cases are effected, then, through the unity of aim, the direction toward the goal, the obligation of subordination to the goal. This triple element imposes essential demands on the personal action of the individual participants and marks it with a particular stamp.

The Judge

The judge, who is, as it were, the personification of justice, reaches the culmination of his work in pronouncing the sentence. Juridically it certifies and fixes the truth and gives it legal value, in all that concerns the actual fact under judgment as well as in all that refers to the law to be applied in the case. To this clarification and service of truth the whole trial is directed. Therefore, by the objective direction toward this goal, the judge finds a sure directive norm in every personal inquiry, judgment, prescription, prohibition, which the unfolding of the case brings with it. From this it becomes evident that the juridical-moral obligation to which the judge is subject is identical with the obligation already mentioned as deriving from divine law, that is to say, to search and determine according to the truth whether a bond which has been contracted by external signs exists in reality, or whether the necessary prerequisites for its dissolution exist. Once the truth is established, the judge has to pronounce the sentence in conformity with it. In this resides the great importance and personal responsibility of the judge in the direction and conclusion of the trial.

The Defender of the Bond

To the Defender of the bond falls the duty of sustaining the existence, or the continuation, of the conjugal bond, not, however, in the absolute sense, but in subordination to the aim of the trial, which is the search for and establishment of objective truth.

Hence, the Defender of the bond must collaborate toward the common goal, by investigating, explaining, and throwing light on whatever can be adduced in favor of the bond. So that he, who must be considered as *Pars necessaria ad iudicii validitatem et integritatem*—a party necessary for the validity and integrity of the trial, may effectively fulfill his office, the trial procedure has attributed to him particular rights and assigned him definite duties. And just as it would not be compatible with the importance of his position and the careful and faithful performance of his duty, if he were to content himself with a cursory survey of the facts and with a few superficial observations, similarly, it is not proper that such an office be entrusted to those who lack experience in life and maturity of judgment. The fact that the observations of the Defender of the bond are subjected to the examination of the judges is no exemption from this rule, since the judges must find in the accuracy of his efforts an aid and a complement to their own activity; nor can it be expected that they repeat the labor and the investigation of the Defender; rather must they be able to trust his findings.

On the other hand, one cannot demand of the Defender of the bond that he compose and prepare, at all costs, an artificial defense, without regard to the serious foundation of his affirmations. Such a demand would be contrary to reason; it would place on the Defender of the bond the burden of fruitless labor; it would bring no clarification, but rather confuse the issue; it would be damaging by dragging out the trial indefinitely. In the interest of truth itself and because of the dignity of his office, one must grant to the Defender of the bond, should the case require it, the right to declare that after diligent, accurate, and conscientious examination of the facts, he has found no reasonable objection to raise against the request of the plaintiff or the petitioner.

This fact and this consciousness, of not having to sustain unconditionally a thesis imposed upon him, but to be at the service of the truth as existing, will preserve the Defender of the bond from proposing questions which suggest one-sidedly the answer or set traps; from exaggerating and turning possibilities into probabilities or even accomplished facts; from affirming or construing contradictions, where sound judgment does not see them or easily dissolves them; from impugning the veracity of witnesses because of discrepancies or inexactness in nonessential points, or without importance for the object of the case—discrepancies or inexactitudes which, as the psychology of the depositions of witnesses teaches, are within the limits of the normal margin of error and do not detract from the value of the substance of the deposition itself. The consciousness of having to serve the end of truth will prevent the Defender of the bond from asking for new evidence when that on hand is already fully sufficient to establish the truth: on another occasion We have designated this as not to be approved.

Nor should it be objected that the Defender of the bond must put his animadversions on record not *pro rei veritate* but *pro validate matrimonii.* If by this one means that he, on his part, must emphasize all that speaks in favor and not that which is against the existence or the continuation of the bond, that is entirely correct. If, instead, it is meant to affirm that the Defender of the bond, in the performance of his task, is not also required to serve, as his ultimate goal, the ascertaining of the objective truth, but should unconditionally and independently from the evidence and the outcome of the trial sustain the obligated thesis of the existence, or of the necessary continuation, of the bond, this assertion must be considered false. In this sense, all those who take part in the trial must without exception make their action converge on the only goal: *pro rei veritate!*

The Promoter of Justice

We would not wish to omit some brief observations also concerning the Promoter of justice. It is possible that the public good requires a declaration of the nullity of a marriage and that the Promoter of justice makes a regular petition to the competent tribunal. At no other point would one be so much inclined to place in doubt the unity of purpose and collaboration of everyone involved in the matrimonial trial as here, where two public officers appear to take positions against each other before the tribunal: one, the Defender of the bond, must because of his office deny that which the other, also by his office, is called upon to promote. Instead, it is precisely here that the unity of purpose and the joint effort of all toward this end becomes most evident; for both, despite their apparent opposition, place before the judge basically the same request: to pronounce a verdict according to the truth and reality of the objective fact itself. The unity of purpose and collaboration would be broken only if the Defender of the bond and the Promoter of justice were to consider their own immediate and opposing aims as absolutes and were to free and separate them from their connection and subordination to the final common goal.

The Lawyer

But the unity of purpose, the direction toward the goal, and the obligation of subordination to the goal of the matrimonial trial must be considered and pondered with particular attention as regards the legal consultant or lawyer who serves the plaintiff, the defendant, or the petitioner, because more than anyone else he is in danger of losing sight of them.

The lawyer assists his client in formulating the introductory petition of the case; in clearly determining the object and the foundation of the controversy; in highlighting the decisive points of the fact to be judged; he indicates to him the evidence to put forward, the documents to exhibit; he suggests to him which witnesses are to be summoned to the trial and what points in the deposition of witnesses are unassailable; during the trial he helps him justly to evaluate the exceptions and counter-arguments and to confute them; in a word, he brings together and puts forward everything that may be adduced as evidence in favor of the request of his client.

In this manifold activity the lawyer may well make every effort to win the case for his client; but in all his action he cannot evade the single and common final aim: the legal discovery, the ascertainment and affirmation of truth, and of the objective fact. The consciousness of such subordination must guide the lawyer in his reflections, in his counsels, in his assertions, and in his proofs. It not only cautions him against artificially constructing or taking on a case without any serious foundation, from employing fraud or deceit, from inducing the parties and the witnesses to make false depositions, from having recourse to any other dishonest expedient, but it also positively causes him to proceed, in the entire series of the acts of the trial, according to the dictates of conscience. To the supreme end of making truth manifest, it is necessary that the efforts of the lawyer as well as the Defender of the bond develop in convergence, because both, though moving from opposite points with different immediate objectives, must tend toward the same final goal.

From this is apparent what must be thought of the principle unfortunately frequently affirmed or, in fact, followed. "The lawyer," it is said, "has the right and the duty to produce all that helps his thesis, no less than the Defender of the bond does in respect to the opposite thesis; for neither of the two is the norm *pro rei veritate* valid. The appraisal of the truth is exclusively the office of the judge; to burden the lawyer with such a task would mean impeding or even completely paralyzing his activity." Such an observation is based on a theoretical and practical error; it fails to recognize the innate nature and the essential final objective of the juridical controversy. In matrimonial cases this cannot be compared to a contest or a joust where the two contestants do not have a common final objective, but where each follows his particular and absolute aim, without regard, and actually in opposition, to that of his antagonist; the sole aim is to defeat the adversary and win a victory. In such a case the victor, by the success which crowns his struggle, creates the objective fact, which for the judge of the combat or the contest is the determining motive for conferring the prize, because for him it is law; to the winner, the prize. Quite the opposite occurs in the juridical contention of a matrimonial trial. Here one does not seek to create a fact with eloquence or dialectics, but to place in evidence and give value to an already existing fact. The above-mentioned principle attempts to separate the activity of the lawyer from the service of objective truth, and would somehow attribute to able argumentation the power to create a right, such as the victorious participant in a contest acquires.

The same consideration of the unconditional obligation to the truth also applies in the simple informative procedure following a request for the dissolution of the bond. The hearing of the case in the ecclesiastical forum does not provide for the intervention of a legal defender of the petitioner; but it is the natural right of the latter to make use on his own of the advice and assistance of a jurist in the preparation of the motivation of the petition, in the selection and presentation of witnesses, and in the overcoming of any difficulties that may arise. The legal consultant or the lawyer may put into operation here also all his knowledge and ability in favor of his client; but even in this extrajudicial activity he must bear in mind the obligation which binds him to the service of truth, his subjection to the common objective and to his part in obtaining it, as he participates in the common effort for the attainment of this objective.

From what We have expounded it appears clear that, in the handling of matrimonial cases in the ecclesiastical forum, the judge, the Defender of the bond, the Promoter of justice, and the lawyer must, as it were, make common cause and collaborate together, without interfering with the specific duty of each, but in conscious and desired union, and in submission to the same purpose.

The Parties, the Witnesses, the Experts

It is superfluous to add that the same fundamental law—to investigate, to clarify, and to give legal value to the truth—is also binding for the other participants in the trial. In order to assure attainment of this goal they are placed under oath. In this subordination to the end they find a clear norm for their interior orientation and their external action, and derive from it certainty of judgment and peace of conscience. Neither to the parties, the witnesses, nor the experts is it permissible to fabricate nonexistent facts, give to existent ones an unfounded interpretation, deny them, confuse them, or hide them. All this would be in contrast with the service they owe to truth, to which they are obligated by the law of God and the oath they have taken.

The Matrimonial Trial in Its Disposition and Subordination to the Universal Aim of the Church: the Salvation of the Soul

If we now pass in review what has already been said, we perceive clearly how the matrimonial trial represents a unity of purpose and action, in which the individual participants must exercise their particular office in reciprocal co-ordination and in common direction toward the same end; like the members of a body each of which, to be sure, has its own function and its own activity, but all of which are reciprocally co-ordinated and arranged together for the attainment of the final design, which is that of the entire organism.

Still, this consideration of the intimate nature of the matrimonial trial would remain incomplete without a look at its external relations.

The matrimonial trial in the ecclesiastical forum is a function of the juridical life of the Church. In Our Encyclical on the mystical body of Christ We expounded how the so-called "Juridical Church" is assuredly of divine origin, but is not the whole Church; how, in a way, she represents only the body, which must be vivified by the spirit, that is to say the Holy Ghost and Its grace. In the same Encyclical We explained likewise how the entire Church, in her body and her soul, as to the participation in goods and the profit which derives from them, is constituted exclusively for the "salvation of souls," according to the words of the Apostle: "*Omnia vestra sunt*—All are yours." With that is indicated the superior unity and the superior aim toward which are destined and directed the juridical life and every juridical function of the Church. It follows that also the thought, will, and personal effort in the exercise of such activity must tend toward the innate purpose of the Church: the care of souls. In other words, the superior purpose, the superior principle, the superior unity mean nothing other than "care of souls," just as all the labor of Christ on earth was the care of souls, and the care of souls was and is the entire action of the Church.

But the jurist who, as such, looks at naked law and rigid justice, is wont to show himself almost instinctively alien to the ideas and the intentions of the care of souls, and advocates a clear separation between the two forums, the forum of conscience and that of external juridico-social co-existence. Up to a certain point, this tendency toward a clear-cut division between the two fields is legitimate, inasmuch as the judge and his collaborators in the judicial procedure do not have pastoral care as their direct and particular duty. However, it would be a fatal error to affirm that in the final and definitive analysis they, too, are not in the service of souls. Thus they would be placing themselves, in the ecclesiastical judgment, outside the scope and the unity of action proper to the Church by divine institution; they would be like the members of a body which no longer fit themselves into its whole and no longer wish to submit and order their actions to the functioning of the entire organism.

The Effectiveness of Such Disposition and Subordination on Juridical Activity

Juridical activity, and particularly the judiciary, has nothing to fear from such disposition and subordination; rather, it is fecundated and promoted by it. The necessary breadth of vision and decision is assured by it, since, while unilateral juridical effort always hides within itself the danger of exaggerated formalism and adherence to the letter, the care of souls guarantees a counterweight, keeping awake in the conscience the maxim: "*Leges propter homines, et non homines propter leges*—Laws are instituted for men, and not men for laws." For this reason, on another occasion We warned that where the letter of the law might be an obstacle to the attainment of the truth, the way must always be open for appeal to the law maker.

The idea of being at the service of the purpose of the Church, furthermore, confers on all those who participate in her juridical activity the necessary independence and autonomy before the civil judiciary power. Between Church and State, as We pointed out in the aforementioned Encyclical on the mystical body of Christ, although both are, in the full meaning of the word, perfect societies, there is nevertheless a profound difference. The Church has her own particular character of divine origin and divine imprint. From this there derives also, in her juridical life, a trait particular to herself, an orientation, right to the final consequences, toward thoughts and goods of a higher order, supraworldly, eternal. Therefore, rather than an opinion, for various reasons it must be considered an erroneous judgment to say, as some do, that the ideal of ecclesiastical juridical practice consists in its greatest possible assimilation and conformity to the civil judiciary order. This stand, however, does not exclude the Church from taking advantage of true progress in the science of law even in this field.

Finally, the thought of belonging to this superior unity of the Church and subordination to her universal aim, the *salus animarum*, the salvation of souls, communicates to juridical activity the firmness to proceed on the sure path to truth and right, and preserves it no less from a weak condescension toward the disordinate covetousness of the passions than from a hard and unjustified inflexibility. The salvation of souls possesses as a guide a supreme, absolutely certain norm: the law and the will of God. To this same law and will of God juridical activity, which recognizes and is conscious of having no other aim save that of the Church, will direct itself firmly in handling the particular cases submitted to it, and will thus see confirmed in a superior order that which was already, in its own field, its fundamental maxim: service and affirmation of the truth in ascertaining the true fact and in applying to it the law and the will of God.[†]

† Message for the Inauguration of the Juridical Year of the Sacred Roman Rota (October 2, 1943).

Strength and Weakness, Children and the Aged

The word "infirm"—from the Latin *in-firmus*, not firm, not strong—indicates a being without strength, without firmness. Now in every family there are generally, first of all, two categories of beings that are weak and therefore stand in greater need of attention and affection: children and old people.

Instinct gives even irrational animals tenderness for their young. How, then, could it be necessary to inculcate it in you, young married couples and future Christian parents? It may happen, however, that too much severity, lack of understanding, may raise a sort of barrier between the hearts of children and those of their parents. St. Paul said: "To the weak I became weak…; I became all things to all men, that I might save all." It is a great quality to be able to become small with the small, a child with children, without compromising, by so doing, paternal or maternal authority. Then it will always be fitting within the family circle to ensure the old the respect, the tranquillity, the delicate attentions, as it were, which they need.

The aged! People are sometimes, perhaps unconsciously, hard with regard to their little demands, their innocent manias, wrinkles that time has impressed on their souls, like those that furrow their faces, but that should make them more venerable in the eyes of others. People are easily inclined to reprove them for what they no longer do, instead of reminding them again, as they deserve, of what they *have* done. One smiles, perhaps, at their weakening memory, and one does not always recognize the wisdom of their judgments. In their eyes, blurred by tears, you will look in vain for the flame of enthusiasm, but you can see the light of resignation in which there already burns the desire of eternal splendor…

However, when people speak of compassion for the weak, they usually mean persons of every age, afflicted with a physical infirmity, temporary or chronic.

In the garden of humanity, ever since it ceased to be called the earthly paradise, there has ripened and will always ripen one of the bitter fruits of original sin: pain. Instinctively man abhors it and avoids it; he would like to lose even the recollection and sight of it. But after Christ in the Incarnation "emptied" Himself, taking the form of a servant; after He chose to "elect the weak things of the world, to confound the strong"; after "Jesus, for the joy set before him, endured a cross, despising shame"; after He revealed to men the meaning of pain and the intimate joy of the gift of one's self to those who suffer, the human heart has discovered in itself unsuspected depths of tenderness and pity. Strength, it is true, is still the unchallenged ruler of unreasoning nature in the pagan souls of today, similar to those whom the Apostle St. Paul called in his time *sine affectione*, heartless, and *sine misericordia*, without pity for the poor and the weak. But for genuine Christians weakness has become a title claiming their respect, and infirmity a title claiming their love. For charity, unlike self-interest and selfishness, does not seek itself, but makes a gift of itself; and the weaker, the more miserable, the more needy and eager to receive is a being, the more it appears to the benevolent eye of charity to be an object of predilection.[†]

Faith, Hope, and Charity

If three notes are sufficient to fix with their harmony the tonality of a musical composition, the song of spring for the Christian could be condensed into three notes, the harmony of which brings his soul in tune with God Himself: faith, hope, and charity.

Faith is a theological virtue, through which we believe in God, who cannot be seen with the eyes of the body; in His infinite goodness, which His justice veils sometimes from human shortsightedness; in His omnipotence, which seems, to the premature reasoning of men, to be in contradiction with His mysterious long-suffering.

God, if He sometimes seems changeable, is actually unchangeable, because He is eternal; each of His dispositions arrives in its turn; each of His designs is accomplished at the time fixed by His Providence.

In the supernatural order, hope is, like faith, a theological virtue, that is, it links man personally with God. It does not yet raise the veil of faith, to show our eyes the eternal and divine object of celestial contemplations. But it brings

† Address to Married Couples (July 14, 1940).

the soul that co-operates with grace the assurance of its future possession, in the infallible promise of the Redeemer. It gives it a pledge and, as it were, a foretaste in the resurrection of God made man, which took place in a spring dawn.

Charity is above all a hymn of love. Real, pure love is the gift of oneself; it is the desire of diffusion and complete donation that is an essential part of goodness, and because of which God, infinite goodness, substantial charity, was moved to diffuse Himself in creation. This expansive force of love is so great that it admits of no limits. As the Creator has loved for eternity the creatures that He wants, by an omnipotent aspiration of His divine mercy, to call in time from nothingness into being: "*In caritate perpetua dilexi te; ideo attraxi te, miserans*—I have loved thee with an everlasting love; therefore have I drawn thee, taking pity on thee," so also the Word Incarnate, come among men, "*cum dilexisset suos, qui erant in mundo, in finem dilexit eos*—Having loved His own who were in the world, He loved them unto the end."†

Poverty and Charity

Father of all the faithful, We turn on humanity Our look of deep commiseration, moved by the many ills which today are added to its century-long sufferings. But We see, too, that to the trials and tribulations God permits in order to purify the guilty world, He opposes, as a remedy, new and ever more ingenious forms of charity.

The Apostle St. James noted it, one might say, not without a certain amount of irony: "What is the use of saying to those in need: warm yourselves and eat your fill, yet give not the things necessary to life?" And Jesus declares that on the last day all men will be judged on this practical exercise of charity. True charity is not limited to giving; it gives itself. Now, to visit the poor, one must leave one's home, one's comfort, and often renounce the habits and the spirit of the world. The Apostle St. John provides the warning: "If any man love the world, the charity of the Father is not in him."

† Address to Married Couples (April 3, 1940).

The poor man, who has a soul just like the rich man's, has, like him, also a heart; and how little is needed sometimes to console him in his distress or assuage the bitterness of his rebellion! In many a hovel into which a person of active and cheerful dedication has entered, even if with but modest material assistance, the words of Wisdom will come true: "*Melius est vocari ad olera cum caritate, quam ad vitulum saginatum cum odio*—It is better to be invited to herbs with love, than to a fatted calf with hatred." Therefore, stimulating you to translate your feeling of pity into acts of benevolence, the poor man makes you realize at the same time the necessity of accompanying the acts by feeling, without which the gesture would remain cold and the word indifferent. Furthermore, the poor man unites you again to God by his example. Sometimes wonderful virtues blossom under miserable roofs.

O charity! Virgin with shining eyes, consoling Mother, Sister with soothing hands. You alone make this earth inhabitable for the unhappy, the orphans, the oppressed, the homeless. You reveal to man the intimate goodness of his heart, and show the earth the best image of God, which is substantial "charity." The only eternal virtue, it will triumph in glory, when faith and hope no longer exist. May it triumph now also in the world! How beautiful it seems, and more desirable than ever at this time in which violence, the daughter of hatred, seems to want to banish it! How good it seems, and more than ever necessary, to this agitated and tormented humanity, which does not want to believe in truth, no longer dares believe in justice, but cannot reconcile itself to denying charity!

Woe to the madmen whose fury is bent on destroying this immortal virtue! Woe to the Pharisees with arid souls and empty looks, who do not see the splendor in its face! Woe to the learned, with deaf hearts, who hear not the echo of its voice alleviating the sorrows of humanity! Woe to the false prophets of universal happiness, whose eyes consume themselves in a vision of the phantasm of complete and definitive justice on earth, and see in charity nothing but an importunate and intruding defamer of her regal sister!

Because it has failed to recognize charity, the world has lost true peace, nor will it find it again until it has once more raised, on the indispensable foundations of justice, the throne of charity. Threatened by a new flood, humanity is anxiously awaiting the return of the dove, herald of the rainbow of peace. But the winged messenger will not bring universal peace to individuals and nations unless it can gather once more on earth the green branch of the olive tree, with soothing salves, which requires, to grow and bear its fruit, the sunshine of charity.[†]

Man the Machine

One might say that present-day humanity, which has known how to build the admirable, complex machine of the modern world, harnessing massive forces of nature to its service, still shows itself incapable of dominating their course, almost as if the rudder had slipped from its hand and, therefore, it runs the risk of being overwhelmed and crushed by them. Such inability to control should, of itself, suggest to men, who are its victims, not to seek salvation solely from the technicians of production and of organization. Their accomplishments can contribute, and notably so, to resolving the grave and extended problems which afflict the earth, only if bound and directed to bettering and strengthening true human values; but in no case—oh, how We wish that all, on both sides of the ocean, recognize this!—can it succeed in forming a world without misery.

One knows where to search for technology in social thinking: in the giant undertakings of modern industry. We have no intention here to pronounce a judgment on the necessity, the utility, and the conveniences of similar forms of production. Without doubt they are the marvelous realizations of the inventive and constructive power of the human spirit; very rightly these enterprises which, through carefully thought-out norms, succeed in production and administration, in co-ordinating and pooling the action of men and things, are held up to universal admiration; there is no doubt likewise that their solid order and quite frequently the completely new and unique beauty of their external forms are reason for legitimate pride at the present time. However, what We must deny is that they can and must be used as a general model for the conformation and organization of modern social life.

† Address to the Ladies of St. Vincent (March 13, 1940).

First of all, it is a clear principle of wisdom that every progress is truly such if it knows how to add new conquests to the old, new advantages to those acquired in the past, in short, if it knows how to store up experience. Now, history teaches that other forms of national economy have always had a positive influence on the entire social life; an influence of which both essential institutions such as the family, the State, private property, and those institutions formed through free association, have taken advantage. We cite as an example the indisputable advantages which appear wherever agricultural enterprise and the crafts predominated.

Without doubt, modern industrial enterprise also has had beneficial effects; but the problem which presents itself today is this: Will a world which recognizes only the economic forms of an enormous productive organization be capable of exercising a happy influence on social life in general, and on those three fundamental institutions in particular? We must answer that the impersonal character of such a world contrasts with the completely personal tendency of those institutions, which the Creator has given to human society. In fact, matrimony and the family, the State, and private property tend by nature to form and develop man as a person, to protect him, and render him capable of contributing, by his voluntary collaboration and personal responsibility, to the maintenance and development, personal also, of social life. The creative wisdom of God, therefore, remains foreign to that system of impersonal unity which makes attempts on the human person, fount and aim of social life, image of God in His most intimate being.

The Demon of Organization

Unfortunately, We are not dealing here with hypotheses or forecasts; this sad reality is already in being. Wherever the demon of organization invades and tyrannizes the human spirit, signs of false and abnormal orientation of social development come to light at once. In not a few countries the modern State is becoming a giant administrative machine. Its hand reaches into practically all facets of life: it attempts to make the entire scale of political, economic, social, and intellectual sectors its field of administration, even birth and death. No wonder, therefore, if in this impersonal climate which tends to penetrate and envelop all life, the sense of the common good becomes dull in the conscience of individuals, and the State loses more and more its primordial character of a moral community of citizens.

Thus is revealed the origin and the point of departure of the current which sweeps modern man into a state of anguish; his "depersonalization." His face and name have been taken away from him to a large extent; in many of the most important activities of life he has been reduced to a mere object of society, since society, in turn, is transformed into an impersonal system, a cold organization of forces.

Unemployment

Whoever still nourishes doubts about this state of affairs, let him turn his attention to the populous world of misery, and ask the various categories of the needy what answer society usually is wont to give them, oriented as it is toward nonrecognition of the person. Ask the ordinary poor, deprived of all resources, who are certainly not rare to encounter in the cities as in the towns and the country; ask the father of a needy family, assiduous client of the bureau of social assistance, whose children cannot wait for the vague, distant deadlines of a golden era always still to come. Ask also an entire people on an inferior or extremely low level of existence who, while taking a place in the family of nations beside their brothers who live in sufficiency or even abundance, wait in vain from one international conference to the other for a stable improvement of their plight. What is the answer which present-day society gives to the unemployed person who presents himself at the windows of the Unemployment Office, prepared, perhaps, through habit to be disappointed anew, but still unresigned to the unmerited destiny of considering himself a useless being? And what is the answer given to a whole people which, no matter how much it tries or struggles, does not succeed in freeing itself from the atrophying grip of mass unemployment?

To all of them for a long time now, it has been incessantly repeated that their case cannot be treated as personal or individual; that the solution must be found in an order yet to be established, in a system which will be all-embracing and which, without basic prejudice to liberty, will lead men and things to a more united and growing force of action, making use of an ever more profound exploitation of technical progress. When such a system shall be arrived at, salvation for all—it is said—shall gush forth automatically, ever improving living conditions and providing full employment everywhere.

The Standard of Living

Far from believing that the persistent deferring of men and things to the future powerful organization is a despicable diversion invented by those who do not wish to help; believing instead that it is a solid, sincere promise, intended to instill faith—one still cannot see, however, on what serious foundations it can rest, since the experiences to date induce rather to skepticism toward the chosen system. This skepticism is justified also by a sort of vicious circle, in which the end established and the means adopted pursue one another without ever coming together or reaching an accord; in fact, where there is an attempt to assure full employment by a continuous improvement of living standards, there is reason to ask oneself with anxiety up to what point it can increase without provoking a catastrophe, and, above all, without causing mass unemployment. It seems, therefore, that the effort should be toward the highest possible level of employment, but with a simultaneous attempt to guarantee its stability.

No faith, therefore, can illuminate a similar scene, dominated by the specter of that insoluble contradiction, nor can its spiral be evaded if men persist in counting on the sole element of top productivity. It is necessary to consider the concepts of living standards and employment of labor no longer as purely quantitative factors but rather as human values in the full sense of the word.

Hence, whoever wants to bring succor to the needs of individuals and peoples cannot await salvation from an impersonal system of men and things, even though it may be strongly developed from the technical standpoint. Every plan or program must be inspired by the principle that man, as a subject, custodian, and promoter of human values, is above things, even above the application of technical progress, and that it is necessary, above all, to preserve from unhealthy "depersonalization" the fundamental forms of social order and utilize them to create and develop human relations. If the social forces should be directed to this end, they will not only fulfill one of their natural functions, but will also be a powerful contribution toward satisfying present necessities, because to them belongs the mission of promoting the full, reciprocal solidarity of men and peoples.

We invite you to erect society on the basis of this solidarity, and not on vain and unstable systems. It requires that the strident, irritating disproportions in the living standards of different groups of people disappear. Rather than external compulsion, it is preferable to exert for this urgent purpose the effective action of conscience, which will impose limits on luxury spending and at the same time induce those who are less well off to think, above all, of the necessary and useful, and then to save the rest, if there is any.

The solidarity of men among themselves demands, not only in the name of fraternal sentiment but also for reciprocal convenience itself, that all possibilities be employed to preserve existing jobs and create new ones. Therefore, those who can invest capital should consider, in view of the common good, whether, within the proportion and limits of their economic possibilities, and at opportune moments, they can reconcile with their conscience not making such investments and, through vain caution, withdraw into inactivity. On the other hand, those who, egotistically exploiting their occupations, prevent others from finding work and cause them to join the ranks of the unemployed, act against conscience. Wherever, also, private enterprise is inoperative or insufficient, the public powers are obliged to provide jobs to the largest extent possible by undertaking projects of general utility and to facilitate with recommendations and other help the employment of those who seek it.

But our invitation to fortify the sentiment and obligation of solidarity extends also to peoples as such; each of them should, in the matter of living standards and employment of labor, develop its own possibilities and contribute to the corresponding progress of other peoples who are less favored. Although even the most perfect realization of international solidarity could hardly bring about absolute equality of peoples, nevertheless it must be practiced at least to the extent of noticeably modifying present conditions, which are far from

† Address to the Sacred College (December 24, 1952).

representing harmonious proportions. In other words, the solidarity of peoples demands the end of the notable disproportions in living standards, and also in investments and the degree of productivity of human labor.

However, such a result cannot be obtained through a mechanical arrangement. Human society is not a machine, and must not become one, not even in the economic field. On the contrary, the contribution of the human being and the individuality of peoples must be employed constantly as a lever against the natural and primordial fulcrum from which one must always start toward the goal of public economy, that is to say, to assure permanent satisfaction in material goods and services, which in turn are directed toward strengthening moral, cultural, and religious conditions.[†]

PART TWO

EDUCATION
THE SCIENCES
THE ARTS

The Education of the Child

Our spirit looks upon the innumerable ranks of adolescents, seeing them as buds opening at the first light of dawn. Prodigious and enchanting is this thronging of youth from a generation which seemed almost condemned to extinction; new youth, throbbing with its freshness and vigor, with eyes fixed on the future, with an unswerving impulse toward higher goals, resolved to improve upon the past and to assure more lasting and more valuable conquests for man's journey on earth. Of this unrestrainable and perennial current toward human perfection, directed and guided by divine Providence, the educators are the most direct and responsible moderators, associated with this same Providence to carry out its designs. It depends on them, in great part, whether the tide of civilization advances or retrogresses, whether it strengthens its impetus or languishes from inertia, whether it goes swiftly toward the mouth of the river or, on the contrary, pauses, at least momentarily, in useless byways, or worse, in unhealthy and swampy backwaters.

We Ourselves, by divine disposition Vicar, and thus invested with the same offices as He who on earth loved to be addressed as "Master," We include Ourselves in the number of those who, in various measure, represent the hand of Providence in leading man to his appointed end.

Is not indeed this See of Ours principally a teaching platform? Is not Our first office that of teaching? Did not the Divine Master and Founder of the Church give to Peter and the Apostles the fundamental precept: Go forth and teach, make disciples?

We feel Ourselves to be, and We are, educators of souls. The Church is no less a sublime school, for a great part of the priest's office consists in teaching and educating. Nor could it be otherwise in the new order established by Christ, which is founded entirely on the relationship of the Fatherhood of God, from which all other paternity in Heaven and on earth is derived, and from which, in Christ and through Christ, Our paternity toward all souls extends. Now, a father is an educator by the very fact of being a father since, as the Angelic Doctor so luminously explains, the basic right to teach is based on no other title but that of fatherhood.

Immense is the responsibility we share together; even if in varying degree, but not in entirely different fields: the responsibility for souls, for civilization, for the betterment and the happiness of man on earth and in Heaven.

If at this moment We have turned Our discourse to a wider field, such as that of education, We have done so with the thought that the erroneous doctrine which used to separate the formation of the intellect from that of the heart may by now be said to be surpassed, at least in principle. In fact, We must deplore that in recent years the limits of what is right have been overstepped in interpreting the norm which identifies teacher with educator, and school with life. Having recognized the potent formative value of the school on the conscience, some governments, regimes, and political movements have found in the school one of the most efficient means for winning over to their side that mass of supporters which they need for the triumph of certain conceptions of life. With a tactic as astute as it is insincere, and for reasons which contrast with the natural ends of education itself, some of the movements of the past and present century have pretended to subtract the school from the supervision of those institutions which, besides the State, had a primordial right—the family and the Church—and have attempted, or attempt, to gain exclusive possession of it, imposing a monopoly which is, among other things, gravely damaging to one of the fundamental human liberties.

But this See of Peter, vigilant guardian of the good of souls and of true progress, just as it has never in the past abdicated this essential right, besides admirably exercising it at all times through its institutions, which were often alone in dedicating themselves to it, will never surrender it in the future, either for hope of earthly advantages or through fear of persecution. It will never consent that either the Church, which has received it through divine mandate, or the family, which claims it through natural justice, be deprived of the effective exercise of their native right. The faithful throughout the world are witnesses of the firmness of this Apostolic See in defending the liberty of the school among a great variety of lands, circumstances, and men. For the school, and at the same time for the cult and the sanctity of marriage, the Holy See has not hesitated to face every difficulty and danger with the serene conscience of one who serves a just, holy cause, according to God's will, and with the certainty of performing an inestimable service to civil society itself.

On the other hand, in those countries where the freedom of the school is guaranteed by just laws, it is up to the teachers to know how to make effective use of them, insisting upon their actual application.

The Modern School

If it is excellent practice to prize those systems and methods which have been proven by experience, then it is necessary to weigh with every care the theories and usages of modern teaching institutions before accepting them. The good results which may perhaps have been obtained in countries whose populations have a different outlook and a different level of culture from yours, do not always give sufficient guarantee that those same doctrines may be applied everywhere without distinction.

The school cannot be compared to a chemical laboratory, in which the risk of wasting more or less costly substances is compensated by the probability of a discovery; for every single soul in the school salvation or ruin is at stake. Therefore, those innovations which will be judged opportune will involve, to be sure, the selection of secondary pedagogical means and directions without touching the end and substance, which will always be the same, as the final end of education, its subject, its principal author and inspiration are always identical—namely God our Lord.

The Teacher

The teacher, the educator who draws inspiration from the role of fatherhood, whose final end is the generation of human beings similar to ourselves, will form his students with the example of his life no less than with precepts. If he does not do so, his work will be—in St. Augustine's terms—that of a "merchant of words" and not of a shaper of souls. Moral teachings themselves have only a superficial effect upon the spirit unless they are buttressed by acts. Indeed, the very exposition of school disciplines will not be fully assimilated by the young unless it comes forth from the teacher's lips as live, personal expression: no subject will be profitably received by the student when it is presented without enthusiasm, as a matter extraneous to the life and interests of the person who teaches it.

Educators of the present day, who draw sure guidance from the past, what ideal image of man must you prepare for the future? You find it basically delineated in the perfect Christian. And in saying perfect Christian, We have in mind the Christian of today, a man of his times, who knows and admires all the progress brought about by science and technology, a citizen who is not a stranger to life as it unfolds today in his own country. The world will not regret it if an increasingly large number of such Christians occupy positions in every department of private and public life. It depends largely upon teachers to prepare the ground for this beneficial introduction by directing their students to a discovery of the inexhaustible energies of Christianity in the work of the improvement and renewal of peoples.

The Students

Let the students become accustomed to the difficult work of the intellect, and let them learn the severity and the necessity of work in order to enjoy the rights of living in society in the very same way as the manual laborer does. It is time to enlarge their views on a world less ridden with reciprocally envious factions, with extreme nationalisms and desires for hegemony, for which the present generations have suffered so much. Let the new youth open itself to the spirit of Catholicism, and let it feel the power of that universal love which gathers together all the peoples of the world in the One Lord. Conscious of their personality, and therefore of the greater treasure of freedom; healthily critical; but at the same time, with a sense of Christian humility, rightly subject to the laws and to the duties of solidarity; religious, honest, cultured, open minded, and enterprising: this is how We would like to see youth come forth from the schools.[†]

The Boarding School: Its Effects and Its Purposes

We feel that it is impossible in the education of youth to be satisfied simply with good results, without a reasonable effort being made to strive after perfection with the help of God's grace. Well, then, as One who has a particular love for youth at study, We should like to take this opportunity to set before you some thoughts on the educative work of schools. This We do for your benefit and also for that of so many other young people whose future, and that of society itself, depends upon the few short years spent at school.

Boarding school education has given good results in the past and is still doing so. Recently, however, it has been the object of severe criticism on the part of certain experts in pedagogy. These would like to see it abolished as though it were totally inept. But their criticisms, even when backed by this or that manifest defect, do not constitute a sufficiently good reason for a sweeping condemnation of this type of education in itself.

It is certainly true that the natural milieu of the home, when helped by the Church and its deficiencies made good by the school, is best suited to assure a good and even perfect education. Frequently, however, circumstances of place, of work, or the persons concerned prevent the family from fulfilling this difficult task on its own. In such cases the boarding school becomes a providential institution without which countless young people would be deprived of a great good.

---

† Address to Catholic Action (September 4, 1949).

Parents Still Responsible

But parents are not freed from the duty of caring for their children; rather must their influence be allowed to penetrate the boarding school itself, for they too have their part to play in that general formation which is the objective of the school. Between education within the family circle, which is often impracticable, and full-time education at a boarding school we have the system of part-time board, which combines the advantages of education at home with those proper to boarding schools.

The chief advantages of the latter are that it develops in the character a more rigorous sense of duty, a spirit of discipline and precision, as well as the habit of organizing one's own activity.

To these must be added a sense of responsibility for one's actions. In school a boy in time learns to live in society, thanks to the variety of relations he has with his superiors, his fellow pupils, and those junior to him in age. He is incited to a healthy emulation, a right sense of honor, and the acceptance of inevitable sacrifices. Such dispositions acquired when he is still young will doubtless help him to face life's vicissitudes and will help him to fulfill the duties of his own particular state. Excess and defect in method, however, can compromise the attainment of these results to such an extent that the outcome may be quite the contrary and so give rise to the charge that boarding school education is fruitless and harmful.

Too Rigid Discipline

A communal life away from one's environment, especially if discipline is so rigid as not to distinguish one individual from another, undoubtedly has its dangers. Even small errors in method can produce boys who will have anything but a sense of personal responsibility. Because of their mechanical discharge of their duties, their study, discipline, and prayer unconsciously become mere matters of form. Strict uniformity tends to suffocate personal initiative; a secluded life to restrict a wide vision of the world. An inflexible insistence on rules sometimes gives rise to hypocrisy, or imposes a spiritual level which for one will be too low and for another, on the contrary, unattainable. Excessive severity ends by making rebels of strong characters, while the timid become depressed and secretive.

It is possible and indeed imperative that these dangers be obviated by means of discernment, moderation, and kindness. In the first place one must learn to regard each boy as an individual of specific character. So-called mass education, as likewise mass teaching, is certainly less costly in effort but runs the risk of being of use to only some boys, while all have the right to profit by it.

It is one of the laws of life that children are never quite alike, either in intelligence or in character or in other spiritual qualities. When, therefore, one is arranging their way of life, or correcting or judging them, this individuality must be borne in mind. At least one must avoid that excessive uniformity which sometimes requires hundreds of boys of different ages to study, sleep, dine, and play in the same building—with the same timetable and rules for all.

Individual Attention

One way of obviating the disadvantages of such an arrangement is to divide the boys into homogeneous groups of such proportions as not to make it impossible for those in charge to have a paternal interest in each individual. Each group would have the timetable, rules, and activity best suited to it. It is true that from the complex of moral and spiritual values of which he is made aware through the education he receives at his school, through a judicious choice of books and through good example, the normal youth will choose what he needs for his right formation.

Yet this is not enough. He must further feel himself the object of a special attention on the part of the educator. He should never have the impression of being lost and forgotten in the mass—his own particular requirements disregarded, his needs and weaknesses overlooked—as if only his mere physical presence were of account. This individual attention will stimulate the boy to mold and develop his own personal character. It will develop a spirit of enterprise and a sense of responsibility toward his superiors and his fellows, just as if he were living in the bosom of a large and well-ordered family.

Moderation Necessary, Even in Pious Practices

The second characteristic of school life should be moderation. The old precept "*ne quid nimis,*" which is the same as the other "*in medio stat virtus,*" must inspire every act of the educator, be it when he draws up a rule or insists on its observance. An enlightened sense of discretion should determine the length of study time and of recreation. This same discretion should be in evidence when awarding prizes and when taking disciplinary action, when finding the balance between personal freedom and the enforcement of rules.

Even pious practices must know the right measure, so that they do not become insupportable or tedious to the soul. Not infrequently have deplorable results been noted from an excessive zeal in this matter. Boys of Catholic boarding schools where moderation has not been a guiding principle, but which have sought to impose a tenor of religious practices hardly suitable for young clerics, have been seen to neglect, on their return to their families, the most elementary duties of a Christian, such as going to Mass on Sunday. One should, indeed, help and exhort young men to pray but always in such measure that prayer remains a refreshing need of the soul.

Gentleness with the Young

Thirdly, an aura of gentleness should prevail in every school, of a kind, however, that will not undermine the formation of strong characters. Young people, especially those of good family background, are formed to a sense of duty through personal persuasion, rational arguments, and affection. A boy who is convinced of the love his parents and superiors have for him will not fail to respond, sooner or later, to their solicitude. Therefore the command which cannot be reasonably justified, the reproof which betrays personal rancor, as also purely vindictive punishment, must be rejected.

Gentleness is to be abandoned only as a last resort, for a short time, and in individual cases. It must control our judgment and override strict justice because a boy is rarely mature enough to understand evil fully or so set upon it as not to be able to return to the path of righteousness when once this has been shown him.

Your work in education cannot fail to show excellent results if these general, though practical, norms are diligently applied. You should also bear in mind the helpful recommendations which your knowledge of pedagogy will suggest to you.†

Conscience and Education

THE object of education and its role in the natural order is the development of a child to make a complete man of him; the role and object of Christian education is the formation of a new human being, reborn in baptism, into a perfect Christian.

We would now draw attention to an element which, though it is the basis and lever of education, especially of Christian education, seems to some people, at first sight, almost extraneous thereto. We would like to speak of that which is deepest and most intrinsic in man: conscience. We are led to do this by the fact that some currents of modern thought are beginning to alter its conception and question its value. We will therefore treat of conscience in so far as it forms the subject matter of education.

Conscience is, so to speak, the innermost and most secret nucleus in man. It is there that he takes refuge with his spiritual faculties in absolute solitude: alone with himself or, rather, alone with God—whose voice sounds in conscience—and with himself. There it is that he decides for good or evil; there it is that he chooses between the way of victory and that of defeat. Even if he should wish to do so, a man could never shake off conscience; with it, whether it approves or condemns, he will travel along the whole way of his life, and likewise with it, a truthful and incorruptible witness, he will come up for God's judgment. Hence conscience, to express it with an image as old as it is fitting, is a sanctuary on the threshold of which all must halt, even, in the case of a child, his father and mother. Only the priest enters there, as entrusted

† Address to Students and Faculty of the Convitto Nazionale Maschile di Roma (April 1956).

with the care of souls and as minister in the Sacrament of Penance; nor for this reason does conscience cease to be a jealous sanctuary of which God Himself wishes the secrecy to be preserved through the seal of the most sacred silence.

In which sense can one then talk of the education of conscience?

It will be necessary to call to mind some of the fundamental Catholic doctrinal conceptions in order to understand well that conscience can and must be educated.

Our divine Savior has brought to ignorant and feeble man His truth and grace: truth, to show him the way toward his goal; grace, to give him the strength to reach it.

To go along that way means, in practice, to accept the will and the commandments of Christ and to conform one's life to them, i.e., each single act, inner or exterior, which the free human will chooses and decides upon. Now, what is the spiritual faculty, if not conscience, that, in each particular case, gives guidance to the will so that it may choose and determine its actions in conformance to the divine will? Conscience, then, is the faithful echo, the clear reflection of human action's divine pattern. Therefore, expressions such as "the judgment of the Christian conscience" or, "to judge according to the Christian conscience," mean this: that the pattern of the ultimate and personal decision for a moral action must be taken from the word and will of Christ. In fact, He is the way, the truth, and the life, not only for all men collectively, but for each single one; the mature man, the child, and the youth.

Formation of the Conscience and Christian Morality

From this it follows that the formation of the Christian conscience of a child or a youth consists above all in illuminating his mind with respect to Christ's will, law, and way; acting, besides, on his mind as much as this can be done from outside, so as to induce him freely and constantly to execute the divine will. This is the highest task of education.

But where shall the educator and the youth find in each individual case with ease and certainty the Christian moral law? They will find it in the law of the Creator imprinted in the heart of each one as well as in revelation, that is, in all the truth and precepts taught by the divine Master. Both the law written in the heart, that is, the natural law, and the truth and precepts of supernatural revelation, have been given by Jesus the Redeemer into the hands of His Church as humanity's moral treasure, so that the Church may preach them, intact and protected against any contamination and error, to all creatures, from one generation to another.

Against this doctrine, uncontroverted for many centuries, there are now emerging difficulties and objections which call for clarification.

For dogmatic doctrine as well as for the Catholic moral order the application of an almost radical revision is being advocated, with a view to deducing a new scale of values from it.

The primary step or, rather, the first blow against the edifice of Christian moral canons should be—as is pretended—the redeeming of these rules from the narrow and oppressive guardianship of the authority of the Church, so that, freed from the sophistic subtleties of the casuistic method, morality may be brought back again to its original form and left to the individual's intelligence and determination. Anyone can see to what baneful results such overturning of the very foundations of education would lead.

Omitting to point out the obvious inexperience and immaturity of judgment of those who maintain such opinions, it will be well to bring into light the central flaw of this "new morality." By leaving all ethical judgment to the conscience of the individual, jealously closed in itself and made sole arbiter of its determinations, this morality, far from smoothing the way for it, would make it stray from the main road which is Christ

The divine Redeemer has given His relevation, of which moral obligations are an essential part, not to individual men but to His Church, with the mission to lead men faithfully to accept that sacred deposit.

Likewise, divine assistance, intended to preserve revelation from errors and distortions, was promised to the Church and not to individuals. A wise provision, because the Church, a living organism, may thus illustrate and probe truths, even moral truths, with certainty and flexibility, and apply them to the variable conditions of times and places without altering their substance.

How then is it possible to reconcile the Savior's providential disposition, through which the Church was entrusted with the Christian moral heritage, with a sort of individualistic autonomy of conscience?

Purity of Soul and Body

The "new morality" affirms that the Church, instead of urging the law of human liberty and of love, and enforcing it as the worthy dynamic force of moral life, leans instead almost exclusively and with excessive rigidity on the firmness and the irrevocability of Christian moral laws, resorting frequently to the admonitions "you must" and "it is not lawful," smacking all too often of demeaning pedantry.

The Church wishes instead—and this is expressly emphasized with regard to the forming of consciences—that a Christian should be introduced to the infinite riches of faith and grace in a persuasive manner, so that he may feel inclined to penetrate deeply into them.

The Church, however, cannot give up admonishing the faithful that these riches cannot be acquired and kept without observing some precise moral obligations. A different behavior would only end by putting into oblivion a dominant principle which Jesus, its Lord and Master, always insisted upon. Jesus did in fact teach that it is not enough to say "Lord! Lord!" in order to enter the Kingdom of Heaven, but that it is necessary to do the will of our heavenly Father. He spoke of the "strait gate," of the "narrow way," which leads to life and added: "Strive to enter by the narrow gate; for many shall seek to enter, and shall not be able." He gave as a touchstone and hallmark of love for Himself, Christ, the observance of the commandments. Likewise, to the rich young man questioning Him, He said: "If thou wouldst enter into life, keep the commandments," and to the further question: "Which?" He replied: "Thou shall not kill, thou shalt not commit adultery, thou shalt not steal, thou shalt not bear false witness, thou shalt honor thy father and thy mother, and love thy neighbor as thyself." He has put as a condition to those who want to follow Him that they have to renounce themselves and take up His Cross daily. He demands that man be ready to forsake for Him and for His sake his most cherished possessions, his father, his mother, and his own children, up to his ultimate wealth, his own life. Because, He added: "I say unto ye, my friends; fear not those who kill the body and can do no more. I shall show ye whom ye shall fear: fear Him who, when life has been taken away, has the power to cast into hell."

Thus spoke Jesus Christ, the divine Teacher, who certainly knew better than men how to penetrate into souls and attract them to His love, with the infinite perfection of His heart, *bonitate et amore plenum*—full of goodness and love.

Therefore, taking the words of Christ strictly as a standard, should it not perhaps be said that the Church of today is inclined to lenience rather than to severity? Thus, the accusation of oppressive harshness which the "new morality" raises against the Church in reality attacks first and foremost the Person of Christ.

The Moral Obligations of Youth

Therefore, being conscious of the right and of the duty of the Apostolic See to intervene authoritatively, when necessary, on moral questions, We declare to educators and to youth: the divine commandment to be pure in soul and body applies without diminution also to today's youth. The youth of today has also the moral obligation and the possibility of keeping itself pure with the aid of grace. We reject, therefore, as erroneous the claim of those who consider inevitable the failings of the age of puberty, considered by them of no great import and almost as if they were not a grave fault, because, they add, passion cancels the liberty which is required to make a person morally responsible for an act.

On the contrary, it is required from a wise educator that, without neglecting to impress on his youthful charges the noble qualities of purity so as to induce them to love and desire it for its own sake, he should at the same time clearly inculcate the commandment as it stands, in all its gravity and earnestness as a divine order. He will thus urge them to avoid immediate occasions, he will comfort them in the struggle, of which he shall not hide the hardness, he will induce them to embrace courageously the sacrifices demanded by virtue, and he will exhort them to persevere and not to fall into the danger of surrendering from the very beginning and thus succumbing passively to perverse habits.

General Validity of Christian Moral Laws

Even more than from the field of private behavior many today would like to exclude the dominion of moral law from public, social, and economic life, from the action of internal and external public powers, in war and in peace, as if God had nothing to say there, at least nothing binding.

The emancipation of outward human activities such as the sciences, politics, and art from morality is sometimes motivated from a philosophical point of view by the autonomy which belongs to them, in their own field, to be governed exclusively by their own laws, although it is admitted that, as a rule, these laws agree with the moral laws. The example usually given is art, for which not only any dependence but also any connection with morality is denied since "Art is only art and not morality or anything else, and is subject therefore only to aesthetic laws; these, however, if truly aesthetic, will not lend themselves to serve lust." In a similar way one speaks of politics and economy, which do not require the counsel of other sciences and therefore of ethics, but, being guided by their own laws, are for that very reason good and just.

This evidently is a subtle way of removing consciences from the dominion of moral laws. One cannot deny that such autonomies are justified, inasmuch as they express the method peculiar to each activity and the boundaries which separate their various forms in theory. But the separation of method should not signify that the scientist, the artist, the politician, are independent from moral responsibilities in the carrying out of their activities, especially if these have an immediate repercussion in the field of ethics, as in the case of art, politics, and economy. A clear-cut and theoretical separation has no sense in life, which is always a synthesis, because the sole subject of any kind of activity is man himself, whose free and conscious acts cannot avoid moral evaluation. Furthermore, considering the problem from a wide and practical viewpoint which is sometimes wanting even in outstanding philosophers, it can be said that such distinctions and autonomies are perverted by decadent human nature in such a way as to make appear as the laws of art, politics, and economy what in reality serves lust, selfishness, and greed. Thus, the theoretical independence from morality becomes, in practice, rebellion against morality and the harmony inherent in the sciences and arts, which even the philosophers of that school of thought clearly detect but call accidental, is thereby destroyed, while, instead, it is essential when considered in relation to the subject, which is man, and to its Creator, which is God.

We have never ceased to insist on the principle that the order of God embraces the whole of life, with the inclusion of public life, in all of its manifestations, being convinced that in this principle there is no restriction of genuine human freedom or any intrusion into the province of the State, but a shield against errors and abuses from which Christian morality, if rightly applied, is able to protect. These truths must be taught to youth and inculcated in the youthful consciences by those who, in the family or in the school, have the obligation to attend to their education, sowing thus the seed of a better future.†

Fundamental Rights of the Christian Family

Time and time again We have insisted—in connection with various problems—on the sanctity of the family, on its rights, on its tasks as the fundamental cell of human society. Its life, its health, its vigor, its activities ensure the life, health, vigor, and activities of society as a whole. For its existence, its dignity, its social function derived from God, the family must answer to God. Its rights and privileges are inalienable, intangible; it is its duty, above all before God, and in the second place before society, to defend, to claim, to promote effectively these rights and privileges, not only for its own benefit but for the glory of God, for the welfare of the community at large.

How often have been sung the praises of the mother, considered the very heart, the sun of the family! But if the mother is its heart, the father is its head; the health and efficiency of the family depend, therefore, first of all upon the ability, the virtues, the activities of the father.

For the Christian there is a rule which enables him to determine with certitude the extent of the rights and duties of the family within the community of the State. This is the rule: The family does not exist for society, but society exists for the family. The family is the fundamental cell, the element which constitutes the community of the State, since, to use the very expressions of Our predecessor Pius XI, of happy memory, "The State is such as the

† Broadcast on "Family Day" (March 24, 1952).

families and the men by whom it is formed make it, as the body is formed by its members." By virtue, so to speak, of the instinct of preservation, the State should consequently fulfill what is, essentially and according to the design of God, Creator and Savior, its first duty: to guarantee fully those values which ensure for the family order, human dignity, health, happiness. These values, which are the very elements of common welfare, can never rightly be sacrificed to what might, in appearance, seem to be a common good. Let us mention as examples, some of which are greatly threatened at the present day: the indissolubility of marriage; the protection of human life before birth; sufficient housing for the family, not that composed of one or two children or the childless family, but for the normal more numerous type of family; the possibility of working, because unemployment in the case of the father is the bitterest of hardships for the family; the rights of parents over their children with respect to the State; the full freedom of parents to educate their children in the true faith and therefore the right of Catholic parents to Catholic schools; social conditions that will guarantee that families, and particularly young people, need not have the moral certainty of being subjected to corruption.

In these and yet other points which more closely affect family life there is no difference whatsoever between families; as regards some other economic and political questions, however, they may find themselves in very different and unequal conditions, and sometimes in competition or even in conflict. Particularly here, every effort should be made—and Catholics will wish to give a good example—to promote an equilibrium, even at the cost of sacrificing particular interests, for the sake of internal peace and a healthy economy.

But, with regard to the essential rights of families, true followers of the Church will do their utmost to defend them. Perhaps here or there, on some points, it may be necessary to yield before the superiority of political forces, but in such cases there will be no surrender, only the exercise of patience. Moreover, in cases of this sort, it is necessary that doctrine be safe, that all efficient means be adopted to achieve step by step the end that has never been forgone.

Among such efficacious means, though not of immediate effect, one of the most powerful is the union of fathers, firm in the same convictions, in the same will.

Another means which, even though it may not bring immediately the desired results, is never wasted and always bears fruit, is the care taken by this coalition of fathers to endeavor to enlighten public opinion, to persuade it little by little to favor the triumph of truth and justice. No effort to act upon that public opinion should be spared or neglected.

Literature on Sexual Initiation

There is a field where the necessity for this education and a healthy influencing of public opinion is making itself felt with tragic urgency. In that field it has been perverted by propaganda which might unhesitatingly be called evil.

We refer to writings, books, and articles concerning sexual initiation, which nowadays often reach enormous sales and flood the whole world, invading infancy, submerging the new generation, disturbing the minds of those engaged to be married and of young married couples.

The Church has treated, with all the gravity, attention, and dignity which the question requires, the problem of instruction in this subject as made advisable or needful by the normal physical and psychic development of adolescents as well as in specific cases demanded by special conditions. The Church may with good reason proclaim that, with the deepest respect for the sanctity of matrimony, in theory and practice, she has granted freedom to husband and wife in what is permitted by the impulse of a healthy and decent nature, without offending the Creator.

The intolerable impudence of such literature is appalling: whereas the pagan world itself seemed to halt with respect before the secret intimacy of married life, today we witness the violation of that mystery, which is offered to the public at large, even to the young, as a vivid, sensual spectacle. There is truly reason to wonder whether there still remains a sufficiently clear-cut borderline between this initiation—so-called Catholic—and the erotic or obscene literature and illustrations which aim deliberately at corruption or which, for base motives of interest, shamefully exploit the basest instincts of fallen nature.

But there is more. Such propaganda also threatens the Catholic world with a twofold calamity, not to use a stronger expression. First of all it exaggerates beyond measure the importance and significance, in life, of the sexual element. Even if it be admitted that these authors, purely theoretically speaking, keep within the limits of Catholic ethics, it is, however, no less true that their manner of explaining sexual life is such that it acquires, in the mind of the reader and in his practical judgment, the meaning and value of something which is an end in itself. It makes him lose sight of the true original aim of matrimony, which is the procreation and the education of children, and the serious duty of husband and wife with regard to this end; the literature of which we are speaking leaves this too much in the background.

Furthermore, this so-called literature seems not to take into account the universal experience which is of yesterday, of today, and of all times, because it is based on nature itself, and which attests that in moral education neither initiation nor instruction brings of itself any advantage; that it is in fact seriously harmful and detrimental if not firmly supported by constant discipline, by strong self-control, and, above all, by resort to the supernatural force of prayer and the Sacraments. All Catholic educators worthy of the name and of their mission are fully conscious of the preponderant importance of supernatural energies in the sanctification of the individual, young or adult, unmarried or married. In writings of the kind mentioned, barely a word is said about all this when it is not altogether passed over in silence. The very principles so wisely illustrated by Our predecessor Pius XI in his Encyclical *Divini Illius Magistri* on the subject of sexual education and its interrelated problems, are set aside—sad sign of the times!—with a simple wave of the hand or with a smile. Pius XI, it is said, wrote these things twenty years ago for his own times; much ground has been covered since then!

Fathers, join together, under the guidance of your Bishops, of course; call to your help all Catholic women and mothers to fight together, without any wavering or false shame, in order to thwart and disrupt these movements, whatever may be the name or the authority with which they cloak themselves or which may have been lent to them.[†]

† Address to French Fathers (September 18, 1951).

Immorality

Just as any Christian, any person endowed with decency and natural common sense is astonished and appalled at the sight of the rising tide of immorality which, even in these exceptionally grave times, threatens to submerge society. No one hesitates to recognize the cause of it, particularly in the licentious publications and the indecent shows which are offered to the eyes and ears of adolescents and adults, of the young and old, of mothers and daughters. And what should be said about art, fashions, the public and private behavior of both men and women? One can hardly believe that writers, publishers, artists, managers, and promoters of certain artistic and theatrical displays do not hesitate to sink to such low levels of corruption, converting the use of the pen and art itself, the industrial progress and the wondrous modern inventions, into tools, weapons, and allurements of immorality. Writings and stage productions, though unworthy of the honor due to art and literature, find, nonetheless, readers and spectators by the thousands. And you see teenagers throw themselves at such a diet of the mind and eye with all the impulsiveness of the awakened passions; you see parents taking with them to such sorry spectacles boys and girls, in whose tender hearts and eyes are impressed fatal images and cravings, which often are never erased, instead of innocent and pious visions.

What, then, should we think? That human nature is universally and profoundly depraved and that its craving for scandal is without remedy? Certainly not. As a foundation, God has placed, in the human heart, righteousness which, however, is threatened by the Spirit of Evil and unbridled concupiscence. Except for a small minority, people would not spontaneously seek, and still less demand, unwholesome entertainment, if it were not offered to them and sometimes almost imposed upon them by surprise.

On Art

Consequently, it is extremely important to take the field in defense of public and social morals. It is not a battle waged with material weapons and bloodshed, but a conflict of ideas and feelings, between good and evil. It is proper that all who can do so should direct all their efforts and employ all their talents toward creating and promoting a type of literature, theater, and motion picture which constitutes genuine art, in concept and content elevating, wholesome, and at the same time interesting and attractive. We could never adequately commend and encourage the well-deserving intellectuals who devote themselves to this task like apostles of righteousness. It is evident, however, that not all can shoulder the burden of such an apostolate.

Is there, then, anything the others should do? Are they simply to lull themselves with the hope that the attractiveness of good and beautiful works will universally succeed in arousing and spreading an invincible disgust and repudiation of all turpitude? None is so naive on this point as to cherish such vain hopes. In the face of the unscrupulous exploiters of the press, of stage and screen, shall decent people simply stand helplessly aside? This would be unjust, and so it would appear to whoever knows and considers the laudable legislation which honors the country. To respectable citizens, heads of families, and educators the way is open to ensure the enforcement of these provident laws and of the effective sanctions they envisage, by submitting to the civil authorities, in the prescribed form, reports based on facts and accurate in their references to persons, things, or expressions, so that whatever of an objectionable nature should be presented to the public may be prevented and suppressed.

We do not conceal that this is a vast and varied task. Because of its vastness, it offers a wide field to all people of good will; and because of its variety, it is suitable for people of varying aptitudes. But its amplitude, though it may frighten and discourage the fainthearted, serves also to kindle ever more vividly the ardor of generous souls.[†]

Eyes and Ears Are Broad Avenues

And now let us examine our subject more closely, because much remains to be done and much is expected by the Church.

Ever louder and more urgently resound from the soil of Europe and from beyond the seas the pleas for help in the unfortunate conditions of the family and of the young generation.

† Address to Catholic Women (February 20, 1942).

That war bears the major burden of guilt is well known. It is responsible, above all, for the violent and sorrowful separation of millions of couples and families and for the destruction of innumerable homes.

But it is equally certain that the real and true cause of such a great evil is even more profound. It must be sought in what, by a composite term, is called materialism, in the negation or at least in the neglect and contempt of all that is religion, Christianity, submission to God and to His law, the life to come, and eternity. Like a pestiferous breath, materialism pervades more and more the entire life and produces its evil fruits in matrimony, in the family, and in the youth.

It may be said that according to unanimous judgment the morality of youth in general is in continuous decline. And not only of youth in the cities. In that of the country also, where once a robust and healthy respect for morality flourished, the moral degradation is hardly less pronounced, while much of what spurs to luxury and pleasure in the city has obtained free entry in the village, too.

It is superfluous to recall how much the radio and the movies have been used and abused in the spreading of that materialism, and how much they, the bad book, the licentious illustrated periodical, the indecent show, the immoral dance, and immodesty on the beaches, have contributed to increase superficiality, worldliness, and the sensuality of youth. Reports coming from the most diverse regions signal those areas as centers of youth's religious and moral abandonment. But primarily responsible is the breakup of marriage, of which the moral debasement of youth is the hallmark and deplorable consequence.[‡]

Movies and Morality

One wonders at times if the leaders of the motion picture industries fully appreciate the vast power they wield in affecting social life, whether in the family or the larger civic groups. The eyes and ears are like broad avenues that lead directly to the soul of man; and they are opened wide, most often without challenge, by the spectators of your films. What is it that enters from

‡ Address to Women of Catholic Action (July 24, 1949).

the screen into the inner recesses of the mind, where youth's fund of knowledge is growing and where norms and motives of conduct that will mold the definitive character are being shaped and sharpened? Is it something that will contribute to the formation of a better citizen, industrious, law-abiding, God-fearing, who finds his joy and recreation in wholesome pleasure and amusement? St. Paul was quoting Menander, an ancient Greek poet, when he wrote to the faithful of his church in Corinth that "bad conversation corrupts good manners." What was true then is no less true today; because human nature changes little with the centuries. And if it is true, as it is, that bad conversation corrupts morals, how much more effectively are they corrupted by bad conversation when accompanied by conduct, vividly depicted, which flouts the laws of God and civilized decency? Oh, the immense amount of good the motion picture can effect! That is why the evil spirit, always so active in this world, wishes to pervert this instrument for his own impious purposes; and it is encouraging to know that your committee is aware of the danger, and more and more conscious of its grave responsibility before society and God. It is for public opinion to sustain wholeheartedly and effectively every legitimate effort made by men of integrity and honor to purify the movies and keep them clean, to improve them and increase their usefulness.[†]

The Essence and Mission of Art

So much has been said about art, an inexhaustible subject!

The agitations of a world shaken in its very foundations, the divergencies of minds, the conflict of interests, the suspiciousness of a hypersensitive individualism have accentuated individual isolation and extended and deepened moral distances despite the multiplying of material contacts. Little by little, the excess of this evil has ended in placing the spotlight on the need for uniting in a common action all the isolated forces of nations and peoples earnestly desiring peace.

† Address to U.S. Movie Producers (July 14, 1945).

Persevering and discerning attempts to reach an understanding or co-operation between the different countries are neither of today nor of yesterday. Current events have underlined not, indeed, their inconsistency and uselessness, but rather their insufficiency and instability. All have therefore endeavored with praiseworthy eagerness to promote, notwithstanding all sorts of difficulties, international unions of a political, juridical, economic, and social nature. Very soon, however, it became evident that something more intimate and more human was still needed, and so, in the fields of engineering, science, and culture, there have begun to come into being, if not a union, at least partial associations.

In the intellectual order, the union of Catholic artists occupies one of the foremost positions. This is natural because, to begin with, art is, under certain aspects, the most vivid and synthetic expression of the human mind and human feelings, and also the most widely intelligible, since, speaking directly to the senses, art knows no diversity of languages, but only the extremely attractive diversity of temperaments and mentalities.

Moreover, with their persuasiveness and delicacy, the auditive and visual arts penetrate the intelligence and the sensitiveness of the spectator or of the listener to depths which the written or spoken word with its insufficiently colored analytical precision could never reach.

For these two reasons art helps men, notwithstanding all the differences of character, education, and civilization, to become acquainted with and understand each other, or at least to get an intuitive knowledge of one another, and consequently to pool their respective resources in order to complement one another.

In order that art may produce so desirable a result, it is necessary in the first place for it to have an expressive value, without which it ceases to be true art. This remark is not superfluous these days when, too often, in certain schools, a work of art is not sufficient of itself to express the thought, to disclose the sentiment, to reveal the soul of its author. But when a work of art needs to be explained verbally, it loses its peculiar value and only serves to give to the senses purely physical enjoyment and to the spirit the enjoyment of a subtle and empty game. Another condition, if art is to accomplish with dignity and fruitfulness its glorious mission consisting in the promotion of understanding, harmony, and peace, is that through art the senses, far from weighing down the soul and nailing it to the earth, should serve it as wings on which to rise above transient trifles and paltriness toward that which is eternal, true, beautiful, toward the only real good, the only center where union is accomplished, where unity is achieved, toward God. Is it not here that the splendid vision of the Apostle, "*Invisibilia enim ipsius a creatura mundi per ea quae facta sunt, intellecta conspiciuntur, sempiterna quoque eius virtus et divinitas*—For the invisible things of Him, from the creation of the world, are clearly seen, being understood by the things that are made; His eternal power also, and divinity," literally applies?

All the maxims which bring art down from its sublime office profane it, therefore, and make it barren. "Art for art's sake": as if art could be an end in itself, condemned to move, to crawl, at the level of sensible and material things; as if through art man's senses did not follow a call going beyond the simple knowledge of material nature, the call to awaken in his intellect and soul, because of the transparency of this nature, the wish for "things that the eye hath not seen, nor the ear heard and that have not reached his heart."

We will say nothing here about an immoral art which aims to debase and enslave the spiritual powers of the soul to the passion of the flesh. Furthermore, "art" and "immoral" are two terms in strident contradiction. Therefore, make the reflection of the divine beauty and light smile upon the earth, upon humanity; helping man to love "all that which is true, pure, just, saintly, lovable," and you will have made a great contribution to peace "*et Deus pacis erit vobiscum*—and the God of Peace will be with you."[†]

The Duty of Physicians

The Christian physician never loses sight of the fact that his ailing or wounded patient, who, thanks to his care, will continue to live for a time either short or longer, or, notwithstanding his attention, will die, is on the way toward immortal life, and that his misery or eternal happiness is also dependent upon him.

† Address to the First Congress of Catholic Artists (March 9, 1950).

Compounded of matter and spirit, himself an element in the universal order of beings, man on his journey here is in reality moving toward an end exceeding the limits of time, toward a goal set above nature. Because of this interpenetration of matter and spirit in the perfectly compounded unity of man, because of this participation in the movement of all visible creation, it follows that the physician is often called upon to give advice, to make decisions and formulate principles which, though aiming directly at the cure of the body, its members and organs, nevertheless have their bearing upon the spirit and its faculties, the supernatural destiny of man and his social mission.

Now, if he does not always take into account this composition of man, his place and his function in the universal order of beings, and his spiritual and supernatural destiny, the physician easily runs the risk of becoming entangled in more or less materialistic prejudices, of following the fatal consequences of utilitarianism, of hedonism, and absolute autonomy in respect to moral law.

Man Is Only the Usufructuary of His Body

The complexity of this compound of matter and spirit, and of the universal order as well, is such that man cannot guide himself toward the total and unique goal of his being and his personality except by the harmonious action of his multiple corporal and spiritual faculties, and he cannot maintain his place either by isolating himself from the rest of the world or by losing himself as thousands of identical molecules lose themselves in an amorphous agglomeration. Now, this very real complexity and this necessary harmony present their difficulties and dictate his duty to the physician.

In shaping man, God regulated each of his functions; He distributed them among his various organs; He established the distinction between those which are essential to life and those which concern only the integrity of the body, however precious may be its activity, its well-being, and its beauty. At the same time, He fixed, prescribed, and limited the use of each function. Therefore, man is not permitted to order his life and the functions of his organs according to his desire, in a way contrary to the internal and inherent purposes assigned to them. Actually, man is not the owner and absolute lord of his body, but only its usufructuary. From this fact is derived a whole series of principles and rules which regulate the use and the right to dispose of the organs and members of the body, and which are equally binding to the interested person himself and the physician called to advise him...

The same rules should, moreover, guide the solution of conflicts between divergent interests, according to the scale of values, save, always, the Commandments of God. Therefore, man is never allowed to sacrifice his eternal interests to temporal goods, even the most highly valued, nor is he permitted to cast aside these goods in favor of vulgar caprice and the exigencies of passion. In such—sometimes tragic—crises the physician is often the counsellor and almost the final arbiter.

Though circumscribed and restricted to the person himself, complex as he is in his unity, the inevitable conflicts among divergent interests give rise to extremely delicate problems. How much more difficult are those, then, which society poses when it asserts its rights upon the body, its integrity, and upon the life of man itself! Now, it is sometimes quite difficult to determine the limits in theory; in practice, the physician, no less than the individual directly concerned, may find himself in the necessity of examining and analyzing such exigencies and claims, of measuring and evaluating their morality and binding ethical force...

The Integrity of the Body

Here reason and faith equally draw the line between the respective rights of society and the individual. There is no doubt that man by his own nature is destined to live in society; but even as reason alone teaches us, in principle society is made for man and not man for society. Not from society but from the Creator Himself has he the right to his body and his life, and to the Creator he is responsible for the use he makes of them. From this it follows that society cannot directly deprive him of that right, until he has rendered himself punishable with such a privation by a grave and proportionate crime.

Regarding the body, the life, and the bodily integrity of single individuals, the juridical position of society is essentially different from that of the individuals themselves. Though it is limited, man's power over his members and organs is a direct power, as they are constitutional parts of his physical being. Indeed, it is clear that since their differentiation in a perfect unity has no other purpose than the good of the entire organism, each of these organs and members may be sacrificed, if it places the whole in a danger which cannot otherwise be avoided. Quite different is the case of society, since it is not a physical being whose parts would be the individual men, but a simple community of purpose and action; for which reason it may demand of those who compose it, and who are called its members, all the services necessary to the common good.

These are the bases upon which must be founded every judgment which concerns the moral value of the acts or interventions permitted or imposed by public power upon the human body, the life, and the integrity of the person…

Suffering and Death

The truths so far set forth may be known only by the light of reason. But there is a fundamental law which presents itself more to the attention of the physician than the others, and whose integral meaning and purpose can be clarified and made manifest only by the light of revelation: We mean to say suffering and death.

Undoubtedly, physical pain has also a natural and salutary function: it is a signal of alarm which reveals the beginning and development, often insidious, of a hidden disease and induces and urges the search for a remedy. But the physician inevitably encounters pain and death in the course of his scientific research, as a problem to which his spirit does not possess the key, and in the exercise of his profession, as an ineluctable and mysterious law, before which his skill often remains impotent and his compassion sterile. He can indeed establish his diagnosis according to all laboratory and clinical findings and formulate his prognosis according to all the dictates of science; but in the depths of his conscience, of his heart of man and scientist, he feels that the explanation of that enigma persists in escaping him. He suffers because of it; anguish holds him inexorably in its viselike grip until he asks faith for an answer which, even if incomplete, as it is in the mystery of God's design and will be revealed only in eternity, nevertheless serves to pacify his soul.

Here is the reply. God, in creating man, had exempted him, through the gift of grace, from that natural law of every living and sensitive body, and had not designed to include pain and death in his destiny. It was sin that brought them upon him. But He, the Father of mercy, took them into His hands and caused them to pass through the body, the veins, and the heart of His beloved Son, who was God like unto Himself, made into man to be the Savior of the world. Thus pain and death have become the means of redemption and sanctification for every man who does not deny Christ. Thus the path of the human race, which unfolds in its entire length under the Sign of the Cross and under the law of pain and death, while it matures and purifies the soul here on earth, leads it to unlimited happiness of a life without end.

To suffer, to die: it is really, to use the daring expression of the Apostle of all nations, the "foolishness of God," a foolishness wiser than all the wisdom of men... In the light of revelation the pious author of *The Imitation of Christ* was able to write the sublime twelfth chapter of his second book, "*De regia via sanctae Crucis*—Of the Royal Road of the Cross," all resplendent with the most admirable understanding and the highest Christian wisdom of life.

In the face of the imperious problem of pain, what reply, then, can the physician give to himself? And what to the unfortunate man whom sickness has reduced to a gloomy torpor, or who rises in vain rebellion against suffering and death? Only a heart imbued with a vivid and profound faith can find accents of intimacy, sincerity, and conviction capable of making acceptable the reply of the divine Master Himself: It is necessary to suffer and die, in order to enter this way into glory. He will fight with all the means and resources of his science and his ability against sickness and death, not with the resignation of a desperate pessimism, nor with the exasperated resoluteness which a modern philosophy believes it must exalt, but rather with the calm serenity of one who sees and knows what pain and death represent in the designs of salvation of the omniscient and infinitely good and merciful Lord.

Is There Such a Thing as Christian Medical Science?

It is manifest, therefore, that the person of the physician and all his activities move constantly in the sphere of moral order and under the dominion of its laws. In no statement, in no advice, in no action, in no intervention may the physician keep outside the sphere of morals, free and independent from the fundamental principles of ethics and religion; nor is there any act or word for which he is not responsible before God and his own conscience.

It is true indeed that there are some who reject as an absurdity and a chimera the concept of a "Christian medical science," in theory and in practice. In their opinion there cannot be a Christian medicine, just as there is not a Christian physics or a Christian chemistry, theoretical or applied. The realm of the exact and experimental sciences—they say—extends beyond the religious and ethical area, and therefore they know and recognize only their own immanent laws. Strange and unjustified contraction of the field of vision of the problem! Do they not see that the objects of those sciences are not isolated in space, but are a part of the universal world of creatures; that they have a definite place and level in the order of goods and values; that they are in permanent contact with the objects of the other sciences, and in a special way they come under the law of immanent and transcendent finality which binds them into an ordered whole? Let us admit, though, that when one speaks of the Christian orientation of science, one has in mind not so much science in itself as its representatives and devotees, in whom it lives, develops, and becomes manifest. Physics and chemistry also, which conscientious scientists and professional men put to use to the advantage and benefit of individuals and society, can become agents and instruments of corruption and ruin in the hands of perverse men. It is therefore all the more obvious that in medicine the supreme interest of truth and good is opposed to a presumed objective or subjective freedom from the many relations and ties which relate it to the general order...

Death and Capital Punishment

The Fifth Commandment—*Non occides*—Thou shalt not kill—this synthesis of the duties regarding the life and the integrity of the human body, is rich in lessons both for the teacher in his university chair and for the practicing physician. As long as a man is not guilty, his life is intangible, and, therefore, any act directly tending to destroy it is illicit, whether it be in embryonic form or in its full development, or even at its conclusion. Only God is the lord of the life of a man not guilty of a crime punishable by death! The physician does not have the right to dispose of the life of either a child or its mother; and no one in the world, no private person, no human authority, may authorize him to proceed to its direct destruction. His office is not to destroy lives but to save them. These are fundamental and immutable principles which the Church, in the course of the last ten years, has found it necessary to proclaim repeatedly and with every clarification against opposing opinions and methods. The Catholic physician finds a secure guide in this regard, for his theoretical judgment and his practical conduct, in the resolutions and decrees of the teaching authority of the Church.

But there is in the moral order a vast field which requires of the physician particular clearness of principle and security of action: that in which ferment the mysterious energies immersed by God in the organism of man and woman for the procreation of new lives. It is a natural power, of which the Creator Himself has determined the structure and the essential forms of activity, with a precise purpose and with corresponding duties, to which man is subjected in every conscious use of that faculty. Nature's primary purpose (to which the secondary ends are essentially subordinated) in this use is the propagation of life and the education of the offspring. Only matrimony, regulated by God Himself in its essence and in its properties, assures both of these things in accordance with the welfare and the dignity of the parents no less than the children. This is the only norm which illuminates and supports all this delicate material; the norm to which in all concrete cases, in all special questions, it is necessary to refer; the norm, finally, whose faithful observance guarantees in this matter the moral and physical health of individuals and of society.

The Physician and Temptations

It should not be difficult for the physician to understand this immanent finality profoundly rooted in nature, to affirm it and apply it with intimate conviction in his scientific and practical activity. People often listen to him with more belief than to the theologian himself, when he admonishes and advises that whoever offends and transgresses the laws of nature sooner or later will have to suffer the distressing consequences in his personal value and in his physical and psychical integrity.

There is the youth who, under the impulse of newborn passions, appeals to the physician; here, the betrothed, who on the eve of their approaching marriage ask advice, which all too often they want to be contrary to nature and virtue; here, married couples, who seek from him enlightenment and assistance, or, even more, connivance, because they pretend they can find no other solution or way out of the conflicts of life excepting the willful infraction of the ties and duties inherent in the use of matrimonial relations. They try, then, to give weight to all the possible arguments or pretexts (medical, eugenic, social, and moral) to induce the physician to give advice or offer help, which will permit the satisfaction of the natural instinct, but deprive it of the possibility of achieving the aim of the generating force of life. How can he remain firm before all these assaults if he himself should be lacking clear knowledge and conviction that the Creator Himself for the good of mankind has linked the voluntary use of those natural energies to their immanent purpose with an indissoluble bond which admits of no relaxation or rupture?

Is It Permitted to the Physician to Lie?

The Eighth Commandment also has its place in the duty of physicians. Falsehood is permitted to no one according to moral law. There are, however, cases in which the physician, even if questioned, though never saying anything positively false, still cannot crudely expose the whole truth, especially when he knows that the patient would not have the strength to bear it. But there are other cases in which he has, without doubt, the duty to speak clearly; a duty before which every medical or humanitarian consideration must give way. He is not permitted to lull the patient or his relatives in an illusory security, with the danger of compromising in this way the eternal salvation of the patient or the fulfillment of obligations of justice or charity. Anyone would be in error who attempted to justify or excuse such conduct under the pretext that the physician always expresses himself in the way he considers best in the personal interest of the patient and that it is the others' fault if they take his words too literally.

The Professional Secret

Among the duties deriving from the Eighth Commandment one must also list the observance of the professional secret, which should serve and does serve not private interests only but, even more so, the common good. Conflicts may arise in this field, also, between private and public good, or among the various elements and aspects of common welfare; conflicts in which it may become extremely difficult to measure and weigh justly the pros and cons of the reasons for speaking or keeping silent. In such perplexity, the conscientious physician asks of the fundamental principles of Christian ethics the rules which will help him to choose the right path. Indeed, these, while clearly affirming the obligation of the physician to maintain professional secrecy, especially in the interests of the common good, do not, however, recognize in this an absolute value. In fact, it would not be consistent with the common good if this secrecy should be placed at the service of crime or fraud.[†]

Birth Control

God has made all the other things on earth for man, and man, as regards his being and his essence, has been created for God and not for any other creature, though as to his actions he has obligations toward the community as well. Now, the child is "man," even if he is not yet born, in the same degree and by the same title as his mother.

Furthermore, every human being, even a child in his mother's womb, has the right to life directly from God and not from his parents, from any human society or authority. Therefore, there is no man, no human authority, no science, no "indication" whatsoever, medical, eugenic, social, economic, moral, that may lend a valid juridical right for the deliberate direct disposal of an innocent human life, that is, a disposal aiming at its destruction, either as an objective or as a means to another objective, in no way, perhaps, illicit

† Address, Micro-Biological Union of San Luca (November 12, 1943).

of itself. Thus, for example, to save a mother's life is a very noble aim; but the direct killing of the child as a means to that end is not licit. The direct destructions of so-called "worthless lives," before or after birth, practiced in great numbers a few years ago, cannot in any way be justified. Consequently, when that practice began, the Church expressly declared it to be contrary to natural, divine, and positive law, and therefore illicit to kill—even by order of a public authority—those who, though innocent, are nevertheless, on account of a physical or psychical deficiency, not useful to a people, but will, rather, become a burden to it. The life of an innocent creature is intangible, and any direct attempt or aggression against it is a violation of one of the fundamental laws without which safe social living is not possible.

Pains of Childbirth

Even the pains that, since original sin, a mother has to suffer to give birth to her child only draw tighter the bond that binds them: she loves it the more, the more pain it has cost her. This was expressed with a great and touching simplicity by Him who has molded mothers' hearts: "The woman, when delivering, is in pain because her hour has arrived; but when she has given birth to her child she will not even remember the anguish suffered, because of the joy that a man was born into the world." Moreover, the Holy Ghost, through the pen of St. Paul the Apostle, also emphasizes the greatness and joy of maternity. God gives the child to the mother, but along with the gift, He makes her co-operate effectively in the opening of the flower of which He had deposited the germ in her womb, and this co-operation becomes a life which will conduct her to eternal salvation: "Women will be saved by childbearing."

Our predecessor Pius XI, of happy memory, in his Encyclical Letter *Casti connubii,* of December 31, 1930, once again solemnly proclaimed the fundamental law governing the matrimonial act and relations between husband and wife: that any attempt on their part in the performance of the matrimonial act or in the development of its natural consequences, aiming at depriving it of its innate force and hindering the procreation of a new life, is immoral; and that no "indication" or necessity can change an intrinsically immoral act into a moral and licit act.

This precept is in full force today, as it was yesterday, and it will be so tomorrow too, and always, because it is not a simple injunction by a human law, but the expression of a natural and divine law.

Sterilization

It would be much more than a simple want of diligence in the service of life if such human attempts did not regard a single act but touched the organism itself with the intention of depriving it, by means of sterilization, of the faculty to procreate a new life.

Direct sterilization—to wit, that aiming, as a means or as an objective, to render procreation impossible—is a serious infringement of the moral law and is therefore illicit. Even the public authority has no right, on the plea of any "indication," to permit, and much less to enjoin it or have it achieved, to the prejudice of innocent beings. This principle is already asserted in the Encyclical of Pius XI concerning marriage, just referred to. Hence, when, some ten years ago, sterilization began to be ever more widely applied, the Holy See found it necessary expressly and publicly to declare that direct sterilization, permanent or temporary, of either a man or a woman, is illicit, in virtue of the natural law, from which the Church herself, as you know, has not the authority to dispense.

Natural Sterility

Nowadays, another grave problem presents itself, that is, whether, and to what extent, the obligation of being ready for the service of maternity is reconcilable with a constantly spreading recourse to the natural periods of sterility (the so-called "agenesic" periods in woman), which seems to be a clear expression of a will contrary to that precept.

Before anything else, two hypotheses have to be taken into consideration. If the application of that theory does not mean anything beyond the fact that husband and wife may make use of their matrimonial right also during the days of natural sterility, there is nothing to object to; for it is true that, by so doing, they do not prevent or jeopardize in any way the consummation of the natural act and its further natural consequences. It is precisely in this that the application of the theory of which we speak differs essentially from the abuse already mentioned, which consists in the perversion of the act itself. If, instead, one goes further, that is, permitting the performance of the matrimonial act exclusively on those days, then a husband's and wife's conduct has to be examined more attentively. Here again two hypotheses come up for our consideration. If, when contracting marriage, at least one of the couple already had the intention of restricting to the periods of sterility the matrimonial right itself, and not merely its use, so that during the other days the other partner would not even have the right to request the act, then this would imply an essential defect in the marriage consent, which would bring with it invalidation of the marriage itself, because the right deriving from the marriage contract is a permanent one, uninterrupted and not intermittent, in each of the partners with respect to the other.

If, on the other hand, the limitation of the act to the days of natural sterility refers not to the right itself but only to the use of that right, the validity of the marriage is unquestionable; however, the lawfulness of such conduct on the part of a husband and wife should be admitted or denied, according as the intention constantly to observe those periods is or is not based on sufficient and reliable moral motives. The mere fact that the partners do not vitiate the nature of the act and are also ready to accept and to bring up the child that, notwithstanding their precautions, might be born, would not of itself be sufficient to guarantee the uprightness of their intention and the unquestionable morality of their motives.

The reason is that marriage imposes a state of life which, while it confers certain rights, likewise enjoins the accomplishment of a positive task concerning that state. This being so, the general principle may be applied that a positive service may be omitted if grave motives, beyond the control of the good will of those who are under the obligation to perform it, show that its performance is inadvisable and prove that the petitioner (in this case mankind) cannot equitably claim it.

The marriage contract, which confers on husband and wife the right to satisfy the natural inclination, sets them in a specific state of life, the matrimonial status. Now, on husbands and wives, who make use of it through the specific act of their status, nature and the Creator impose the function of providing for the preservation of the human race. That is the characteristic service which gives to their status its peculiar value, the *bonum prolis*—the good of posterity. The individual and society, the people and the State, the Church itself, depend for their existence, in the order established by God, on prolific marriages. Hence, to embrace the matrimonial state, to make use continually of the faculty peculiar to it and licit only therein, and, on the other hand, to avoid its primary duty, always and deliberately, without a serious motive, would be to sin against the very meaning of married life.

Medical, Eugenic, and Social "Indications"

Serious motives, such as those not seldom appearing in medical, eugenic, and social so-called "indications," may exempt some from the positive, obligatory act for a long time and even, if necessary, for the whole duration of marriage. It follows from this that observance of the sterile periods may be licit from the moral standpoint; and in the conditions mentioned it is so indeed. If, however, according to a reasonably and equitably formed judgment, there are no such serious reasons, personal or deriving from external circumstances, the will habitually to avoid the fecundity of their union, though continuing fully to satisfy their sensuality, may only derive from a false evaluation of life and from motives not harmonizing with sound ethical canons.

Abstention

In some very delicate cases, where it cannot be pretended that the risk of maternity should be run, where it has indeed to be absolutely avoided, and where, on the other hand, observance of the agenesic periods either does not afford sufficient guarantee or has to be discarded for other reasons, any preventive manipulation and any direct attempt on the life and development of the seed is in conscience prohibited and excluded, and one course only remains, that is, abstention from any complete exercise of the natural faculty.

It will be objected that such abstention is impossible, that such heroism cannot be put into practice. Nowadays you will hear this objection, you will read it, everywhere raised even by those who, in view of their duties and qualification, ought to be able to judge very differently. The following argument is brought up as a proof: "No one is obliged to do what is impossible, and it is presumable that no reasonable legislator can want to force people by his law to do that which is impossible. For a husband and wife abstention over long periods of time is impossible. Therefore, they are not obliged to abstain; the divine law cannot have this meaning."

In this way, from partially true premises, a false conclusion is made. In order to persuade oneself of this it is sufficient to invert the terms of the argument: "God does not oblige people to do what is impossible. But God enjoins abstinence to a husband and wife if their union cannot be completed according to the rules of nature. Therefore, in these cases abstinence is possible." As confirmation of this argument we also have the doctrine of the Council of Trent, which, in the chapter on the observance, necessary and possible, of the Commandments, referring to a passage from St. Augustine, teaches: "God does not command impossible things, but while commanding, He warns you to do what you can and to ask what you cannot do, and He helps you so that you may be able."†

Heredity, Eugenics, and Painless Birth

THE laws of heredity are full of meaning for man. From the first moment and at the first stage of its existence, the initial cell of the new man is already astonishing in its structure and incredibly rich in the specificity of its dispositions. It is full of teleological dynamism governed by the genes, and these genes are the bases of so much happiness or unhappiness, of vitality or weakness, of achievement or failure. This consideration explains why research on heredity meets with more and more interest and points of application. An attempt is made to preserve what is good and sound, to strengthen it, promote it, and perfect it. Deterioration of hereditary factors must be prevented; deficiencies

† Address to Obstetricians (October 29, 1951).

already present must, as far as is possible, be corrected, and care must be taken to prevent hereditary factors of a negative character from becoming accentuated by combination with those of a similarly oriented inferior tendency in the partner. Vice versa, factors of a positive character should be united with a similar hereditary patrimony.

Genetics

The science of genetics does not have a merely theoretical importance; it is also extremely practical. It aims at contributing to the welfare of individuals and to that of the community, to the common good. It seeks to carry out this task in two fields, genetic physiology and genetic pathology.

Experience has demonstrated that natural dispositions, good or faulty, have great influence on the upbringing of man and his future behavior. Doubtless the body with its aptitudes and organs is only the instrument, whereas the soul is the artist who plays the instrument; doubtless the skill of the artist may compensate for many a defect in the instrument; but it is better and easier to play on a perfect instrument; and when its quality falls below a set limit, it becomes quite impossible to use it—without taking into consideration the fact that, leaving comparisons aside, matter and spirit are joined into a substantial unity in man.

But, to take up this comparison once again, the science of genetics does enable us better to understand the structure and variations of the instrument and hence improve the playing. An examination of a man's lineage makes it possible, within certain limits, to diagnose the dispositions he has received in his patrimony and to prognosticate the inherited positive characteristics and, more important still, those, too, which reveal some hereditary blemish.

However limited direct influence may be on the hereditary patrimony, practical genetics is not at all reduced to the role of passive spectator. Daily life already demonstrates the extremely harmful effects of certain practices of parents in the natural transmission of life. Such proceedings, with the poisonings and the infections they cause, are to be forbidden as far as possible, and genetics looks for and points out the means of reaching this goal. Its conclusions deal particularly with combinations of patrimonies of different origins:

it points out those to be encouraged, those that can be tolerated, and those that should be rejected from the point of view of genetics and eugenics. Permit Us to quote the declarations of one of the most important geneticists of the present time: in a letter that he has just sent Us, he expresses his regret that, in spite of the enormous progress it has made, genetics "from the technical and analytical point of view is floundering in a mire of doctrinal errors, such as racism, mutationism applied to phylogenesis to explain in modern terms the evolutionism of Darwin, birth control in the case of all those who have, or are presumed to have, diseases or grave defects that are hereditary, either by preventive means or by abortive practices, the compulsory prenuptial certificate, etc."

There are, in fact, certain genetic and eugenic defense measures that common morality, and Christian morality especially, must reject in principle and in practice.

Eugenic Sterilization and the Right to Marry

Among the measures that are offensive to morality is the "racism" already mentioned: *eugenic sterilization.* Our predecessor Pius XI and We Ourselves have expressly declared contrary to natural law not only eugenic sterilization, but all sterilization whatsoever of an innocent person, whether it be temporary or final, of a man or woman. Our opposition to sterilization was and remains unchangeable, for the aim and desire to suppress by sterilization a lineage bearing hereditary diseases has not disappeared with the end of "racism."

Another path leads to the same goal: *forbidding marriage,* or making it a physical impossibility, by interning those with undesirable hereditary factors. It likewise is to be rejected. The end in view is good in itself, but the means of obtaining it is an attack on the right of the individual to contract and enjoy marriage. When the bearer of some hereditary disease or deficiency is unable to conduct himself as a human being, and consequently to contract marriage, or when later he has become incapable of claiming by an act of free will the right acquired by a valid marriage, he can legitimately be prevented from begetting a new life. Outside of these cases, the forbidding of marriage and matrimonial intercourse for biological, genetic, and eugenic motives is an injustice, no matter who does the forbidding, whether an individual or public authority.

It is certainly right, and in most cases an obligation, to point out to those who are bearers of extremely undesirable hereditary factors what a burden they are about to impose on themselves, their mates, and their offspring; a burden which might become intolerable. But to advise against something is not to forbid it. There may be other reasons, especially moral and personal ones, which are so imperious that they give the right to contract and enjoy marriage even in the circumstances indicated.

To justify direct eugenic sterilization, or the alternative of internment, it is claimed that the right to marriage and to the acts which it implies is not interfered with by sterilization, even when it is prenuptial, total, and certainly final. This attempt at justification is doomed to failure. If, for a person of common sense, the fact in question is doubtful, the unfitness for marriage is also doubtful; that is the time to apply the principle that the right to marry persists as long as the contrary is not proved beyond all doubt. And so, in this case, the marriage must be permitted; but the question of its objective validity remains open. If, on the other hand, there is no doubt whatsoever as to the above-mentioned fact of sterilization, it is premature to affirm that the right to marriage is not thereby called in question and, in any case, there are good grounds for challenging the truth of this assertion.[†]

Painless Childbirth

The laws, the theory, and the technique of natural childbirth, without pain, are undoubtedly valid, but they have been elaborated by scholars who, to a great extent, profess an ideology belonging to a materialistic culture; this latter is not valid simply because the scientific results mentioned above are. It is even much less accurate to say that the scientific results are true and demonstrated as such, because their authors and the cultures from which they derive have a materialistic orientation. The criteria of truth lie elsewhere.

† Address to the Participants of the Primum Symposium Geneticae Medicae (September 8, 1953).

The convinced Christian finds nothing in his philosophical ideas and his culture that prevents him from occupying himself seriously, in theory and in practice, with the psychoprophylactic method.

There are two points which deserve to be emphasized here: Christianity does not interpret suffering and the Cross in a merely negative fashion. If the new technique spares her the sufferings of childbirth, the mother can accept it without any scruple of conscience; but she is not obliged to do so. In the case of partial success or failure, she knows that suffering can be a source of good, if she bears it with God and in obedience to His will. The life and sufferings of Our Savior, the pains which so many great men have borne and even sought and through which they have matured and risen to the summits of Christian heroism, the daily examples we see of acceptance of the Cross with resignation: all this reveals the meaning of suffering, of the patient acceptance of pain in the present plan of salvation, for the duration of this earthly life.[‡]

Artificial Insemination

WHETHER he is concerned with the human body or with man as a whole, the Christian doctor must always beware of the fascination of technology, of the temptation to use his own science and ability for purposes other than the curing of the patients entrusted to him. He will also have to guard against another temptation—this one criminal—to make the gifts of God hidden in the depth of nature subservient to ignoble interests, unavowable passions, or inhuman experiments. Unfortunately, we need not reach back very far in time to find concrete proof of these deplorable abuses.

For example, the disintegration of the atom and the production of atomic energy is one thing; quite another is its use as destroyer, which is kept beyond any control. The magnificent technical progress of modern aviation is one thing, quite another the mass use of squadrons of bombers when there is no

‡ Address to a Group of Physicians of the International Secretariat of Catholic Physicians and of the AMCI (January 8, 1956).

possibility of limiting their action to strategic and military objectives. One thing, above all, is the respectful research which reveals the beauty of God in the mirror of His works, and His power in the forces of nature; quite another thing, the deification of this nature and of material forces in the negation of their Author.

The Duties of the Physician

What, instead, does the doctor who is worthy of his vocation do? He gains possession of these same forces, of these properties of nature, in order to procure with them healing, health, vigor, and often, what is still more precious, to prevent disease, contagion, and epidemics. In his hands the terrifying force of radioactivity is imprisoned, aimed at healing ills rebellious to any other treatment; the properties of the most virulent poisons serve to prepare efficacious remedies; better still, the germs of the most dangerous infections are variously used in serum therapy and in vaccination.

Natural and Christian morals, finally, keep their own incontrovertible rights and from them, and not from considerations of sentiment, of materialistic, naturalistic philanthropy, are derived the essential principles of medical deontology: dignity of the human body, pre-eminence of the soul over the body, brotherhood among all men, sovereign rule of God over life and destiny. An important problem which requires, no less urgently than the others, the light of Catholic moral doctrine is artificial insemination. We cannot let this occasion pass without indicating briefly, along general lines, the moral judgment which is called for on this subject.

The practice of artificial insemination, when it refers to man, cannot be considered, either exclusively or principally, from the biological and medical point of view, ignoring the moral and legal one.

Artificial insemination, outside of marriage, must be condemned as essentially and strictly immoral.

Natural law and divine positive law establish, in fact, that the procreation of a new life cannot but be the fruit of marriage. Only marriage safeguards the dignity of the spouses (principally of the wife in the present case) and their personal good. It alone provides for the well-being and education of the child.

It follows that no divergence of opinion among Catholics is admitted on the condemnation of artificial insemination outside of marriage. The child conceived in those conditions would be, by that very fact, illegitimate.

Artificial insemination produced in a marriage by the active element of a third party is equally immoral and consequently to be condemned without appeal.

Only the spouses have a reciprocal right upon each other's body to generate a new life: an exclusive, inalienable right, which cannot be ceded. And so it must be, even out of consideration for the child. On whoever gives life to a small being, nature imposes, by the very strength of that tie, the duty to keep and educate it. But no ties of origin, no moral or legal bonds of conjugal procreation, exist between the legitimate husband and the child who is the fruit of the active element of a third party (even if the husband has given his consent).

As far as the legitimacy of artificial insemination in marriage is concerned, it suffices, for the moment, to recall these principles of natural law: the simple fact that the result desired is obtained by this means does not justify the use of the means itself; nor does the desire of the husband and wife, in itself perfectly legitimate, to have a child, suffice to establish the legitimacy of resorting to the artificial insemination which would satisfy this desire.

It would be erroneous, therefore, to think that the possibility of resorting to this means might render valid a marriage between persons unable to contract it because of the *impedimentum impotentiae.*

On the other hand, it is superfluous to mention that the active element can never be obtained legitimately by means of acts against nature.

Although new methods cannot be ruled out a priori for the sole reason of their novelty, nonetheless, as far as artificial impregnation is concerned, extreme caution is not enough; it must be absolutely excluded. Saying this does not necessarily proscribe the use of certain artificial means destined only to facilitate the natural act, or to assure the accomplishment of the end of the natural act regularly performed.

Let it never be forgotten that only the procreation of a new life according to the will and the designs of the Creator brings with it, to a marvelous degree of perfection, the accomplishment of the proposed ends. It is at the same time in conformity with corporeal and spiritual nature and the dignity of the married couple, as well as with the healthy, normal development of the child.†

Moral Obligations of Catholic Jurists

WITHOUT doubt the jurist is not called upon by his profession to dedicate himself to theological speculation in order to know the object of his study; but if he knows not how to rise to the vision of supreme and transcendent reality, from whose will is derived the order of the visible universe and of that small part of it which is the human race with its immanent and morally necessary laws, it will be impossible for him to see in all its admirable unity and its most intimate spiritual depths the intricate pattern of social relationships, over which law presides, and the norms which regulate them. As the great Roman jurisconsult and orator affirmed, "*natura iuris... ab hominis repetenda (est) natura*—nature and the essence of law cannot but be derived from the nature of man himself." On the other hand, this nature of man cannot be known, even approximately, in its perfection, dignity, and loftiness, and in the ends which command and subordinate its actions to themselves, without recognition of the ontological connection by which it is bound to its transcendent cause. It is therefore clear that it will not be possible for the jurist to arrive at a sound conception of law, nor to achieve his own systematic arrangement of it, unless he ceases regarding man and human things without the light emanating from divinity to illuminate for him the arduous path of his research.

The error of modern rationalism has consisted precisely in the pretension to want to build the system of human laws and the general theory of law, considering the nature of man as an independent entity, which lacks every necessary reference to a superior Being, on whose creative and controlling will he depends, in essence and action. One knows in what an inextricable maze of difficulties contemporary juridical thought has become entangled because of this initial deviation, and how the jurist who conformed to the

† Address to Physicians (September 29, 1949).

canon set up by the so-called positivism has failed in his task, losing, with the proper knowledge of human nature, a sound conception of law, which came to lack that compelling power on man's conscience which is its primary and principal effect. Divine and human matters, which, according to Ulpian's definition, form the most general object of jurisprudence, are so closely linked that it is impossible to ignore the former without losing the exact notion of the latter.

The Specific Object of Jurisprudence

This is all the more true in that the more specific object of jurisprudence is justice and injustice, "*iusti atque iniusti scientia*," or justice, in its high function of preserving the balance between individual and social exigencies within the bosom of the human family. Justice is not only an abstract concept, an exterior ideal, which institutions must seek to embody as far as is possible at a given historical moment; it is also and above all something immanent to man, to society and its fundamental institutions, because of that sum total of practical principles that it dictates and imposes, of those more universal rules of conduct which form part of the objective, human, and civil order established by the lofty mind of the first Maker. The knowledge of justice and injustice presupposes, therefore, a higher wisdom, which consists in knowing the order of creation and consequently its Ordainer. Law, as Thomas Aquinas taught, *est obiectum iustitiae*, is the norm in which the great fruitful idea of justice takes concrete form and expression, and as such, if it leads to God, eternal and unchangeable justice in His essence, receives from God light and clarity, vigor and strength, meaning and content.

In the exercise of his profession, the jurist moves, therefore, between the infinite and the finite, between the divine and the human, and in this necessary movement lies the nobility of the science he cultivates. His other claims to respect in the eyes of human society can be regarded as the consequence of the one already mentioned.

The Subject of Jurisprudence: Man

If the objects of his investigations are juridical norms, the subject for whom these are intended is man, the human being, who thus falls into his field of competence. And, let it be noted, not man in his lower and less noble part, who is studied by other sciences, also useful and worthy of admiration, but man in his specific capacity as a rational agent who, in order to conform to the laws of his rationality, must act guided by certain rules of conduct, either directly dictated to him by his conscience—reflection and herald of a higher law—or prescribed for him by the human authority that regulates the life of society. It is true that man does not always present himself to the jurist in the higher aspects of his rational nature, but often offers for his study his least commendable sides, his bad inclinations, his wicked perversities, guilt, and crime; yet even where the splendor of his rationality appears tarnished, the real jurist must always see that ground of humanity from which guilt and crime can never erase the seal stamped on it by the Creator's hand.

If, then, we look at the subject of law with the eyes of the Christian faith, what a crown of light we see round his head, that crown set on him by the redemption of Christ, the blood shed to redeem him, supernatural life, to which it restored him and of which it made him a participant, and the final goal assigned to him as the end of his journey on earth. In the light of Christian faith, the subject of law is not man in his pure nature, but man raised by the Savior's grace to the supernatural order, and therefore in contact with divinity through a new life, which is the very life of God, in which man shares. His dignity, therefore, grows to infinite proportions and, in like measure, increases the nobility of the jurist who makes him the object of his science.

Conflicts of Conscience

The irreconcilable contrasts between the lofty conception of man and of law according to the Christian principles, which We have attempted to expound briefly, and juridical positivism may become the source of inner bitterness in professional life. We know well how conflicts not infrequently arise in the conscience of the Catholic jurist, desirous of remaining true to the Christian conception of law, especially when he finds himself in the position of having to apply a law which his conscience condemns as unjust. As a matter of fact, from the end of the eighteenth century—especially in the regions where persecution of the Church was rife—there have been numerous cases of Catholic magistrates who found themselves faced with the painful problem of the application of unjust laws. Therefore, We take this opportunity to enlighten the conscience of Catholic jurists by enunciating some fundamental norms.

For every sentence passed, the principle holds good that the judge cannot purely and simply disclaim all responsibility for his decision, placing it totally on the law and on its authors. These are certainly principally responsible for the effects of the law itself. But the judge, who with his sentence applies it to the particular case, is a party to it, and therefore shares the responsibility for those effects.

The judge may never with his decision oblige anyone to commit any intrinsically immoral act, that is, an act which is by its nature contrary to the law of God and of the Church.

He may in no case expressly recognize and approve of an unjust law (which, in any case, would never constitute the basis of a valid judgment before his conscience and before God). He cannot therefore pronounce a penal sentence which would be tantamount to such an approval. His responsibility would be even more grave if his sentence were to cause a public scandal.

However, not every application of an unjust law is equivalent to recognizing and approving it. In this case, the judge may—and sometimes, perhaps, must—let the unjust law take its course, when that is the only way to avoid a still greater evil. In order to avoid harm or to ensure a good of much greater importance, he may inflict a penalty for the transgression of an unjust law if it is of such a nature that the person involved is reasonably disposed to endure it, and provided the judge knows and can prudently suppose that such a sanction will be readily accepted by the transgressor, for superior reasons. In times of persecution, both priests and laymen have permitted themselves to be sentenced, without putting up any resistance, and even by Catholic magistrates, to pay fines or be deprived of their personal freedom, for infraction of unjust laws, when by so doing it was possible to preserve for the people an honest magistrature and ward off from the Church and from the faithful much more terrible calamities.

Capital Punishment and Divorce

Of course, the more gravid of consequences is the judicial sentence, the more important and general must be the good it aims to protect or the evil it aims to avoid. There are, however, cases in which the idea of compensation through the attainment of superior benefits or the banishment of greater evils cannot apply, as for instance in the death sentence. In particular, the Catholic judge may not pronounce, unless for motives of great moment, a sentence of civil divorce (where it exists) for a marriage which is valid before God and the Church. He must not forget that such a sentence, in practice, has not civil effects only, but in reality leads rather to the erroneous belief that the present bond is broken and the new one valid and binding.[†]

Science and Religion

The marvel of creation has challenged the admiration and intellect of all peoples for centuries... The ways and means of deciphering it have caused heated arguments between the learned investigators of nature, matter, and spirit. These efforts and arguments are nothing other than the search for the truth hidden within the enigma of creation. What else, what more, does the human soul desire than truth?

Just as we do not create nature, neither do we create the truth: our doubts, our opinions, our assertions or denials do not change it. We are not the measure of truth in the world, nor of ourselves, nor of the high objective to which we are destined. Our sagacious art measures the reliability of our tools and instruments, of our apparatus and contrivances, transforms and fetters and subdues the materials which nature offers us, but it does not create them; and it must be satisfied to follow nature as the disciple follows the master whose work he imitates. When our intellect does not conform to the reality of things or is deaf to the voice of nature, it wanders in the illusion of dreams and pursues a phantom.

† Address to the First National Congress of Italian Catholic Jurists (November 6, 1949).

The Church and Scientific Progress

But not only our technical arts come from God, but also the perception of truth in our intellect, since, in the scale of creation, it stands, as it were, on the third degree in descending order, below nature and below God.

As a friend of truth, the Church admires and loves the progress of knowledge, as she does that of the arts and of everything connected with learning.

Is not the Church herself the divine progress in the world and the mother of the highest intellectual and moral progress of mankind and the civilized life of the peoples of the earth? She advances through the centuries, teacher of truth and virtue, contending against error and not against those who have wandered from the fold, not destroying but constructing...

As with every art, every science serves God, because God is *scientiarum dominus*—Master of sciences—and *docet hominem scientiam*—Teacher of sciences to mankind. In His school, man has two textbooks. In the book of the universe, human reason in search of the truth studies the good things made by God; in the book of the Bible, the human intellect and good will search for a truth higher than reason, sublime as the intimate mystery of God, known only to Him. The school of God is the meeting place of philosophy and theology, of the divine word and paleontology, of the division of the light from darkness and astronomy, of the earth set in its appointed place and its rotation around the sun, of the view of God and the view of man. God's goodness, like a mother's, takes on, as it were, the hesitations of the human language to help man retain the lofty truth which He reveals to him in order to exalt him and in his study of nature and faith make him a disciple of God. The Church has also made this school her school and the platform from which she teaches...

Reason and Faith

No, the homage which reason renders faith does not humiliate reason but honors it and exalts it, for the highest achievement of the progress of human civilization is that it facilitates the path of faith as it evangelizes the world. Faith is not proud, it is not a lord that tyrannizes over reason, nor does it contradict it: the seal of truth is impressed by God no differently upon faith than upon reason. Indeed, not only do they not dissent, but they help one another in turn, as We have already pointed out, since clear reason demonstrates the foundations of faith and clarifies its terms with its light, while faith preserves reason from error, widens its horizon, and enlarges it with various knowledge.[†]

It is a fact that a considerable number of men of great culture are separated from Christian thought. The universities and the general studies are not of today or of yesterday; they were born in the Middle Ages in the bosom and under the protection of the Church. Even then one sometimes found errors, heresies, antisocial theories; however, in those days, Christian thought spread its wings at the universities, forming and directing the mind. The torch of faith radiated its light, a faith that does not humiliate the intellect, and when it makes it kneel down in reverence, rather exalts it before the truth and truthfulness of God. For it is God Who, in the admirable accord of the science of reason with divine science, renders the human intellect angelic. But what have been the results of the slow work of spiritual dissolution originating in pagan humanism, in the Enlightenment, in the philosophies of the eighteenth century, in the idealism and positivism of the nineteenth, against which the reality of the world and of man cries out? What advantages and progress have society, the family, and the human individual derived from them? Look at university culture. How many fields of study and scientific research have developed and expanded without any contact with Catholic thought, without taking into account the great fact of supernatural revelation, expanding in a sphere which, if not always antireligious, at least ignores religion? Out of them has come a de-Christianization of the spirit in many of the older generation who are called upon to guide their brothers, to enlighten others, to think for them and direct them in life, a de-Christianization of which we taste today the bitter fruit.

By this divorce and antagonism between science and religion, truth cannot be obscured or cast down from her throne of light, because she herself is light and throne, vestige and radiance of the inaccessible light in which God has His throne, and from which, like two streams from the same source, the truths of reason and the truths of faith descend to man. There is never a

† Address at the Inauguration of the Fourth Year of the Pontifical Academy of Sciences (December 3, 1939).

quarrel between them, they are sisters of unequal beauty. They do not disdain, nay, they love to show themselves friends in the human mind, eager for all flashes of truth, manifest and hidden: thus the great and sublime geniuses of the Christian centuries were content to make their intellects the handmaid of faith and bow their heads before "the shame that was Golgotha."‡

Rediscovery of God Through Science

Contrary to rash statements in the past, the more true science advances, the more it discovers God, almost as though He were standing, vigilant and waiting, behind every door which science opens. Furthermore, We wish to say that not only does the philosophical thinker benefit from this progressive discovery of God, achieved in the increase of knowledge—and how could he do otherwise?—but those also profit who participate in the new discoveries or who make them the object of their considerations. The genuine philosophers especially benefit from it, since, by using the scientific advances as a springboard for their rational speculations, they can achieve greater security in their conclusions, clearer illustrations in possible obscurity, more convincing support in finding ever more satisfactory answers to difficulties and objections.

Nature and Basis of Proofs for the Existence of God

Thus directed and guided, the human intellect moves to meet that demonstration of the existence of God, which Christian wisdom recognizes in the philosophical arguments weighed through the centuries by giants of learning and, which is well known in the presentation of the "five paths" which the Angelic Doctor St. Thomas offers as the sure and expeditious itinerary of the mind to God. Philosophical arguments, We have said; but not for that aprioristic, as an ungenerous and self-contradictory positivism has accused them of being. They are based upon concrete realities ascertained by the senses and sciences, even if they acquire conclusive strength only from the vigor of natural reason.

‡ Address to University Youth (April 20, 1941).

In this manner, philosophy and the sciences develop with analogous and compatible methods, taking advantage of empirical and reasonable elements in differing measures and working together in harmonious unity toward the discovery of the truth.

But if the primitive experience of the ancients was able to offer sufficient arguments to reason to demonstrate the existence of God, now, with the amplification and deepening of the field of experience itself, the imprint of the Eternal upon the visible world is all the more splendid and radiantly visible. It seems profitable, therefore, to re-examine the classical proofs of St. Thomas on the basis of the new scientific discoveries, especially those based upon the movement and order of the universe; to consider, that is, if and to what extent the more profound knowledge of the structure of the macrocosm and the microcosm contributes to the reinforcement of philosophic arguments. On the other hand, it is not unprofitable to see if and to what point these arguments, as is not infrequently affirmed, have been shaken by the fact that modern physics has formulated new fundamental principles, abolished or modified ancient concepts, whose meaning was perhaps in the past adjudged fixed and definite, as, for example, time, space, movement, causality, substance, concepts of the greatest importance for the question that now holds our attention. Rather than a revision of the philosophic proofs, it is a question of scrutinizing the physical bases from which those arguments derive—and We must necessarily limit Ourselves to only a few for reasons of space. But there is no fear of surprises: science itself remains firmly grounded in that world which today, as yesterday, presents itself in those five "modes of being" from which the philosophic demonstration of the existence of God takes its motives and force.

Two Essential Hallmarks of the Cosmos

Of these "modes of being" of the world which surrounds us, perceived with more or less understanding, but with equal evidence, by the philosopher and the common intelligence, there are two which the modern sciences have sounded, verified, and probed wonderfully and beyond all expectation: the mutability of things, including their beginning and their end; the order of finality which shines in every corner of the cosmos.

The contribution made by the sciences to the two philosophical demonstrations is truly notable; and upon them hinge and are constituted the first and fifth ways. Physics especially has contributed to the first an inexhaustible mine of experience, revealing the fact of mutability in the profound recesses of nature, where before now no human mind could ever even suspect its existence and amplitude, and furnishing a multiplicity of empirical facts which gave highly valid support to the philosophical reasoning.

We say support, because the very direction of these transformations, while verified by modern physics, seems to Us to surpass the value of a simple confirmation and almost attains the structure and the level of physical argument which is largely new, and more acceptable, persuasive, and agreeable to many minds.

With equal richness, the sciences, especially astronomy and biology, have recently supplied to the argument of order such a wealth of knowledge and such an intoxicating vision, as it were, of the conceptual unity which animates the cosmos, and of the finality which directs its march, as to give to modern man in advance that joy which Dante imagined in the empyrean Heaven when he saw how "all that is dispersed through the universe is united by love in the mind of God."

Providence has disposed that the idea of God, so essential to the life of each man, while it can be easily grasped by a simple glance at the world so that not to comprehend the voice of nature is sheer foolishness, shall receive confirmation from every deepening of the understanding and progress in the field of scientific knowledge.

We wish, therefore, to give a few rapid examples of the precious service which modern sciences render to the demonstration of the existence of God. We limit Ourselves first to the fact of mutations, revealing principally the amplitude, the vastness, and, as it were, the totality which modern physics meets with in the inanimate cosmos. Then we shall pause for a look at the significance of their direction, which has been also ascertained. It will be as though one listened to a concerto within the immense universe, which sings "the glory of Him who moves all things."

The Mutability of the Cosmos

It is truly astonishing at first glance to see how the knowledge of the fact of mutability has steadily gained ground in both the macrocosm and the microcosm as the sciences have gradually progressed, almost confirming with new proofs the theory of Heraclitus: "Everything flows."

Daily experience demonstrates the enormous quantity of transformations in the world, near and far, which surrounds us, especially the local movements of bodies. But in addition to these true and actual local motions, multiform chemicophysical changes are equally easy for us to see, as, for example, the mutation of the physical state of water in its three phases of vapor, liquid, and ice; the profound chemical effects brought about by the use of fire, the knowledge of which goes back to prehistoric ages; the disintegration of stone and the corruption of vegetable and animal bodies. To this common experience natural science was added, which teaches us to understand these and other similar events as processes of destruction or construction of corporeal substances in their chemical elements, that is to say, in their smallest parts, the chemical atoms. It further teaches us that this chemicophysical mutability is in no way restricted to terrestrial bodies, according to the belief of the ancients, but is extended to all bodies of our solar system and the great universe, which the telescope, and, even more, the spectroscope, have shown to be formed of the same kind of atoms.

Against the indisputable mutability of nature, including inanimate beings, there arose the enigma of the unexplored microcosm. It seemed, indeed, that inorganic matter, as opposed to the animated world, was in a certain sense immutable. Its smallest parts, the chemical atoms, could certainly unite among themselves in the most various ways, but it seemed that they enjoyed the privilege of an eternal stability and indestructibility, issuing unchanged from every chemical synthesis and analysis. A hundred years ago, elementary particles were still believed to be simple, indivisible, and indestructible. The same was thought of the energies and material forces of the cosmos, especially on the basis of the fundamental laws of the conservation of mass and energy. Some naturalists considered themselves authorized to the extent of formulating in the name of their science a fantastic monistic philosophy, the inglorious memory of which is bound to the name of Ernst Haeckel, among others. But during his own times, toward the end of the last century, this oversimplified conception of the chemical atom was also upset by modern science. The growing knowledge of the periodical system of chemical elements, the discovery of the corpuscular irradiation of radioactive elements, and many other similar facts have demonstrated that the microcosm of the chemical atom with dimensions in the order of one ten-millionth of a millimeter is a theater of continual mutation, no less than the macrocosm.

Mutability in the Electronic Sphere

The character of mutability was first verified in the electronic sphere. From the electronic structure of the atom, irradiations of light and heat emanate, which are absorbed by external bodies in a manner corresponding to the level of energy of the electronic orbits. In the exterior parts of this sphere the ionization of the atom is carried out as well as the transformation of energy and the analysis of chemical combinations. It was supposed, however, that these chemicophysical transformations still left one refuge for stability, because they had not reached the nucleus itself of the atom, home of the mass and the positive electric charge, by which the place of the chemical atom in the natural system of the elements is determined; and it almost seemed that the type of the absolutely stable and invariable had been met.

Mutability in the Nucleus

But already in the early days of the twentieth century, the observation of radioactive processes which are referable, in a last analysis, to the spontaneous dissolution of the nucleus, indicated that such a type did not exist. With the instability of the known aspects of nature verified as far as its most profound recesses, there was one fact which left investigators perplexed, because it seemed that the atom was impregnable at least to human forces, since in principle all the attempts to accelerate or arrest the natural radioactive dissolution, even the splitting of the nonactive nuclei, had failed. The first rather modest splitting of a nucleus (of nitrogen) goes back a bare three decades, and only for the past few years has it been possible, after great efforts, to bring about, in considerable quantities, processes of formation and decomposition of nuclei. Although this result, which, in so far as it serves the purposes of peace, will certainly be a matter of pride for our century, can be considered only a first step in the field of practical nuclear physics, nevertheless, it lends weight to our consideration: the atomic nuclei are certainly, for many orders of magnitude, less active and more stable than the ordinary chemical compositions, but notwithstanding that, they are also in general subject to similar laws of transformation, and therefore mutable.

At the same time, it has been discovered that such processes have the greatest importance in the economy of the energy of the fixed stars. At the center of our sun, for example, according to Bethe, a temperature which averages around twenty million degrees centigrade is reached, a recurring chain reaction in itself in which four nuclei of hydrogen are joined to a nucleus of helium. The energy which is thus freed compensates for the loss due to the irradiation of the sun itself. In modern physics laboratories also, it is possible to bring about transformations of nuclei by means of a bombardment with particles furnished with great energy, and with neutrons. This has been accomplished with the uranium atom, for example. In this connection, the effects of cosmic radiation should be mentioned, which can split the heaviest atoms, not infrequently giving off entire swarms of subatomic particles.

We wished to cite only a few examples, enough to place beyond doubt the definite mutability of the inorganic world, large and small: the thousandfold transformations of the forms of energy, especially in the chemical decomposition and combinations in the macrocosm, and no less the mutability of the chemical atoms as far as the subatomic particles of their nuclei.

The Eternally Immutable

The scientist of today, penetrating with his investigations more deeply into nature than his predecessor of a hundred years ago, knows that inorganic matter in its very marrow, in a manner of speaking, is stamped with the mark of mutability and therefore its being and its existence demand an entirely different reality and one that is by its nature immutable.

As in a painting in chiaroscuro the figures stand out from the dark background, obtaining in this manner alone the full effect of modelling and of life, so the image of the eternally immutable emerges clear and resplendent from the torrent that carries away with it all the material things in the macro- and microcosms and whirls them into an intrinsic mutability which never stops. The scientist who stands on the edge of this immense torrent finds relief in that cry of truth with which God defines Himself: "I am who am," and whom the Apostle praises as "*Pater luminum, apud quem non est transmutatio neque vicissitudinis obumbratio*—the Father of lights, with whom there is no change nor shadow of alteration."

The Direction of the Transformations

But modern science has not only enlarged and deepened our knowledge of the reality and magnitude of the mutability of the cosmos; it has also offered us valuable indications concerning the direction according to which the processes of nature are carried out. While a hundred years ago, especially after the discovery of the law of constants, it was thought that the natural processes were reversible and therefore, according to the principles of strict causality—or, rather, determination—an ever recurring renewal and rejuvenation of the cosmos was considered possible. With the law of entropy, discovered by Rudolf Clausius, it became known that the spontaneous natural processes are always related to a diminution of the free and utilizable energy, which in a closed material system must finally lead to a cessation of the processes on the macroscopic scale.

This fatal destiny, which only hypotheses, sometimes far too gratuitous ones such as that of the continuous renewal of creation, forcibly try to deny, but which instead comes from positive scientific experience, eloquently postulates the existence of a necessary Being.

In the microcosm, this law, which is actually statistical, is not applicable, and furthermore, at the time of its formulation, hardly anything was known of the structure and behavior of the atom. However, the most recent investigations of the atom and the quite unexpected development of astrophysics have made surprising discoveries possible in this field. Results can be mentioned here only briefly; they indicate that in the atomic and intra-atomic development a sense of direction is clearly noticeable.

In order to illustrate this fact it suffices to recall the already mentioned example of the behavior of solar energy. The electronic structure of the chemical atoms in the photosphere of the sun gives off each second a gigantic quantity of radiant energy into the surrounding space, an energy that does not return. The loss is compensated for from the interior of the sun by means of the formation of helium from hydrogen. The energy which is thus liberated derives from the mass of hydrogen nuclei, of which in this process a small part (seven percent) is converted into equivalent radiation. The process of compensation is carried out, therefore, at the expense of the energy which originally existed as mass in the nuclei of hydrogen. Thus this energy, in the course of billions of years, is slowly but irreparably transformed into radiation. A similar phenomenon occurs in all radioactive processes, whether natural or artificial. Here too, then, in the narrow confines of the microcosm itself, we meet with a law which indicates the direction of evolution and which is analogous to the law of entropy in the macrocosm. The direction of spontaneous evolution is determined by means of the diminution of the energy utilizable in the structure and the nucleus of the atom, and up to now no processes have been noted which could compensate or cancel this diminution by means of spontaneous formation of nuclei of high energetic value.

The Universe and Its Development

If, then, the scientist turns his gaze from the present state of the universe to the future, however far off, he will be forced to realize that the world is growing old, both in the macrocosm and in the microcosm. In the course of billions of years, even the quantity of atomic nuclei, which is apparently inexhaustible, loses its utilizable energy and matter approaches, to speak figuratively, the state of a spent and scorified volcano. And the thought presents itself inescapably: if the present cosmos, today so pulsating with rhythm and life, is not sufficient to account for its existence, as we have seen, how much less will it be the case for that cosmos once the shadow of death shall have passed over it.

We now turn our eyes toward the past. In proportion to the distance in time to which we turn backward, matter is seen to be richer and richer in free energy and the theater of great cosmic upheavals. Thus, everything seems to indicate that the material universe has had, in finite time, a powerful start, provided as it was with an unimaginable abundance of reserves in energy; then, with increasing slowness, it has evolved to its present state.

Two questions spontaneously come to mind:

Is science in a position to say when this powerful beginning of the cosmos took place? And what was the initial, primitive state of the universe?

The most noted experts in atomic physics, in co-operation with the astronomers and the astrophysicists, have put great effort into shedding light on these two difficult but extremely interesting problems.

Beginning of Time

First, to cite some figures, which serve only to express the order of magnitude in the designation of the dawn of our universe, that is, its beginning in time, science has at its disposal several paths of investigation, each fairly independent of the other, though they are convergent, as We indicate briefly:

The Velocity of Travel of the Spiral Nebulae or Galaxies

The examination of numerous spiral nebulae, carried out especially by Edwin E. Hubble at Mount Wilson Observatory, has demonstrated the significant result—though tempered by reserve—that these far-off systems of galaxies tend to rush away from one another at such speed that the space between two such spiral nebulae doubles in the period of about thirteen hundred million years. If one looks back across the period of this process of the "Expanding Universe" the conclusion is that from one to ten billion years ago the matter of all the spiral nebulae was compressed into a relatively narrow space, at the time of the beginning of the cosmic processes.

The Age of the Solid Crust of the Earth

To calculate the age of the original radioactive substances, highly approximate data are deduced from the transmutation of these substances into the corresponding isotope of lead, for instance the transformation of the isotope of uranium 238 into RaG, of the uranium isotope 235 into actinium D, and of the isotope of thorium 232 into thorium D. The mass of helium which is formed thereby can also serve as a check. In this way the average age of the most ancient minerals is indicated at a maximum of five billion years.

The Age of Meteorites

The preceding method, when applied to meteorites to calculate their age, gives about the same figure of five billion years. This result takes on special importance because the meteorites are generally believed to be of interstellar origin and, except for terrestrial minerals, they are the only examples of celestial bodies which can be studied in scientific laboratories.

The Stability of the Systems of Double Stars and Star Masses

The oscillations of gravitation within these systems, like the wearing away of the tides, again restrict their stability within the limits of from five to ten billion years.

Although these figures are astonishing, nevertheless, even the simplest believer would not take them as unheard of and differing from those derived from the first words of Genesis, "In the beginning…," which signify the beginning of things in time. These words take on a concrete and almost mathematical expression, and new comfort is given to those who share with the Apostle an esteem for that Scripture, divinely inspired, which is always useful *"ad docendum, ad arguendum, ad corripiendum, ad erudiendum*—to teach, to prove, to blame, to educate."

The State and Quality of Original Matter

With equal earnestness and freedom of investigation and verification, learned men, in addition to the question of the age of the cosmos, have applied their audacious talents to another question which we have already mentioned and which is certainly much more difficult, and that is the problem concerning the state and quality of primitive matter. According to the theories which are taken as a basis, the relative calculations differ considerably one from the other. Nevertheless, the scientists agree in holding that not only the mass but also the density, the pressure, and the temperature must have attained degrees of enormous intensity, as can be seen in the recent work of A. Unsöld, director of the Observatory in Kiel. Only under these conditions can one comprehend the formation of the heavy nuclei and their relative frequency in the periodical system of the elements.

On the other hand, the eager mind, in its search for truth, rightfully insists upon asking how matter came to be in a state so unlike that of our common experience of today, and what preceded it. One waits in vain for an answer from natural science, which honestly declares that this is an insoluble enigma. It is true that this is asking too much of natural science as such; but it is also true that the human spirit versed in philosophical speculation is able to penetrate the problem more profoundly.

It is undeniable that a mind illuminated and enriched by modern scientific knowledge, which calmly evaluates this problem, is led to break the circle of a matter preconceived as completely independent and autochthonous—either because uncreated or self-created—and to acknowledge a Creative Spirit. With the same clear and critical gaze with which he examines and judges facts, he also catches sight of and recognizes the work of the omnipotent Creator, whose power, aroused by the mighty "fiat" pronounced billions of years ago by the Creative Spirit, unfolded itself in the universe and, with a gesture of generous love, called into existence matter, fraught with energy. Indeed, it seems that the science of today, by going back in one leap millions of centuries, has succeeded in being a witness to that primordial *Fiat Lux*, when, out of nothing, there burst forth with matter a sea of light and radiation, while the particles of chemical elements split and reunited in millions of galaxies.

It is true that the facts verified up to now are not arguments of absolute proof of creation in time as are those which are drawn from metaphysics and revelation, in so far as they concern creation in its widest sense, and from revelation alone in so far as they concern creation in time. The facts pertinent to natural sciences, to which We have referred, still wait for further investigation and confirmation, and the theories founded upon them have need of new developments and proofs, in order to offer a secure basis to a line of reasoning which is, of itself, outside the sphere of the natural sciences.

Notwithstanding this, it is worth noting that modern exponents of the natural sciences consider the idea of the creation of the universe entirely reconcilable with their scientific conception, and indeed they are spontaneously brought to it by their researches, though only a few decades ago such a "hypothesis" was rejected as absolutely irreconcilable with the present status of science. As late as 1911, the celebrated physicist Svante Arrhenius declared that "the opinion that something can proceed from nothing is in contrast with the present status of science, according to which matter is immutable." Similar to this is Plate's affirmation: "Matter exists. Nothing proceeds from nothing: in consequence matter is eternal. We cannot admit the creation of matter."

Conclusion

What, then, is the importance of modern science in the argument for the existence of God drawn from the mutability of the cosmos? By means of exact and detailed investigations into the macrocosm and the microcosm, it has widened and deepened to a considerable extent the empirical foundation upon which the argument is based and from which we conclude a self-existent Being immutable by nature. Further, it has followed the course and the direction of cosmic developments, and just as it has envisioned the fatal termination, so it has indicated their beginning in time at a period about five billion years ago, confirming with the concreteness of physical proofs the contingency of the universe and the well-founded deduction that about that time the cosmos issued from the hand of the Creator.

Creation, therefore, in time, and therefore, a Creator; and consequently, God! This is the statement, even though not explicit or complete, that We demand of science, and that the present generation of man expects from it. It is a statement which rises from the mature and calm consideration of a single aspect of the universe, that is, of its mutability; but it is sufficient because all mankind, the apex and rational expression of the macrocosm and the microcosm, is made conscious of its sublime Creator and feels His presence in space and in time, and, falling to its knees before His sovereign Majesty, begins to call upon the name "*Rerum Deus, tenax vigor,—Immotus in te permanens—lucis diurnae tempora—successibus determinans.*"

The knowledge of God as unique Creator, a conviction shared by many modern scientists, is certainly the extreme limit which natural reason is capable of reaching; but it does not constitute the last frontier of truth. Science, which has encountered the Creator in its path, philosophy, and, much more, revelation, in harmonious collaboration because all three are instruments of truth, like rays of the same sun, contemplate the substance, reveal the outlines, and portray the lineaments of the same Creator. Revelation especially renders the presence almost immediate, full of life and love, which is what the simple believer and the scientist are aware of in the intimacy of their spirits when they repeat without hesitation the concise words of the ancient Creed of the Apostles: "*Credo in Deum, Patrem omnipotentem, Creatorem caeli et terrae!*"†

The World of Today

The System of Natural Laws

If until recently two constant laws were known—that of the conservation of mass and that of the conservation of energy—the most recent research has proved with ever more convincing facts and arguments that every mass is equivalent to a determined quantity of energy and vice versa. Therefore, the two ancient laws of conservation are, in effect, special applications of a more

† Address, Pontifical Academy of Sciences (November 22, 1951).

general higher law, which says: In a closed system, despite all changes, even where there is a considerable transformation of mass into energy or vice versa, the sum of both remains constant. This higher law of constancy is one of the keys the atomic physicist employs today to penetrate the mysteries of the atomic nucleus.

Such a scientific system of the macrocosm, rich in internal connections and well organized, contains beyond all doubt many laws of statics, which, however, because of the multitude of elements—atoms, molecules, electrons, protons, etc.—are not, as regards certainty and accuracy, inferior to strictly dynamic laws. In any case, they are founded and anchored, as it were, in rigidly dynamic laws of the microcosm, although knowledge of the microcosmic laws is in its details still almost completely hidden from us, despite the formidable efforts made by recent research to penetrate the mysterious activity within the atom. Gradually these veils may fall; then the apparently noncausal character of microcosmic phenomena will disappear: a wonderful new kingdom of order, of order even in the smallest particles, will be discovered.

Max Planck's Investigation of the Atom

And these intimate processes of the investigation of the atom will appear as really surprising to us, not only because they open up before our eyes a world hitherto unknown, whose richness, multiplicity, and regularity seem somehow to vie with the sublime grandeur of the firmament, but also for the unpredictably grandiose effects that technology itself can expect from them. In this connection We cannot abstain from mentioning an astonishing phenomenon about which the Nestor of theoretical physics, Max Planck, Our Academician, has written in a recent article of his, *Sinn und Grenzen der exakten Wissenschaft* (*Meaning and Limits of the Exact Sciences*). The curious transformations of the atom have for many years occupied only research workers in pure science. The amount of energy sometimes developed in it was undoubtedly surprising; but, since atoms are extremely small, it was never seriously thought that they might become important even from a practical point of view. Today, on the other hand, this question has taken on an unexpected aspect as a consequence of the results of artificial radioactivity. It has in fact been established that in the splitting a uranium atom undergoes if it is bombarded by a neutron, two or three neutrons are freed, each of which may meet and smash another uranium atom. In this way the effects are multiplied, and it may happen that the growing number of collisions of neutrons with uranium atoms increases in a short time the number of freed neutrons and, proportionally, the sum of energy developed from them, to an extent so great that it is almost inconceivable. A special calculation shows that, by this reaction, a cubic meter of uranium oxide powder, in less than a hundredth of a second, develops enough energy to lift a weight of a billion tons to a height of twenty-seven kilometers: an amount of energy which could supplant for many years the activity of all the great electric power stations in the world. Planck ends with the observation that, although the technical utilization of such a tempestuous process cannot yet be envisaged, it nevertheless opens the way to serious possibilities, so that the thought of the construction of a uranium machine cannot be regarded as merely utopian. It is important above all, however, to prevent this reaction from taking place as an explosion, and to brake its course by apt precautionary chemical means. Otherwise, a dangerous catastrophe might occur, not only in the locality itself but also for our whole planet.

The Higher Laws of Life

If now from the boundless realm of the inorganic we elevate ourselves to the spheres of vegetative and sensitive life, we find there a new world of laws in the property, the multitude, the variety, the beauty, the order, the quality, and the utility of the various forces of nature that are part of our globe. Beside many laws of the inorganic world, we meet also special higher laws, laws peculiar to life, which cannot be reduced to the purely physicochemical ones, so that it is impossible to consider living beings as mere sums of physicochemical components. Nature opens up to us here a marvelous new horizon; let it be enough for Us to mention as examples: the laws of the development of organisms, the laws of external and internal sensations, and, above all, the fundamental pyschophysical law. Higher spiritual life, too, is regulated by natural laws, for the most part of such a quality that to define them precisely becomes more difficult the higher they stand in the order of being.

The Hidden Laws of Nature

This admirable and ordered system of qualitative and quantitative, particular and general laws of the macrocosm and the microcosm, is today largely unveiled in its intricacy to the scientist's eyes. And why do We say unveiled? Because it is not projected or constructed by us into nature, thanks to some innate subjective form of consciousness or of the human intellect, nor is it created purposely on behalf and for the use of such an economy of thought and study, that is, to facilitate our knowledge of things; nor is it, finally, the fruit or the conclusion of agreements or understandings among scientists studying nature. Natural laws exist, so to speak, incarnate and secretly operative within nature, and we, by observation and experiment, look for them and discover them.

It cannot be said that matter is not a reality, but an abstraction fashioned by physics; that nature is in itself unintelligible and that the world that can be apprehended by the senses is a world apart, where the phenomenon, which is appearance of the exterior world, gives us a vague notion only of the reality of the things it hides. No: nature is reality, recognizable reality. If things seem to be and are mute, they have, however, a language that speaks to us, that emerges from their bosom, like water from a perennial spring. This language is their causality which reaches our senses with the sight of colors and movement, with the sound of metals, the roar of whirlwinds, and the cries of animals, with the sweetness and the bitterness of honey and gall, with the scent of flowers, with the weight and temperature of their material substance, impressing upon us an image or likeness which is the vehicle for our intellect to lead us to the reality of things. Hence we speak not of the image or likeness of our intellect, but of the things themselves; and we can distinguish the phenomenon of the world of the senses from the substance of things, the appearance of gold from the gold itself, as the appearance of bread from bread itself, from whose substance we make food in order to assimilate and identify it with the substance of the body itself. The movement of things toward us calls forth an image in us; without an image there can be no conformity of our intellect with real things, and without an image knowledge becomes impossible; and we cannot call anything true unless it has some equivalent in our intellect. The things from which our mind takes its knowledge provide measurements to our mind and to the laws we find in them and take from them; but they, in turn, are measured by that eternal divine intellect which embraces all things created, as the mind of the craftsman embraces every work of his art. What do the hand and the brain of the scientist do? They discover them, reveal them, distinguish them, and classify them, not like one who follows flying birds, but like one who is in possession of them, and is investigating their nature and intrinsic properties.

When, in 1869, Lothar Meyer and Mendeleev arranged the chemical elements in that simple scheme which today is recognized as the natural system of the elements, they were deeply convinced that they had found a regular order, based on their properties and internal tendencies, a classification suggested by nature, the progressive development of which promised the most penetrating discoveries regarding the structure and essence of matter. In fact, modern atomic research began from that point... This is only one example among many, and therefore the most inspired scientists of the past and present have come to the lofty conclusion that they are heralds of a truth identical and the same for all peoples and races that walk the earth and look up at the sky; a truth resting, in its essence, on an *adaequatio rei et intellectus*, which is nothing but the acquired conformity, more or less perfect, more or less complete, of our intellect with the objective reality of natural things, in which the truth of our knowledge consists.

But do not be mistaken, like those philosophers and scientists who thought that our cognitive faculties know only their own mutations and sensations, so that they were induced to say that our intellect arrived at knowledge only from the images of things, and, therefore, that only the images of things, and not the things themselves, were the object of our science and of the laws we formulate with respect to nature. A manifest error!

Science, exalted by a Copernicus and a Galileo, a Kepler and a Newton, a Volta and a Marconi, and other famous and distinguished investigators of the physical world that surrounds us externally, would accordingly amount to a beautiful creation of daydreaming and a beautiful phantasm of physical knowledge; appearance would take the place of the reality and truth of things; and it would be just as true to assert as to deny the same thing. But no; science knows not dreams or images of things, but the things themselves through the images we receive from them, because, as the Angelic Doctor, following

Aristotle, has taught, a stone cannot be in our mind, but the image or figure of the stone can—the image which it produces, a true likeness, in our senses and then in our intellect, so that by this likeness it can be, and is, in our mind and in our study and make us return to it and to reality. Even recent research in experimental psychology testifies, or rather confirms, that these likenesses are not the mere product of autonomous, subjective activity, but psychic reactions to stimuli independent of the subject, coming from the things themselves; reactions in conformity with the different qualities and properties of things, which vary with the variation of the stimulus.

The images, therefore, which natural things, by way of light and heat, or by way of sound, taste, and smell, or by any other means, impress on the organs of our senses and which, through the inner senses, arrive at our intellect, are nothing but the instrument provided us by nature, our first teacher of knowledge, to make herself known to us; but it is no less true that we can examine, study, investigate this instrument and think about these images and how much they present to us of nature, and the way in which they become our sources of knowledge of the world which surrounds us. From the act of cognition by which our intellect understands a stone, we pass on to the act of understanding how our intellect understands a stone: an act which follows the first, since man, born without innate ideas and without recollections of a previous life, enters the world devoid of images and knowledge—born and created, as We have already recalled, "with his senses only, to learn what he later will do in the light of reason."

The Spectacle of the Earth

Admire, O probers of nature and of the laws that govern it, in the center of the material universe the greatness of man, to whose first encounter with light, greeted by his infant wailing, God holds open the spectacle of the earth and the firmament with all the marvels to enchant him and attract his innocent eyes! What is this spectacle if not the fundamental and first object of all human knowledge, which embarks from there with thousands upon thousands of inquiries with which the teacher nature entices again and again the avidity of our senses?

You wonder at yourselves; you scrutinize your inner acts, you withdraw within yourselves to seek their sources, and you find them in these internal senses, in these powers and faculties, which you make the object of a new science of yourselves, of your intimate rational nature, of your feeling, your intellect, and your will. And so we have the science of man and of his corporal and psychic laws, anatomy, physiology, medicine, psychology, ethics, politics, and that sum total of sciences which, even with all its errors, is a hymn to God Who, when He molded man, breathed into him a vital spirit, superior to that of other living beings, making him into His image and likeness. Thus the material extrinsic macrocosm has a great deal to say to the spiritual intrinsic microcosm: one and the other in their operating power are supremely regulated by the Author of the laws of matter and spirit. But the changes of the spirit, which listens to the voice and the marvels of the universe, are sometimes terrible, sometimes give it vertigo, sometimes raise it powerfully and make it take strides, also in the progress of science, which are more gigantic than the regular movements of the planets and the constellations in the heavens, to the point of sublimating it from the material physical world of its study to the spiritual world beyond the created one to praise "Love that moves the sun and all the other stars."

This love, which has created, moves, and governs the universe, also rules and directs the history and progress of all humanity, and guides everything toward an end, hidden from our thought by the mist of time, but fixed forever by Him for that glory which the heavens show forth and which He awaits from the love of man, whom He has permitted to fill the earth and subdue it with his labor. May this love arouse and direct the desire and the good will of the powerful and of all men to become brethren, to act in peace and justice, to be inflamed by the fire of the immense, beneficial charity of God, and cease drenching in blood and filling with devastation and tears this earth, on which all of us, under whatever sky, have been placed to struggle as the children of God, for an eternal life of happiness.[†]

† Address at the Inauguration of the Seventh Year of the Pontifical Academy of Sciences (February 22, 1943).

The Atomic Age

On our globe, under our eyes, man appears master and potent above all the natural living creatures—man, to whom God assigned the duty to multiply and to populate the earth and procure the bread on which he lives; therefore, it is not astonishing that the great philosopher Aristotle should compare the human soul to the hand, the organ before all other organs. Everything, in fact, we owe to the hand: cities and fortresses, monuments, books of knowledge, of science, of art and poetry, the inheritance and patrimony of libraries and of human civilization. Similarly, the soul has been given to man, one might say, in place of all sorts of things so that he might procure, in some way, all these things, inasmuch as our soul can receive through the senses and intellect all the shapes or images of the things themselves.

Knowledge of Natural Laws and Domination of Natural Forces

The genuine law of nature which the scientist formulates with patient observation and diligence in his laboratory is much more and better than a mere description or intellectual calculation, which considers only phenomena and not the real substances with their properties. It does not stop at, nor is it satisfied by, the appearance and the image of senses, but penetrates into the depths of reality, searches and discovers the intimate hidden forces of the phenomena, manifests their activity and relationships.

It is therefore easy to understand that the knowledge of the laws of nature makes it possible for man to dominate the natural forces and place them at his service in the highly advanced modern technology. Only in this way can human thought elevate itself to understand how the regular order of the spectroscopic lines, which the physicist observes and distinguishes today in his laboratory, will disclose perhaps tomorrow to the astrophysicist a deeper vision and knowledge of the mysteries of the composition and development of the celestial bodies.

Thus, from the foundation of the law of nature, with the active help of modern technological means, and by the positive and true knowledge of the internal tendencies of the elements and of their effects in the natural phenomena, the scientist proceeds, against all difficulties and obstacles, to further discoveries, pursuing his research with constancy and perseverance.

The most grandiose example of the results of such intense activity seems to be found in the fact that man's relentless efforts have finally succeeded in reaching a deeper knowledge of the laws which concern the formation and disintegration of the atom, and in that way to master experimentally, up to a certain point, the release of the powerful energy which emanates from many such processes, and all this not in submicroscopic quantity, but in truly gigantic measure.

The use of a great part of the internal energy of the nucleus of uranium has become a reality and has had its application in the making of the "atom bomb" or "nuclear energy bomb," the most terrible weapon which human mind has conceived up to date.

In this state of affairs We cannot refrain from expressing a thought which constantly weighs upon Our soul, as well as upon that of all who have a true sense of humanity; and in this connection We recall the words of St. Augustine in his treatise *De Civitate Dei*, where he talks about the horrors of war, even of a just war: "Of which evils"—he writes—"if I were to narrate, as it should be, the many and manifold devastations, the harsh and cruel sufferings, although it would be impossible to do justice to the subject, when would we reach the end of the long dispute? Whoever considers with sorrow these horrible and fatal evils, must confess their misery; but whoever endures them and thinks of them without anguish in his soul, much more miserably believes himself to be happy, because he has also lost human feeling." But if the wars of that period already justify such a severe judgment of the Great Doctor, with what words should We judge at present those which struck our generations and bent to the service of their work of destruction and extermination a technology incomparably more advanced? What misfortunes should humanity expect from a future conflict, if it should prove to be impossible to arrest or curb the use of ever newer and ever more surprising scientific inventions?

Conquests of the Human Intellect

But putting aside, for the moment, the use of atomic energy in war, and in the confident hope that it be directed instead solely to projects of peace, it must be considered as a truly inspired investigation and application of those laws of nature which regulate the intimate essence and activity of inorganic matter.

In truth, properly speaking, this involves only one single great law of nature, which manifests itself above all in the so-called "periodic system of the elements."

Up to a short time ago, science and technology had been interested almost exclusively in the problems regarding the synthesis and analysis of molecules and chemical compounds; now, instead, the interest is concentrated on the analysis and synthesis of the atom and of its nucleus. Above all, furthermore, the work of the scientists will have no rest until it finds an easy and sure way to govern the process of splitting the atomic nucleus, in order to make its very rich sources of energy serve the progress of civilization.

Amazing conquests of the human intellect, which scrutinizes and investigates the laws of nature, carrying humanity with it along new paths! Can one envisage a more exalted concept?

Idea and Design of God

But law means order; and universal law means order in great things as well as small. It is an order deriving immediately from the intimate tendencies innate in natural things; an order that nothing can create by itself or give of itself to itself, as no being can give itself to itself; an order that signifies the Order of Reason in a Spirit which has created the universe and on which "depend Heaven and the whole of nature"; an order which those tendencies and energies received as they came into being and through which both collaborate for a well-ordered world.

This marvelous assemblage of natural laws, which the human spirit, with tireless observation and accurate study, discovered, adding victories upon victories over the occult resistances of the forces of nature, what else is it but an image, though pale and imperfect, of the great idea and of the great divine design, which in the mind of God the Creator is conceived as a law of this universe since the days of His eternity? Then, in the inexhaustible thinking of His wisdom, He prepared the heavens and the earth, and then, creating the light on the abysses of chaos, cradle of the universe also created by Him, He gave a beginning to motion and to the flight of time and of centuries, and called into being, into life and activity, all things according to their species and their kind, to the most imponderable atom. How rightly every intellect which contemplates and penetrates the heavens and weighs the stars and earth should exclaim, turning to God: "*Omnia in mensura et numero et pondere disposuisti*—You have disposed everything in measure and number and weight!"

The scientist almost feels the palpitation of this eternal wisdom, when his research reveals to him that the universe is formed as in one casting in the boundless foundry of time and space. Not only the starry heavens shine, composed of the same elements, but they even obey the same great and fundamental cosmic laws, always and wherever they appear, in their internal and external action. The same laws of gravitation and of the pressure of radiation determine the quantity of mass for the formation of the solar bodies in the immensity of the universe up to the farthest nebulous spirals; the same mysterious laws of the atomic nucleus regulate, through atomic composition and disintegration, the economy of the energy of all fixed stars.

This absolute unity of design and government which manifests itself in the inorganic world you find no less grandiose in the living organisms. What else does a simple look at the universal and common structure of the organisms and at the most recent discoveries and conclusions of anatomy and comparative physiology show you? Take the construction of a skeleton of a higher living being with analogous organs, and especially the disposition and function of sensitive organs—for instance, of the eye from the simplest forms to the very perfect visual organ of man; take, in the whole realm of living creatures, the fundamental laws of assimilation, metabolism, and generation. Does not all this indeed show a general and magnificent unified concept, realized and resplendent in various forms and in very many different ways? Is this not perhaps the closed and absolutely fixed unity of natural laws?

Divine Government of the Universe and Miracles

Yes; it is a unity closed with the key of that universal order of things against which, inasmuch as it depends on the first Cause of a Creative God, God Himself cannot act; because, if He should do so, He would operate against His own prescience or His will or His goodness; now, in Him "there is no change, nor the shadow of variation." But if this order is considered as dependent on secondary causes, God possesses its key and can leave it closed or open it and operate beyond it. Could it be that God, in creating the universe, made Himself subject to the order of secondary inferior causes? Is not this order, indeed, subject to Him, emanating from Him, not as a necessity of nature, but from arbitrary will? Hence He can act beyond the instituted order when He pleases; for instance, by working the effects of secondary causes without recourse to them, or producing other effects, to which they do not extend. What works then are these? They are works of which God alone holds the key in His secret and which He reserved for Himself in the passage of time amid the particular order of subordinated causes.

Before such works, extraordinary either because of the substance of the fact itself, or because of the person in which they manifest themselves, or because of the manner and order in which they are accomplished, people and scientists stand astonished. The miracle is born when the effects are manifest and the cause concealed. But the ignorance of the hidden cause, which astonishes the unbeliever, sharpens the eye of the faithful and of the learned, who, within certain limits, know and measure how far the work of nature, with its laws and forces, reaches; beyond that reach they see the work of a superior hidden and omnipotent hand, that hand which created the universal order of things, and in the process of the particular orders of cause and effect marked the moment and circumstances of its marvelous intervention.

This divine government of the universe certainly cannot but arouse a feeling of admiration and enthusiasm in the scientist, who in his research discovers and recognizes the traces of the wisdom of the Creator and supreme Legislator of Heaven and earth, who with the hand of an invisible pilot guides all the creatures "to different ports—through the great sea of being—each one endowed with the instinct that carries it."

Yet, what are the tremendous laws of nature if not a shadow and mere idea of the depth and immensity of the divine design in the grandiose temple of the universe? Often—We have to confess Our human weakness—before the vision of the things and images of Our senses, that thought becomes dim and retreats; but if the thought of God enters the work of the scientist, he does not confuse it with the movements or images that he sees in or outside of himself; and that disposition of soul to search for and recognize God gives him, in his laborious study, the proper enthusiasm and copious compensation for all the labors endured in the interest of research and discovery, and, far from making him proud and conceited, teaches him humility and modesty.

Certainly, the more deeply the cultivator of knowledge and science pushes his research into the wonders of nature, the more he feels his insufficiency to penetrate and exhaust the wealth of the design of the divine construction and of the laws and norms which govern it...

Further Progress of Science

Incessant is the progress of science. It is true that the successive states of its progress have not always followed the path which from first observations and discoveries leads directly to the hypothesis, from the hypothesis to the theory, and finally to the certain and unquestionable attainment of the truth. There are, instead, cases where the investigation follows a sort of curve; cases, namely, in which theories that seemed to have already conquered the world and reached the apex of undisputed doctrines, acceptance of which brought esteem in the realm of science, fall again to the level of hypotheses, to remain perhaps, later, completely abandoned.

Notwithstanding, however, the inevitable uncertainties and deviations that any human effort brings with it, the progress of science knows no pauses nor leaps.

Through new and broader avenues, humanity is advancing, but always like a pilgrim, toward deeper knowledge of the laws of the explored or unexplored universe, as it is spurred on by the natural thirst for truth; however, even after thousands of years human knowledge of the internal principles of the moving forces of the growth and processes of the world, and even more of the design and divine impulse which penetrates, moves, and directs everything, will be and will remain an imperfect and pale image of the divine conception. In the face of the prodigies of eternal wisdom which, in the sea of the living, govern everything with undeviating order and direct all things toward hidden harbors, the investigating thoughts of the scientist are blind and mute, and give way to that humble admiring adoration that sees before it the marvel of creation, in which the hand of man was not present and which it cannot imitate, but in which his eye can discern a sudden flash of the power of God. Before the many inscrutable enigmas of the order and concatenation of the laws of the immensely great and immensely small cosmos, the human mind must repeat the exclamation: "*O altitudo divitiarum sapientiae et scientiae Dei: quam incomprehensibilia sunt indicia eius et investigabiles viae eius!*—O the depth of the riches of the wisdom and of the knowledge of God! How incomprehensible are His judgments, and how inscrutable His ways!"†

On the "New" World Order

On the eve of the first coming of Christ, when the Roman world seemed to embrace the entire globe, a new order was already expected, and Virgil sang of the great hope and the return of the virgin goddess of justice: "*Magnus ab integro saeculorum nascitur ordo; iam redit et Virgo*—Great and newly is born the order of the centuries; now returns the Virgin." Even today the entire world feels the need of a rebirth of order, in which each may work in his own way, in his rightful place, and according to his own ability. Look at the statesmen: what is and must be their mission? Is it not, certainly, to provide for the common good and temporal order, in harmony, obviously, with the exigencies of eternal and supernatural order? On the other hand, look at the Church. She has an even higher mission: to restore, promote, and extend, in the realm of human society, the Kingdom of God, outside of which there can

† Message, Inauguration of the Twelfth Year of the Pontifical Academy of Sciences (February 8, 1948).

never be consolidated that true, sincere, permanent, calm order, which is the correct definition of peace.‡

Christian Moral Law a Prerequisite

The new order, which after the suffering and destruction of this past war all the peoples long to see realized, must be built upon the firm, immutable rock of moral law, manifested by the Creator Himself through the natural order, and engraved by Him, with indelible characters, in the hearts of men; moral law, whose observance must be inculcated and promoted by public opinion in all nations and all States with such unanimity of voice and force that no one can dare to put it in question or weaken its obliging bond.

Like a wonderful beacon, it must with the rays of its principles direct the course of the labors of men and nations, which must follow its admonishing, salutary, and profitable signals, if they do not want to condemn to storm and shipwreck every labor and effort to establish a new order. Summing up, therefore, and integrating what We expounded on other occasions, We still insist on certain essential prerequisites for an international order, which, while assuring a just and lasting peace to all peoples, will bring forth well-being and prosperity.

The Right to Neutrality

In the field of a new order founded on moral principles, there is no place for prejudice to the liberty, integrity, and security of other nations, whatever their territorial extension or capacity for defense. While it is inevitable that the great nations, because of their greater potential power, trace the path for the establishment of economic groups between themselves and the smaller, weaker nations, the right of these to have their liberty respected in the political field is no less incontestable than their right to effective protection of that neutrality in disputes among States which belongs to them according to natural as well

‡ Address to Men of Catholic Action (September 20, 1942).

as international law. Furthermore, the right to protection of their economic development, since only in this way can they adequately attain the common good, the material and spiritual well-being, of their own people.

The Right of Minorities

In the field of a new order founded on moral principles, there is no place for open or camouflaged oppression of the cultural and linguistic peculiarities of national minorities, for hindering or curtailing their economic capacity, for limiting or abolishing their natural fecundity. The more conscientiously the competent authorities of the State respect the rights of the minority, the more surely and effectively can it demand of its members that they carry out loyally the civic duties which are shared with other citizens.

Access to Basic Materials

In the field of a new order founded on moral principles, there is no place for narrow, egotistical calculations tending to corner sources of economic supply and basic materials to the exclusion of nations less favored by nature. In this connection, it is a great consolation to Us to see affirmed the necessity that all partake of the goods of the earth, even among those nations which in the realization of this principle would belong to the category of the givers and not of the receivers.

But it is a matter of equity to find a solution to this question—so decisive for world economics—which would proceed methodically and progressively with the necessary guarantees, and would take a lesson from the shortcomings and failures of the past. If, in the future peace, this point should not be faced squarely, it would remain in international relations as a germ capable of sprouting bitter contrasts and exasperating jealousies, leading in the end to new conflicts. It is necessary, however, to observe how a satisfactory solution of this problem is closely connected with another fundamental rule of the new order, of which We shall now speak.

Limitation of Armaments

In the field of a new order founded on moral principles, once the most dangerous igniters of an armed conflict are eliminated, there is no place for total war or an unchecked arms race. It must not be permitted that the tragedy of a world war, with its economic and social ruin and its moral aberrations and disturbances, should fall upon humanity for a third time. In order to stave off such a scourge, it is necessary to proceed seriously and honestly toward progressive and adequate limitation of armaments. The want of balance between the excessive armaments of the powerful States and the deficient armaments of the weak constitutes a threat to the preservation of the tranquillity and peace of the peoples, and calls for a firm proportionate limitation of the manufacture and possession of offensive weapons.

In keeping with the measure in which disarmament may take place, appropriate means, honorable and effective for all, must be established to give back to the principle "*pacta sunt servanda*—pacts must be observed," the vital and moral function which rightfully belongs to it in the juridical relations among States. This principle, which in the past has suffered alarming crises and undeniable infractions, now encounters an almost insuperable mistrust among the various peoples and their respective leaders. In order to restore reciprocal trust, institutions are called for which, after acquiring general respect, should dedicate themselves to the noble office of both guaranteeing the sincere implementation of treaties and promoting, according to the principles of right and equity, the desirable corrections or revisions.

We are not unaware of the quantity of difficulties to be surmounted, and the almost superhuman effort and good will needed on all sides in order to bring about a happy solution to the double undertaking outlined here. But this common labor is so essential for a lasting peace that nothing must deter responsible statesmen from undertaking it and co-operating with the forces of good will, which, looking toward the future good, will overcome the painful memories of attempts which failed in the past, and will not be deterred by the realization of the gigantic effort which such an undertaking entails.

Persecution of Religion

In the field of a new order founded on moral principles, there is no place for persecution of religion and of the Church. Living faith in a personal, transcending God releases a pure and enduring moral force which governs the whole course of life; because faith is not only a virtue, but also the divine entrance through which all virtues enter into the temple of the soul and form that strong and tenacious character which does not vacillate even in the severest tests of reason and justice. This is an eternally valid truth; but it is especially resplendent when, from the statesmen as from the least of citizens, the utmost in courage and moral energy are demanded in order to reconstruct a new Europe and a new world upon the ruins piled high by the violence, hatred, and schisms of world conflict.[†]

Propaganda of Hatred

Another indispensable prerequisite for such a new order is: victory over the hate which today divides the peoples; the renunciation, therefore, of systems and practices from which it constantly receives new nourishment. There is indeed in some countries at present an unrestrained propaganda which does not refrain from openly altering the truth and day by day, and almost hour by hour, presenting opposing nations in a false, outrageous light to public opinion. But whoever truly desires the well-being of the people, whoever longs to contribute to preserving the spiritual and moral foundation of future collaboration among peoples from incalculable damage, will consider it a sacred duty and lofty mission to prevent the loss, in the thoughts and feelings of men, of the natural ideals of truth, justice, courtesy, and co-operation for good, and, above all, of the sublime supernatural ideal of fraternal love brought by Christ into the world.

† Radio Message to the World (December 24, 1941).

Absolute Autonomy of the State

The conception which assigns to the State unlimited authority is not only pernicious to the internal life of the nation, to its prosperity, and to the orderly increase of its well-being; it also damages relations between peoples, because it breaks the unity of international society, it rips out the foundations and the value of the rights of people, opens the way to the violation of the rights of others, and renders difficult understanding and peaceful coexistence.

In fact, although humanity, by disposition of the natural order established by God, divides itself into social groups, nations, or States, independent one from the other in the way they organize and direct their internal life, it is nonetheless linked by moral and juridical bonds into a huge community intended for the good of all peoples and regulated by special laws which safeguard its unity and promote its prosperity.

Now, it is evident to all that the so-called absolute autonomy of the State is in open contrast with that inherent natural law, that it actually radically denies it, leaving the stability of international relations at the mercy of the whim of the leaders and eliminating the possibility of a true union and a fruitful collaboration in the general interest.

Since for the existence of harmonious and lasting contacts and fruitful relations it is indispensable that peoples recognize and observe those principles of natural international law which regulate their normal development and function, such principles demand the respect of related rights to independence, life, and the possibility of progressive development in the ways of civilization; they further demand loyalty to the pacts, stipulated and sanctioned in keeping with the norms of international law.

International Law and Divine Law

There is no doubt that the indispensable condition of any peaceful coexistence between peoples is mutual good faith, anticipation and conviction of reciprocal faithfulness to the given word, the certainty that both sides are convinced that wisdom is better than weapons of war, and that they are prepared to discuss without relying on force or the threat of force in the case of delays, impediments, changes, and disputes, all of which can occur not from lack of good will but from changed circumstances or actual conflicting interests.

But, on the other hand, separating international law from the anchor of divine law and founding it on the autonomous will of States is to dethrone that very law and take away its most noble and valid titles, abandoning it to the inauspicious dynamics of private interest and collective egotism, all intent on promoting their own rights and ignoring those of others.

Revision of Treaties

It is also true that, with the passing of time and substantial change of circumstance, unforeseen and perhaps unforeseeable at the time of its stipulation, a treaty or some of its clauses may become or appear unjust or impractical, or too onerous for one of the parties; it is clear that, when this happens, one should immediately proceed with an honest discussion to modify or substitute the pact. But to consider pacts ephemeral, in principle, and tacitly to attribute to one's self the faculty to abrogate them unilaterally when they are no longer convenient, would destroy all reciprocal faith among States. Thus natural order would be upset and unbridgeable chasms would be dug to separate the various peoples and nations.

Today, all observe with fear the abyss to which the errors We have pointed out and their natural consequences have brought man. The proud illusions of infinite progress have collapsed and whoever should not yet be awake to this, the tragic present, will shake with the words of the prophet: "Listen, O you deaf, and look, O you blind." That which appeared to be external order was no more than invading confusion: derangement of the norms of moral life, which, divided from the majesty of divine law, had distorted all the fields of human endeavor.

Re-education of Mankind

But let us leave the past and turn our eyes toward that future which, according to the promises of the powerful in this world once the bloody clashes are done, will consist of a new order founded on justice and prosperity. Will such a future be truly different; will it, above all, be better? Will the peace treaties, the new international order, be inspired by justice and equity toward all, by that spirit which frees and pacifies, or will there be a lamentable repetition of ancient and recent errors? To hope for a decisive change exclusively from the clash of war and its final outcome is vain, and experience demonstrates it to us. The hour of victory is an hour of external triumph for the side which succeeds in attaining it; but at the same time, it is the hour of temptation, in which the angel of justice struggles with the demon of violence; the heart of the victor is too easily hardened; moderation and farsighted wisdom appear to him to be weakness; the heat of popular passions, excited by the sacrifices and suffering endured, often veils the eyes even of responsible persons and causes them to ignore the admonishing voice of humanity and equity, overcome or silenced by inhumanity: Woe to the vanquished! Resolutions and decisions born under such conditions risk being no more than injustice in the guise of justice.

No, the salvation of peoples does not come by the external means of the sword, which can impose conditions of peace but does not create peace. The energies which must renew the face of the earth must proceed from the interior, the spirit. Once the bitterness and cruelty of the present struggle have cleared, the new world order of national and international life must no longer rest on the quicksands of changing, ephemeral regulations, left to the will of collective and individual egotism. Rather, they must rest on an unshakable foundation, the immovable rock of natural law and divine revelation. There the human legislator must draw that spirit of equilibrium, that acute sense of moral responsibility, without which it is easy to mistake the limits between legitimate use and abuse of power. Only in this way will his decisions have internal consistency, noble dignity, and religious sanction, and not be at the mercy of egotism and passion. Because, if it is true that the ills which beset present-day humanity are partly caused by economic imbalance and the struggle between interests for the equitable distribution of the goods which God has conceded to man to use for his sustenance and progress, it is no less true that their root is more profound and internal. It is found in religious faith and moral convictions, which have been perverted by the progressive detachment of peoples from the unity of doctrine and faith, and from customs and morals, once fostered by the unceasing, beneficent labor of the Church. The re-education of humanity, if it wishes to have any effect, must, above all, be spiritual and religious; and, therefore, it must arise from Christ as its indispensable foundation, be realized by justice, and be crowned by charity.

Among the laws which regulate the life of believing Christians and the postulates of genuine humanity there is no contrast, but common interest and mutual support. In the interest of a suffering humanity, materially and spiritually deeply shaken, We have no more ardent desire than this: that the present afflictions may open the eyes of many so that they may consider in their true light the Lord Jesus Christ and the mission of His Church on this earth, and that all those who exercise power resolve to leave to the Church a free path to work for the formation of the generations, according to the principles of justice and peace.

Unity of Religious Doctrine and Moral Code

If, on the one hand, the Church cannot renounce exercising this mission of hers, which has as its final goal the realization here on earth of the divine design to restore all things in Christ, whether they be celestial or terrestrial, on the other hand her work today appears to be more necessary than at any other time, since sad experience teaches that mere external means, human provisions, and political expedients do not bring about an efficacious mitigation of the ills which beset humanity.

Taking cognizance of the painful failure of human methods to calm the storms which threaten to engulf civilization, many turn their gaze with renewed hope to the Church, rock of truth and love, to this Chair of Peter, whence they feel may be given back to humanity that unity of religious doctrine and moral code which in other times gave consistency to peaceful relations among peoples.[†]

† Encyclical *Summi Pontificatus* (October 20, 1939).

The Lessons of War

We preserve the hope that the nations which have passed through the school of suffering will retain its bitter lessons. In this hope We are comforted by the words of men who more than others have endured the suffering of war and with generous words have expressed, together with the affirmations of their own needs for security against all future aggression, their respect for the vital rights of other peoples and their aversion toward all usurpation of these same rights. It would be vain to expect that this wise judgment, dictated by the experience of history and lofty political sentiment, might be generally accepted by public opinion, or even a majority, as long as feelings run high. Among the peoples who have fought one another, hate and the incapacity for reciprocal understanding have given rise to a fog so dense that it cannot be hoped that the hour has already arrived in which a ray of light may rise to clear up the tragic darkness on both sides of the wall. But one thing We do know, and it is that the moment will come, perhaps earlier than people think, when both sides will recognize how, everything considered, there is only one way out of the entanglements in which struggle and hate have enveloped the world, namely, the return to a solidarity too long forgotten, solidarity not restricted to this or that people, but universal, founded on the intimate connection of their destinies and the rights belonging equally to them all.

At a time when peoples find themselves confronted with tasks which they may never have encountered before in their history, they feel stirring in their tormented hearts the impatient, somehow innate desire to take up the reins of their own destiny with greater autonomy than in the past, hoping that in this manner it will be easier for them to defend themselves against the periodic eruptions of the spirit of violence, which, like a torrent of flaming lava, spares nothing of what is dear and sacred to them.

By its very existence, the Church raises before the world a splendid beacon which constantly recalls this divine order. Her history clearly reflects her providential mission. The struggles which, forced by the abuse of power, she has had to sustain to defend the liberty which she received from God have been, at the same time, struggles for the liberty of man.

The Church has the mission to announce to the world, longing for better and more perfect forms of democracy, the highest and most necessary message there can possibly be: the dignity of man, the vocation to be children of God.†

The Limits of Science

It is only a little more than a century and a half ago that, starting from purely rational premises, the first hypotheses were formulated about the discontinuous structure of matter and the existence of the elementary particles of matter, considered to be the final components of bodies. From that time onward, the molecules were counted, weighed, analyzed; then the atom, at first thought to be indivisible, was divided into its elements, examined, and its most intimate structures probed; the elementary electric charge, the mass of the proton were determined; the neutron, positron, and many other elementary particles were identified and their characteristics made known. A means was found to guide these particles, to accelerate them, and to bombard the atomic nuclei with them. But it was especially by utilizing neutrons that success was attained in producing artificial radioactivity, the fission of nuclei, the transformation of one element into other elements, and the release of enormous quantities of energy.

Ingenious theories and conceptions concerning the phenomena of the world were developed; new mathematical and geometrical systems were created. We cite only the special and the general theory of relativity, the quantum theory, wave mechanics, recent theories about the nature of nuclear forces, theories about the origin of cosmic rays, hypotheses about the source of stellar energy.

But the optimism aroused by such results soon meets with a setback: for anyone with a sense of responsibility who follows the course of events is filled with confusion and anguish. Anguish and confusion in the highest sense of the word, the sign of aspiration toward an ever more perfect organization of thought, an ever clearer view of the perspectives opening before us. The

† Radio Message to the World (December 24, 1944).

triumphs of science themselves call for two requirements to which We have already referred.

The question is, above all, to penetrate the innermost structure of material beings and examine the problems connected with the material foundation of their being and activity. Then the question arises: Can experimental science in itself solve these problems? Are they within its province, and do they fall within the field in which its methods of investigation can be applied? The answer must be no. Science starts out from sense perceptions, which are by their nature external; applying to them the workings of intelligence, it penetrates further and further into the secret recesses of things; but it has to stop short at a certain point, when questions arise which cannot be answered by the observation of the senses.

When the scientist interprets experimental data and applies himself to explaining phenomena that have their origin in material nature as such, he needs a light to show him the way in reverse, going from the absolute to the relative, from the necessary to the contingent, which can reveal to him the truth that science cannot reach by its own methods, because it completely eludes the senses. This light is philosophy, that is, the science of general laws, valid for every being, and therefore also for the sphere of natural sciences, beyond the laws that are known empirically.

The second requirement springs from the very nature of the human spirit, which desires a coherent and unified view of truth. If the different disciplines and their branches are merely juxtaposed like a kind of mosaic, the result obtained is an anatomical composition of knowledge, from which all life seems to have fled. Man, however, demands that a breath of living unity should quicken his knowledge: only thus does science become fruitful and culture breed an organic doctrine. Thence a second question arises: Can science accomplish, merely with its own characteristic means, this universal synthesis of thought? And in any case, since that knowledge is divided into innumerable particular disciplines, which one, among so many varieties, could achieve this synthesis? Here again We believe that science, by its very nature, is not able to provide such a universal synthesis.

This synthesis requires a solid and deeply rooted foundation, from which to draw its unity, and which may serve as a basis for the most general truths. The different parts of the construction, thus unified, must find in this foundation the elements which constitute their essential nature. A superior force is required here: unifying by its *universality*, clear in its *depth*, solid because of its *absolute character*, efficacious by its *necessity*. Once again, this force is philosophy.

Science and Philosophy

Alas! For some time now science and philosophy have been separated. It would be difficult to assess the causes and the responsibility of such a damaging fact. It is certain that the cause of this divorce is not to be sought in the nature itself of the two paths which lead to truth, but in historical contingencies and in people who did not always possess the good will and competence necessary.

Men of science believed, at a certain moment, that natural philosophy was a useless burden and refused to be directed by it. On the other hand, philosophers no longer followed the progress of science, and clung to formal positions that they should have abandoned. But when, as We have shown, the necessity of establishing a serious interpretation of the facts and of elaborating a comprehensive synthesis imposed itself, the scientists succumbed to the philosophies current at the moment. Many of them, perhaps, were not even fully aware that their scientific research was being guided by particular philosophical tendencies.

Hence, for example, mechanistic thought directed for a long time the scientific interpretation of phenomena observed. The defenders of this philosophical position believed that all natural phenomena could be reduced to a mass of physical, chemical, and mechanical forces, in which change and activity were the result merely of a different arrangement of the particles in space and of the forces or displacements to which each of them was subjected. It followed that, theoretically, any future effect whatever could be predicted with absolute certainty, provided that, at the outset, all the geometrical and mechanical data were known. According to this doctrine, the world is merely an enormous machine, composed of an innumerable series of other machines joined together.

Further progress in experimental research, however, demonstrated the inaccuracy of these hypotheses. Mechanics deduced from the facts of the macrocosm are unable to explain and interpret all the phenomena of the microcosm: other elements enter here which are beyond the scope of mechanistic interpretation.

The failure of mechanistic theory has led thinkers to entirely different hypotheses, distinguished rather by a kind of scientific idealism, in which consideration of the active observer plays the main part. For example, quantum mechanics and its fundamental principle of indeterminism, with the criticism of the principle of causality it presupposes, seem to be scientific hypotheses influenced by philosophical thought.

But because these hypotheses themselves do not satisfy completely the desire for total enlightenment, many noted thinkers are reduced to skepticism on the philosophical problems of science. They claim that we must be content to ascertain facts, and try to fit them into comprehensive and simple formulas, as prerequisites to calculating from the initial facts the possible developments of a physical system. This state of mind means renouncing conceptual introspection and losing the hope of establishing ingenious universal syntheses. We do not believe, however, that such pessimism is justified: We are rather of the opinion that the natural sciences, in permanent contact with a philosophy of critical realism, which was always that of the *philosophia perennis* in its most eminent representatives, may reach a general vision of the visible world capable of satisfying, to some extent, the search and the longing for truth.

But it is necessary to stress another point: if it is the duty of science to look for coherence and draw inspiration from sound philosophy, the latter may not arrogate to itself the claim to determine truths which belong exclusively to the sphere of experience and scientific method. For only experience, in the widest sense of the word, can indicate which, among the infinite variety of possible magnitudes and material laws, are those which the Creator really chose to realize.[†]

† Address to the Pontifical Academy of Sciences (April 24, 1955).

Radio and Television

The radio can be one of the most powerful means for spreading true civilization and culture. Today its services have become almost indispensable for educating men in the sense of solidarity, for the life of the State and the people; it is capable of creating a lively force of cohesion in peoples and between nations. It can bear witness before the whole world to the truth and glory of God, promote the victory of equity, bring light, consolation, hope, reconciliation, and love on this earth, and draw men and nations closer together. It can carry the voice of Christ, the truth of the Gospel, the spirit of the Gospel, and the charity of the Gospel to the ends of the earth. It gives also to Us, common Father of the faithful, the joy of being, at one and the same time, present to all Our children in the whole world, every time We send out Our messages and impart Our blessing.

All this the radio can do. But in the hands of blind or wicked men it can also lend itself to error and falsehood, base passions, sensuality, pride, covetousness, and hate; it can be turned into that open sepulcher full of malediction and bitterness of which St. Paul speaks and which swallows up the Christian virtues, sound civilization, peace, and human happiness…

At the service of the dignity of life and Christian ethics: It should hold sacred the child's innocence, the youth's purity, the holy chastity of matrimony, and the happiness of a family life based on the fear and the love of God.

At the service of justice: It should hold sacred the inviolable human rights no less than the right of the authorities to exact from the individual and the community the duties necessary for the common good; the right of peoples to existence, in particular of the weaker members, and alike the right of the great family of nations to request the sacrifices necessary for the peace of the world; the right of the Church to bring, in the fullness of liberty, to all men and all peoples the wealth of the grace and the peace of Christ.

At the service of love: This is the duty of the present hour. At all costs it is necessary to overcome dissension and hate, of which the radio, too, has many times been made the instrument and agent. May it put its far-reaching powerful influence to the service of the noble ideal of Christian charity…

Finally, We wish to draw attention to the understanding of the true needs of humanity and its spiritual nature, which the radio should serve by its musical transmissions. We have no intention of speaking now of those programs in which it would be very difficult to find any artistic merit, any educational value... Rather, We refer to the recital of sacred music, as well as to the efforts to make accessible to the public the works, sacred and profane, of the great modern and ancient composers, whose masterpieces arouse in the mind and soul the lofty sentiments by which they were themselves animated.†

The responsibility of those people who make of the radio an instrument of intellectual or moral corruption presents no problem; it merely calls for the brand of infamy. That of the indifferent, the apathetic, the skeptical, very great by reason of the serious and often imperceptible consequences, calls for something else; it confronts us with the difficulty—a difficulty rather than a problem—of making him understand that he is doing wrong.

The problem arises when it is a question of presenting, with honest and often praiseworthy intentions, arguments, events, or questions legitimately interesting and useful from a literary, artistic, psychological, moral, or social point of view. And this is what then perplexes the mind: Should we hold our peace when it might be fitting or necessary to speak, or should we speak and run the risk of alarming certain ears, perturbing certain souls, but above all of contaminating the candid innocence of childish hearts? Adults have only themselves to blame for their indiscreet or unwise curiosity; but what about the children who, thoughtlessly and without serious malice, so easily evade on this point their parents' supervision? It is the duty of a speaker over the radio to use a language of such tact and reticence that he may be understood by adults without rousing the imagination or troubling the simplicity of the young.‡

Who can praise sufficiently the tremendous services rendered by the radio in cases of urgent need and extreme danger? Who can tell the social usefulness of information in the mutual exchange of news by all the members of the great human family? Who can assess the contribution to culture in general made by the possibility of bringing to our ears lectures and lessons of the most varied nature and allowing us to enjoy the delight of fine diction and elevating music?

† Address to the Congress of the 50th Anniversary of the Convenzione Marconiane Radio (October 3, 1947).

‡ Address to Radio Announcers (April 22, 1948).

The Church, We said, takes an interest in all this. And is there reason to wonder? She stands above national diversities, she is universal. In the radio she sees a singularly valuable element for the fulfillment of her mission. It is true that listening to a Mass on the radio is not the same as taking part personally in the divine Sacrifice. The radio is not a complete substitute for personal contacts; but what an advantage it means for the Head of the Church and other shepherds of souls, allowing them to speak directly to their spiritual sons and daughters and to pray with them!

What intimate force and what religious stimulation can come from the microphone, which for many is the only comfort and the only support arriving from without! Think of the thousands of sick people confined to their beds; of the communities who have no church or priest. By means of the radio, they can at least still communicate with the sources of faith and grace.

Quite rightly, the radio may consider itself entrusted with an educational mission, provided, always, that it does not neglect the main object: being made in the image of God, man has the duty of perfecting this divine likeness in his way of thinking, wishing, and acting. Every form of education must tend to help him in this. The body of man, his temporal and material life, as We have often repeated, must be the object of respect and care. But his soul and his intellectual and spiritual life are incomparably more worthy of attention; they are, in reality, the final and supreme reason for all instruction and education. How, therefore, could the radio exclude religious teaching from the multifarious duties and aims it pursues?[†]

Television

The rapid advances which television has now made in many countries keep Our attention ever more alert to this marvelous gift of science and technology, at once precious and dangerous by reason of the profound reverberations which it is destined to provoke in the private and public life of nations.

† Address to the Members of the International Radio Transmission Conference (May 5, 1950).

We fully recognize the value of this brilliant conquest of science, which is a further manifestation of the wonderful splendors of God, who "has given science to men that He may be honored in its marvels." Television too, therefore, imposes on all of us the duty of gratefulness which the Church tirelessly recommends to her children in the daily Holy Sacrifice of the Altar, with the admonition that "it is truly meet and just, right and salutary, always and everywhere, to give thanks" to God for His gifts.

In any case, it is not difficult to realize the innumerable advantages of television whenever it is placed at the service of man for his perfection.

In recent years, the movies and sports, to say nothing of the necessity of daily work, have tended to draw the members of the family increasingly away from home, upsetting the natural development of domestic life. How can We not rejoice to see television efficaciously contributing to the restoration of the balance, offering the whole family the chance of enjoying together pleasant recreation far from the dangers of unhealthy company and places?

Nor can We be indifferent to the beneficent influence which television is able to exercise from the social point of view in respect to culture, popular education, scholastic teaching, and the very life of peoples, who through that instrument will certainly be helped to know and understand one another better and to reach friendly concord and better mutual co-operation.

Such considerations, however, must not blind us to another aspect of this delicate and important question. Although, in fact, television properly controlled may constitute an effective means of wise and Christian education, it is equally true that it is not exempt from dangers which may be the result of abuses and profanation brought about by human weakness and malice—dangers all the more serious since the suggestive power of this instrument is greater and the public toward whom it is directed is wider and more indiscriminate. Unlike the theater and the movies, whose spectacles are limited to those who choose to enter, television is directed, above all, to family groups of every age and sex and of various cultural levels, bringing to them the daily news, sundry news items, and all kinds of spectacles. Like the radio, it can enter any house and go to any place, at any time, bringing with it not only sounds and words but also the concreteness and mobility of its images, which gives it greater emotional influence, particularly in respect to the young. To this must be added the fact that television programs are based, in great part, on films and plays, which, as experience has shown, all too frequently do not satisfy the requirements of natural and Christian ethics. Lastly, it should be pointed out that television finds its keenest and most attentive audience among children and adolescents, who, by reason of their age, can more easily fall prey to its fascination and, consciously or unconsciously, transmute into living reality the images they absorb from the animated picture on the screen. It is obvious, therefore, how intimately television affects the education of the young and the Christian spirit of family life.

If We consider the inestimable value of the family, which is the primary cell of society, and if We reflect that within the walls of the home not only the bodily but also the spiritual development of the child must begin and grow—precious hope of the Church and of its country—We cannot but proclaim to all those who share the responsibilities of television that the duties and responsibilities which rest on their shoulders are extremely serious before God and society.

Public authorities, above all, must take every precaution, so that the atmosphere of decency and restraint which should surround family life may not be offended or troubled.

Ever present in Our mind is the sad picture of the perturbing and evil power of the movies. But how can We help being horrified by the thought that through television the poisoned atmosphere of materialism, superficiality, and luxuriousness, which too often pervades the motion picture theaters, may penetrate the walls of the home? Truly, it would be impossible to imagine anything more fatal to the spiritual forces of a nation than that, before so many innocent souls, in the bosom of the family itself, there should be repeated those sensational revelations of pleasure-seeking, of passion, and of evil which can shake and ruin for all time a whole edifice of purity, goodness, and healthy individual and social education.

For these reasons, We deem it advisable to point out that the normal supervision which has to be exercised by the authorities responsible for public shows is not sufficient, in the case of television transmissions, to ensure satisfactory service from the moral point of view; there is need for a different criterion, as it is here a question of spectacles destined to reach into the family sanctuary. Thus we see, particularly in this field, that there is no foundation in the supposed right to indiscriminate liberty in art and in the plea that thought and the imparting of information are free; higher values are at stake, the violators of which would not be able to escape the heavy penalties threatened by the divine Savior, "Woe to the world because of scandals!... Woe to the man by whom the scandal cometh!"

We cherish a profound trust that the lofty sense of responsibility of those who preside over public life will prevail in the prevention of those sad possibilities which We have previously deplored. We are pleased to hope, rather, that as far as the programs are concerned, suitable instructions will be issued, so that television may serve for the healthy recreation of the citizens and likewise contribute in all circumstances to their education and moral elevation. But in order that such desirable measures may find their full application, a careful and active vigilance will have to be exercised by all.[†]

The Theater

An old and rather widespread prejudice puts in opposition, almost as if reciprocally hostile, the Church and the dramatic profession. That erroneous conception is unfounded and unfair.

What, then, must the theater—or the movie theater—do to fulfill its mission of doing good? Theirs must be a work of art, but a work of art in the fullest and at the same time highest meaning of the word...

The public, fascinated and forgetting that it has come to see and to hear, itself lives the scene of which it comes to be in a way the actor more than the witness; it lives, hears, thrills, shudders, with all the power of its faculties, in all the liveliness of its impressions. And this turmoil of all its being is moved and sustained by the authors, and by the actors and actresses of the theater and the movies. More often than not the impression is lasting, sometimes indelible. The spectator leaves the hall carrying with him and within him deep convictions or tenacious prejudices, lofty aspirations or abject cupidities.

† Apostolic Letter (January 1, 1954).

If, in the evocation of the same facts, history, handled by different authors, may become tendentious and partial and serve for the propagation of opposite theses, what shall we say of the drama, which acts so directly on the soul of the spectator, and on his senses, imagination, and receptivity, even more than upon his reason and judgment?

This creates a formidable responsibility, but at the same time a noble and elevated one. How is it possible, then, that some take it lightly and without any scruples, and use their action and influence on the human spirit and heart, especially on the young and on adolescents, only to corrupt and degrade them?

For this fatal disorder We seem to see two main causes: The first is a lack of character and energy, which induces some to yield to the desires of a spoiled public, to flatter and even incite its passions and base instincts, and to beg of it in return applause and loud laughter and above all the large profits which it pays for such entertainments. Easy and big successes bring with them the inducement to offer continually new and similar ones; it requires so little talent to produce such spectacles and so little grace and ability to stage them. But, meanwhile, taste, already vulgar, becomes steadily coarser and requires increasingly potent poison, sinking thus to ever lower depths.

The other cause of the evil might seem less dangerous and harmful, so subtle is it and so human! There is a truly great temptation for an author to stress the acuity and depth of his psychological insight, carrying his analysis of characters, of their most delicate sentiments, their most impetuous passions, to the utmost limits and lavishing the riches of his palette on the representation of actions and customs. The temptation is equally strong for actors or actresses to force or attenuate their interpretation of the work of another according to their own personalities, often running close, if not surpassing, the limits of discretion in showing off their personal gifts and attractions, even the physical ones. In a novel, such moral anatomies, such realistic "exhibitionisms," such descriptions of luxury or misery, are liable to disturb the heart of the reader. What will happen, then, when, in the atmosphere and collective excitement of the hall, facts develop sensibly as in reality, but, as it were, condensed, compressed, rendered more intense by the surprising resources of the movies, or at the theater, in characters of flesh and blood, so easily identifiable with their parts that the thoughts, feelings, and passions which sway them really make their eyes sparkle, make them laugh and cry and their hearts throb?

It is therefore quite clear that every co-operator in a dramatic performance who surrenders to the whims of the public instead of dominating them, that is, who gives in to the inanities of vanity or allows himself to be conquered by the greed for profits which his conscience reproves, not only loses something of his own dignity, but also offends art—that art which he shows he does not love courageously enough to resist the caprices of bad taste nor with sufficient integrity to prefer it to the incentives of vainglory or money.

What a magnificent field of activity is offered, therefore, to dramatic authors, producers, and theatrical critics! It belongs to them to re-establish contact between the public and the beautiful and elevated creations of human genius, to work for the re-education of good taste and decent feelings...

As to actors and actresses, the intense emotion of joy and pride that pervades the soul before a public all tense, eager, applauding, is very natural and easily understandable. Honor to those who, aware of their great responsibility, conscious of the nobility of their mission, see in their influence on souls only a means to elevate them above the earth and make them soar toward the ideal. Such are the actors and actresses who do not come upon the scene without having raised their thoughts and intentions to God, and it is no longer a surprise to see how sometimes Christ chooses from their ranks superior spirits that He illuminates and guides toward the mystic heights of a life of perfection.[†]

The Mission of Publishers

The first man who, desirous of communicating his thought to other men in a more lasting form than the fleeting sound of words, carved, perhaps with a rough flint, on the walls of a cave, certain signs of which he determined and explained the interpretation, invented, at the same time, writing and the art of reading. Reading is to penetrate by means of more or less complicated graphic signs into the thoughts of others. Now, since "the thoughts of the just

† Address to Catholic Theater Center (August 26, 1945).

are justice, and the counsels of the wicked are impious," it follows that some books, like some words, are sources of light, strength, intellectual and moral freedom, while others bring only snares and temptations of sin; such is the teaching of the Holy Scriptures: "*Cogitationes iustorum indicia, et consilia impiorum fraudulenta. Verba impiorum insidiantur sanguini; os iustorum liberabit eos*—The thoughts of the just are judgments; and the counsels of the wicked are deceitful. The words of the wicked lie in wait for blood: the mouth of the just shall deliver them." There are, therefore, good and bad things to read, just as there are good and bad words...

Withdraw a moment within yourselves and ask yourselves sincerely whence comes the best that is in you. Why do you believe in God, in His Son become flesh for the redemption of the world, in His Mother Mary, whom He has made your Mother? Why do you obey His commandments, love your parents, your country, your neighbor? Why have you decided to found a family of which Jesus is the King, and in which you may transmit to your children the treasure of Christian virtues? Certainly because faith was infused into you in holy baptism; because your parents, your priest, your teachers, men and women, taught you by word of mouth and with their example to do good and to avoid evil. But delve further into your memories: among the best and the most decisive you will probably find that of some beneficial book; the catechism, sacred history, the Holy Gospel, the Roman Missal, the parish bulletin, *The Imitation of Christ,* the lives of the saints.

The Index

You know, however, that there are also bad books that are bad for everybody, like those poisons against which nobody can declare himself immune. As in every man the flesh is subject to weaknesses and the spirit is ready for rebellion, so such reading constitutes a danger for everybody. The Acts of the Apostles tells us that, during the preaching of St. Paul in Ephesus, many of those who had been addicted to vain and superstitious arts brought their books and publicly burned them; when the value of these writings on magic, thus reduced to cinders, was calculated, it was found to amount to over fifty thousand dinars. Afterwards, in the course of the centuries, the Roman Pontiffs took care to have a catalogue or *Index* published of books which the faithful are forbidden to read.

It is to be considered that many others, although not expressly enumerated, fall under the same condemnation and prohibition because they are harmful to faith and to morals...

If We remind you of this, it is because of the extension of the evil, which is at present facilitated by the continuous growth of book production, and also by the freedom which many people attribute to themselves to read everything. Now, there cannot be freedom to read everything, just as there is not a freedom to eat and drink anything at hand, including perhaps even cocaine or prussic acid.

Certainly it is not forbidden you to enjoy the charm of stories of pure, wholesome human tenderness; the Holy Scriptures themselves offer similar scenes that have kept throughout the centuries their idyllic freshness: the meeting of Jacob and Rachel, and the engagement of young Tobias. And there have always been writers of great talent who have written good, morally sound novels.

But do not believe, young men and women, who allow yourselves to be at times led to reading, perhaps secretly, harmful books, do not believe that their poison will have no effect on you; rather be afraid that this effect, if it is not immediate, will be all the more deadly.

The danger of bad literature is, indeed, under certain aspects, more fatal than that of bad company, because it can render itself more treacherously familiar. How many girls or young women, alone in their room, with the latest bestseller, allow themselves to be told by it the crude things they would not permit others to mention in their presence, or allow scenes to be described of which they would not want to be the victims or the actors for anything in the world! Alas! they are in this way preparing to become so tomorrow! Others, Christian men or women, who from their childhood have followed the straight and narrow path, also complain of the sudden increase of temptations which oppress them and of their growing weakness to resist them. Perhaps if they sincerely examined their consciences, they would have to admit that they had read a sensual novel, glanced through an immoral magazine, or let their eyes rest on indecent illustrations.[†]

† Address to Newlyweds (July 31, 1940).

Books in the Era of Movies and Television

We are living in the era of the motion picture and television. Without doubt both absorb a considerable part of the time which before used to belong to the printed word. Yet it happens that they are the very ones to increase the value of a good book. For, though we fully recognize the importance of the technique and art of the motion picture, yet the unilateral influence it exercises on man and especially on youth, with its almost purely visual action, carries with it such a danger of intellectual decay that it is already beginning to be considered as a danger for the people. It is all the more the duty of the good book, therefore, to educate the people to a deeper understanding of things, to make them think and ponder.[†]

The Duty and Responsibility of the Literary Critic

THE special joy which We feel in receiving you to Our presence, dear Sons and book critics, is equal to the solicitude that belongs to Our duties as shepherd. Among other cares, We are much concerned with this matter, in order to bring to the children of Christ verdant pastures of the spirit, which today are found especially in reading.

We are grateful, therefore, for your gathering, because We see in each one of you a competent and faithful fellow laborer in Our pastoral ministry; collectively, you are a powerful barrier against the overflowing tide of useless literature. Such reading matter threatens to drag the great dignity of human nature into the mud of error and perversion. We need not point out here the necessity, the nobility, and the importance of right criticism. Your own firm persuasion of the great influence of reading on the habits and the lot of individuals and the community has inspired you to take up the difficult task,

† Message to the International Meeting of Publishers of Books and Magazines (December 10, 1950).

which is imposed on the critic by the vast literary production of our day. In a society like our own, so jealous to exercise the right of free press, the criticism of good people, based on a much more sacred right, is certainly one of the most proper means to prevent the spread of evil. This is all the more necessary, because such evil spreads under the appearance or pretext of good. In such matters, of the gravest danger to souls, the intervention of some higher authority is justified and necessary. Criticism, however, that is based on the norms of truth and morality is better adapted, perhaps, to the mentality of the modern man, who wishes to judge things for himself, though welcoming the assistance of a critic in whom he has confidence.

You do not confine your work, however, to the moral aspects of a book; but your criticism takes in the scientific, the literary, and the artistic qualities of a work. Thoroughgoing criticism, such as is expected by the public and by experts, is possible, though it involves much work. Such thoroughness in Catholic critics not only strengthens their authority with the public, but contributes a praiseworthy addition to culture, in line with the perennial tradition of the Church, always ready to assimilate the development of thought and expression. The heights or the depths reached by literature, especially that of the present day, depend largely on the clear judgment, the moral integrity, and the intellectual strength of the critics.

Recognizing this great responsibility resting on the critic, We deem it opportune to point out some fundamental principles to which his work must conform, if it is efficaciously to attain its end of guiding souls into secure paths.

The intention of guiding and advising others in the selection and evaluation of their reading is to no purpose unless we assume in the readers a disposition of spirit to accept the suggestions of others. Every effort of a critic is useless with people who of set purpose refuse to admit the critic's knowledge and competence, and who, consequently, have no confidence in him or in his judgment. There are readers with whom the critic has no success because, by nature or through faulty training, they rely on their own superior appraisal of their mental ability. Dominated by the suggestion of their own sufficiency, they expect from the critic only the confirmation of their own judgment, which they take to be certain and unchangeable. Rejection of objective criticism by such persons, often based on false ideological prejudices, must not discourage the critic. Such rejection only reflects the psychological deficiencies of such persons. With a public of good dispositions, the critic will work much more efficaciously if he knows how to gain their confidence. In fact, this is the starting point and the goal of all criticism, whether there is question of an individual critic or of magazines—and here all the more—that make criticism their collective aim. If the reader turns to a critic, it is because he believes in the critic's knowledge, integrity, and maturity, when expounding the contents of a book or passing a well-founded and unanswerable judgment. How is the critic to gain successfully the confidence of the reader? What is the function of the critic, and what can be rightly asked of the public?

The first requirement in the critic is the mental ability to read and properly understand the book in question. The mention of such a norm seems superfluous; it is not, however, a rare thing to meet reviewers who do not measure up to this first, elementary requisite. Evidently, a close reading, very often boring and fatiguing, must be free from prejudice; and the critic must be reading in subject matter that is sufficiently well known to him. Therefore, the critic must have a many-sided culture; the special knowledge required in a given subject; and a broad general culture that will enable him to place the book properly and to expound its principal contents.

Mere intellectual understanding, however, is not sufficient. The critic must be able to form a judgment which when stated shows his mental competency.

The critic must be able to judge and to evaluate; in other words, to apply wisely his general culture and specialized knowledge to the subject at hand. For this, he must have broad-mindedness, versatility; the ability to see and comprehend the relative bearings of a work, and to point out errors, shortcomings, and contradictions. From this impartial consideration of the good and the bad in a given work there will come limitation and distinction, the Yes and No in each case. Only then does the criticism reach its final form as ready for publication.

In applying the above-mentioned qualities of mind, the critic is influenced by the will, by the sensibility, and by character. This makes it necessary for the critic to have other characteristics. To prevent the will and emotions from negatively influencing his judgments, the critic must first of all be objective. He must show a liking for the author and confidence in him; unless, for positively grave and certain reasons, he is obliged to speak otherwise. A critic habitually subject to partiality should never attempt to write. Nobility of character and goodness of heart are always the best weapons of combat. This holds for the field of criticism, when ideas and opinions are in conflict. Nobility and kindness, however, are not to be confused with the ingenuity and credulity of a child, whose experience of life has not matured. A critic may have some of the qualities indicated, but they must always be joined to probity, integrity, and firmness of character. The critic must not write to please the author, or the publisher, or the public—often subject to strange sympathies or antipathies—or to follow his own inclination. Against his own better knowledge and conscience, against objective truth, a critic can make a false criticism. This false judgment may arise from a wrong interpretation of the meaning or of the questionable teaching of the author; or it may come by deliberately omitting important and relevant portions that should not be concealed. To each critic should apply the testimony given to our Redeemer by His enemies, hypocritically and yet truthfully: "Master, we know that Thou art truthful and that Thou teachest the way of God in truth and that Thou carest nought for any man; for Thou dost not regard the person of men" (Matthew 22:16).

Firmness of character in a critic is shown especially when he writes with serenity and without fear of his own judgment; and when he defends his judgment, keeping always to strict justice. As a judge who lacks the courage to sustain the law should resign, so should a critic, if he loves an easy life more than the truth. Firmness, however, must always avoid arrogance; for this is an a priori presumption of the truth's being in favor of the critic and against the author. Both are subject to the same law in the service of truth; but the critic has the added duty of serving the truth with the maximum loyalty. In every case, the author and the critic should know that the truth is higher than either of them. An unjust criticism, as the word indicates, is not only an error of intellect but a real injury to the author. In such cases, the reputation of the author may greatly suffer; and, moreover, as is often the case, his rightful interests suffer loss. In such cases, the critic has a clear obligation of retraction. On the other hand, a justified criticism should not be withdrawn through fear of a powerful opponent. Such action would argue a deplorable lack of character and courage; it would also undermine the necessary confidence of the public, which rightly expects the critic to hold fast to his word, when it has been delivered according to the truth.[†]

† Address to Ecclesiastics Employed as Book Critics (February 13, 1956).

On Movies

The extraordinary influence of the movies on present-day society is shown by the growing thirst which this society has for them, and which, reduced to numbers, constitute a quite new and remarkable phenomenon. What is the source of the fascination of this new art, which, sixty years after its first appearance, has arrived at the almost magical power of summoning into the darkness of its halls, and not without pay, crowds that are numbered by the billions? What is the secret of the spell which makes these same crowds its constant devotees? In the answer to such questions lie the fundamental causes which bring about the great importance and the wide popularity of the motion picture.

The first power of attraction of a film springs from its technical qualities, which perform the prodigy of transferring the spectator into an imaginary world, or, in a documentary film, of bringing reality, distant in space and time, right before his eyes. To the technical process, then, belongs the first place in the origin and development of the movies. It preceded the film, and first made it possible; it also makes it every day more attractive, adaptable, alive. The chief technical elements of a movie show were already in existence before the film was born; then gradually the film was taken under their control until at length it arrived at the point where it exacts from the technical process the invention of new methods to be placed at its service.

But to understand thoroughly the power of motion pictures, and to make a more exact evaluation of the movie, it is necessary to take note of the important part played in them by the laws of psychology, either in so far as they explain how the film influences the mind, or in so far as they are deliberately applied to produce a stronger impression on the viewer. With careful observation devotees of this science study the process of action and reaction produced by viewing the picture, applying the method of research and analysis, the fruits of experimental psychology, studying the hidden recesses of the subconscious and the unconscious. They investigate the film's influence not only as it is passively received by the viewer, but also by analyzing its related psychical "activation," according to immanent laws, that is, its power to grip the mind through the enchantment of the representation. If, through one or the other influence, the spectator remains truly a prisoner of the world unfolding before his eyes, he is forced to transfer somehow to the person of the actor his own ego, with its psychic tendencies, its personal experiences, its hidden and ill-defined desires. Through the duration of this sort of enchantment, owing in large part to the suggestion of the actor, the viewer moves in the actor's world as though it were his own, and even, to some degree, lives in his place, and almost within him, in perfect harmony of feeling, sometimes even being drawn by the action to suggest words and phrases. This procedure, which modern directors are well aware of and try to make use of, has been compared with the dream state, with this difference, that the visions and images of dreams come only from the intimate world of the one dreaming, whereas they come from the screen to the spectator, but in such a way that they arouse from the depths of his consciousness images that are more vivid and dearer to him. Often enough then it happens that the spectator, through pictures of persons and things, sees as real that which never actually happened, but which he has frequently pondered over deep within himself, and desired or feared. With cause, therefore, does the extraordinary power of the motion picture find its profoundest explanation in the internal structure of the psychic process, and the spectacle will be all the more gripping in proportion to the degree it stimulates these processes.

As a result, the director is constantly forced to sharpen his own psychological sensibility and his own insight by the efforts he must make to find the most effective form to give to a film the power described above, which may have a good or a bad moral effect. In fact, the internal dynamisms of the spectator's ego, in the depths of his nature, of his subconscious and unconscious, can lead him thus to the realm of light, of the noble and beautiful, just as they can bring him under the sway of darkness and depravation, at the mercy of powerful and uncontrolled instincts, depending on whether the picture plays up and arouses the qualities of one or the other camp, and focuses on it the attention, the desires and psychic impulses. Human nature's condition is such, in fact, that not always do the spectators possess or preserve the spiritual energy, the interior detachment, and frequently, too, the strength of will, to resist a captivating suggestion, and thus the capacity to control and direct themselves.

Along with these fundamental causes and reasons for the attractiveness and importance of motion pictures, another active psychic element has been amply brought to light. It is the free and personal interpretation of the viewer, and his anticipation of the action's subsequent development; it is this which obtains, in some degree, the delight proper to one who creates an event. From this element, too, the director draws profit, through apparently insignificant but skillful movements, as, for example, the gesture of a hand, a shrug of the shoulders, a half-open door.

Because of this inner power of the motion picture, and because of its wide influence on the masses of men and even on moral practices, it has drawn the attention not only of competent civil and ecclesiastical authority, but also of all groups possessed of calm judgment and a genuine sense of responsibility.

In truth, how could an instrument, in itself most noble, but so apt to uplift or degrade men, and so quick to produce good or spread evil, be left to its own devices, or made dependent on purely economic interests?

The watchfulness and response of public authorities, fully justified by law to defend the common civil and moral heritage, is made manifest in various ways: through the civil and ecclesiastical censure of pictures, and, if necessary, through banning them; through the listing of films by appropriate examining boards, which qualify them according to merit for the information of the public, and as a norm to be followed. It is indeed true that the spirit of our time, unreasonably intolerant of the intervention of public authority, would prefer censorship coming directly from the people.

It would indeed be desirable if good men would agree to ban corrupt movies wherever they are shown, and to combat them with the legal and moral weapons at their disposal; yet such action is not by itself enough. Private initiative and zeal can wane, and do in fact wane rather quickly, as experience shows. But not so the hostile and aggressive propaganda, which frequently draws rich profits from films, and which often finds a ready ally in the interior of man, that is, in his blind instinct and its allurements, or his brutal and base urges. If, therefore, the civic and moral heritage of peoples and families is to be effectively safeguarded, it is most certainly right for public authority to exercise a due intervention in order to hinder or check the most dangerous influences.

The Ideal Film

The first quality which should mark the ideal film is respect for man. For there is indeed no reason whereby it can be exempted from the general norm which demands that he who deals with men should fully respect man.

However much differences of age, condition, and sex may suggest a difference in conduct and bearing, man is always man, with the dignity and nobility bestowed on him by the Creator, in whose image and likeness he was made (Genesis 1:26). In man there is a spiritual and immortal soul; there is the universe in miniature, with its multiplicity and variety of form, and the marvelous order of all its parts; there is thought and will, with a vast field in which to operate; there is emotional life, with its heights and depths; there is the world of the senses, with its numerous powers, perceptions, and feelings; there is the body, formed even to its minutest parts according to a teleology not yet fully grasped. Man has been made lord in this universe; freely he must direct his actions in accord with the laws of truth, goodness, and beauty, as they are manifested in nature, his social relations with his fellow men, and divine revelation.

Since the motion picture, as has been noted, can incline the soul of the viewer to good or to evil, We will call ideal only that film which not only does not offend what We have just described, but treats it respectfully. Even that is not enough! Rather We should say: that which strengthens and uplifts man in the consciousness of his dignity, that which increases his knowledge and love of the lofty natural position conferred on him by his Creator; that which tells him it is possible for him to increase the gifts of energy and virtue he disposes of within himself; that which strengthens his conviction that he can overcome obstacles and avoid erroneous solutions, that he can rise after every fall and return to the right path, that he can, in sum, progress from good to better through the use of his freedom and his faculties.

Such a motion picture would already contain the basic element of an ideal film; but more still can be attributed to it, if to respect for man is added a loving understanding of him. Recall the touching phrase of the Lord: "I have pity on this people."

The ideal motion picture must speak to the child in language suited to a child, to youth in a way fitted to it, to the adult as he expects to be spoken to, that is, using his own manner of seeing and understanding things.†

† Address to the Representatives of the Italian Movie Industry (June 21, 1955).

Sports

Everything connected with physical exercise—with competition, emulation, sports—interests and attracts the youth of today. But young Christians also know that the race toward intellectual light, the advance into the mysterious and sometimes arduous terrain of revelation, the striving toward goodness and holiness, are proportionately more beautiful, noble, and stirring, as wisdom and virtue of the soul exceed and surpass muscular strength and the transient nimbleness and agility of the limbs.

The vigor of the body, which accompanies and embellishes the flowering of youth, is not diminished or lowered, but rather exalted and ennobled by the striving for religious culture and by the virtue which dominates the passions.[†]

He who reproaches the Church for not caring about the body and physical culture is just as far from the truth as he who would like to restrict her competence and her activity to "purely religious" things, "exclusively spiritual" matters. As if the body, God's creation just as much as is the soul to which it is united, should not have its share in the homage to be paid to the Creator! "Therefore, whether you eat or drink," wrote the Apostle of the Gentiles to the Corinthians, "or whatever else you do, do all to the glory of God." St. Paul speaks here of physical activity; sport comes under the words "whatever else you do." Actually, he often talks about this explicitly; he speaks about racing and wrestling, not with expressions of criticism or condemnation, but as an expert who elevates and ennobles them by a Christian approach.

For what, finally, are sports if not one of the forms of education of the body? Now this education is in strict relationship with morals. How then could the Church be indifferent to them?

Actually, she has always had a consideration and solicitude for the human body which materialism, in its idolatrous cult, has never shown. And that is natural, because it sees and knows in the body only the material flesh, whose vigor and beauty are born and bloom only to fade and die, like grass in the fields. Far different is the Christian conception. The human body is, in itself, the masterpiece of God in the order of visible creation. The Lord had destined it to bloom here below in order to unfold itself immortal in the glory of

† Address to Youth of Catholic Action (November 10, 1940).

Heaven. He joined it to the spirit in the unity of human nature, so that the soul might enjoy the enchantment of God's works, to help it to behold in this mirror their common Creator, to get to know Him, worship Him, love Him! It was not God who made the human body mortal, but sin; only because of sin must the body, taken from dust, one day return to dust. But the Lord will raise it again to recall it to life. Even when they are reduced to dust, the Church respects and honors bodies, dead only to rise again.

But the Apostle Paul leads us to an even higher vision: "Do you not know," he says, "that your body is a temple of the Holy Spirit who is in you, whom you have from God; and you are not your own? For you are bought with a great price. Glorify and bear God in your body."

What, then, is primarily the function and purpose of "sports," in a healthy, Christian sense, if not the cultivation of the dignity and the harmony of the human body, the development of health, vigor, agility, and gracefulness?

Nor should St. Paul be reproached for his energetic expression: "*Castigo corpus meum et in servitutem redigo*—I chastise my body and bring it into subjection," since in that same passage he draws an example from the fervid worshipers of sports. Sports, moderately and conscientiously practiced, strengthen the body, make it healthy, fresh, and vigorous. But to accomplish this task of education, the body is submitted to a rigorous and often harsh discipline which dominates it and keeps it truly in subjection: arduous training, resistance to pain, the habit of continence and strict temperance, all are indispensable conditions for whoever wants to reach for victory. Sports are an effective antidote against softness and easy living; they awaken the sense of order and train one to self-criticism and self-control, to hold danger in contempt, without bragging or cowardice. Thus they already go beyond mere physical robustness, to lead us on the way to moral strength and greatness. From the native country of sports, the proverbial "fair play" had its origin, that chivalrous and courteous emulation which elevates the spirits above the meanness of cheating, the tricks of a touchy and vindictive vanity, and preserves them from the excesses of a narrow, intransigent nationalism. Sports are a school of loyalty, courage, tolerance, resoluteness, universal brotherhood, all natural virtues, but which provide a solid basis for the supernatural virtues, and prepare one to support without flinching the weight of the gravest responsibilities.

To subject the body to healthy fatigue in order to rest the mind and get it ready for new labors, to sharpen the senses in order to acquire a greater intensity of penetration for the intellectual faculties, to exercise the muscles and become accustomed to effort in order to temper the character and to form a will as strong and as flexible as steel: such was the idea that the mountain-climbing priest had formed of sports.[†]

In this sense, sports are not an end, but a means; as such they must be and must remain subordinated to the end, which consists in the perfect, well-balanced formation and education of man as a whole, man whom sports help to carry out his duty readily and joyfully, both at work and in family life.

In the service of a healthy, robust, ardent life, in the service of a more fruitful activity in carrying out the duties of one's own state, sports can and must be also in the service of God. To this end, in fact, it encourages people to direct the physical strength and moral virtues which it develops; but whereas the pagan used to submit to the severe regimen of sport to obtain only a short-lived wreath, the Christian submits to it for a higher purpose, for an immortal prize.

For what would be the use of physical courage and energy of character if the Christian made use of them only for earthly ends, to win a "cup" or to parade as a superman? If he did not know, when necessary, how to cut down his sleep by a half hour or postpone a stadium appointment, rather than neglect assisting at Holy Mass on Sunday; if he did not succeed in overcoming respect of persons in the practice and defense of his religion; if he did not use his presence and his authority to stop or repress—by a look, a word, a gesture—a curse, foul language, an act of indecency; if he did not protect the youngest and the weakest against provocations and suspicious attentions; if he did not foster the habit of concluding his happy successes in sports with praise to God, the Creator and Lord of nature and of all its power? Keep always in mind that the highest honor and the holiest destiny of the body is to be the dwelling of a soul which is resplendent with moral purity and sanctified by divine grace.[‡]

---

† This refers to Pope Pius XI. (TRANSLATOR)

‡ Address to Youth of Catholic Action (May 20, 1945).

PART THREE

CHURCH AND RELIGION

The Church

The Church Is the Mystical Body of Christ

When one reflects on the origin of this doctrine, there come to mind at once the words of the Apostle: "Where sin abounded, grace did more abound." All know that the father of the whole human race was constituted by God in so exalted a state that he was to hand on to his posterity, together with earthly existence, the heavenly life of divine grace. After the unhappy fall of Adam, the whole human race, infected by the hereditary stain, lost its participation in the divine nature, and we were all become "children of wrath." But the all-merciful God "so loved the world as to give His only-begotten Son"; and the Word of the Eternal Father with the same divine love assumed human nature from the race of Adam—but an innocent and spotless nature—so that He, as the new Adam, might be the source whence the grace of the Holy Spirit should flow unto all the children of the first parent. Through the sin of the first man they had been excluded from adoption as children of God; now, however, through the Word incarnate made brothers according to the flesh of the only-begotten Son of God, they receive also the power to become the sons of God. Through His death on the Cross, Christ Jesus not only satisfied the justice of the Eternal Father which had been violated, but He also won for us, His brethren, an ineffable flow of graces. It was possible for Him to impart these graces to mankind directly; but He willed to do so through a visible Church made up of men, so that through her all might co-operate with Him in dispensing the graces of Redemption. As the Word of God willed to make use of our nature, in order to redeem mankind, through His suffering and agony, in the same way throughout the centuries He makes use of the Church that the work begun may endure.

If we would define and describe this true Church of Jesus Christ—which is the One, Holy, Catholic, Apostolic Roman Church—we shall find nothing more noble, more sublime, or more divine than the expression "the mystical body of Jesus Christ." This name springs from and flowers forth, as it were, in frequent teachings of the Sacred Scriptures and the holy Fathers.

The Church Is the Visible Body

That the Church is a body is frequently asserted in the Sacred Scriptures. "Christ," says the Apostle, "is the head of the body, the Church" (Colossians 1:18). If the Church is a body, it must be an unbroken unity, according to the words of Paul: "Though many, we are one body in Christ" (Romans 12:5). But it is not enough that the body of the Church should be an unbroken unity; it must also be something definite and perceptible to the senses as Our predecessor of happy memory, Leo XIII, in his Encyclical *Statis cognitum*, asserts: "The Church is visible because she is a body." Hence they err in a matter of divine truth who imagine the Church to be invisible, intangible, something merely "pneumatological," as they say, through which many Christian communities, though they differ from each other in their profession of faith, are united by an invisible bond.

But a body calls also for a multiplicity of members, which are linked together in such a way as to help one another. And as in the body, when one member suffers, all the other members share its pain, and the healthy members come to the assistance of the ailing, so in the Church the individual members do not live for themselves alone, but also help their fellows, and all work in mutual collaboration for the common comfort and for the more perfect building up of the whole body.

Again, as in nature a body is not formed by any haphazard grouping of members but must be constituted of organs, that is, of members that do not have the same function, and are arranged in due order; so for this reason above all the Church is called a body, because she is constituted by the organic structure of united parts, and consists of a variety of reciprocally dependent members. It is thus that the Apostle describes the Church when he writes: "As in one body we have many members, but all the members have not the same office: so we being many are one body in Christ, and every one members of one another" (Romans 12:4, 5).

One must not think, however, that this ordered or "organic" structure of the body of the Church contains only hierarchical elements and with them is complete; or, as an opposite opinion holds, that it is composed only of those who enjoy charismatic gifts—though members gifted with miraculous powers will never be lacking in the Church. That those who exercise sacred authority in this body are its first and chief members, must be maintained uncompromisingly. It is through them, by commission of the Divine Redeemer Himself, that Christ's apostolate as Teacher, King, and Priest continues forever. At the same time, when the Fathers of the Church exalt this mystical body of Christ, with its ministries, its variety of ranks, its offices, its positions, its orders, its duties, they are thinking not only of those who have received Holy Orders, but of all those, too, who, following the evangelical counsels, spend their lives either actively among men or hidden in the silence of the cloister, or who aim at combining the active and contemplative life according to their rule; as also of those who, though living in the world, consecrate themselves wholeheartedly to spiritual or corporal works of mercy, and of those who live in the state of holy matrimony. Indeed, let this be clearly understood, especially in these our days: fathers and mothers of families, those who are godparents through Baptism, and in particular those members of the laity who collaborate with the ecclesiastical hierarchy in spreading the Kingdom of the Divine Redeemer, occupy an honorable, if often a lowly, place in the Christian community, and even they under the impulse of God and with His help can reach the heights of supreme holiness, which, as Jesus Christ has promised, will never be wanting to the Church.

The Holy Sacraments

Now we see that the human body is given the proper means to provide for its own life, health, and growth, and for that of all its members. Similarly the

Savior of mankind out of His infinite goodness has provided in a wonderful way for His mystical body, endowing it with the Sacraments, so that, as though by an uninterrupted series of graces, its members should be sustained from birth to death, and that generous provision might be made for the social needs of the whole body. Through the waters of Baptism those who are born into this world dead in sin are not only born again and made members of the Church, but, being stamped with a spiritual seal, they become able and fit to receive the other Sacraments. By the chrism of Confirmation, the faithful are given added strength to protect and defend the Church, their Mother, and the faith she has given them. In the Sacrament of Penance, a saving medicine is offered for the members of the Church who have fallen into sin, not only to provide for their own health, but to remove from other members of the mystical body all dangers of contagion, or rather to afford them an incentive to virtue, and the example of a virtuous act.

Nor is that all; for in the Holy Eucharist the faithful are nourished and strengthened at the same banquet and by a divine, ineffable bond are united with each other and with the divine Head of the whole body. Finally, like a devoted mother, the Church is at the bedside of those who are sick unto death; and if it be not always God's will that by the holy anointing she restore health to this mortal body, nevertheless she administers spiritual medicine to the wounded soul and sends new citizens to Heaven, to be her new advocates, who will enjoy forever the happiness of God.

For the social needs of the Church Christ has provided in a particular way by the institution of two other Sacraments. Through Matrimony, in which the contracting parties are ministers of grace to each other, provision is made for the external and duly regulated increase of Christian society, and, what is of greater importance, for the correct religious education of the children, without which this mystical body would be in grave danger. Through Holy Orders men are set aside and consecrated to God, to offer the Sacrifice of the Eucharistic Victim, to nourish the flock of the faithful with the Bread of Angels and the food of doctrine, to guide them in the way of God's commandments and counsels, and to strengthen them with all other supernatural helps.

The Holy Spirit

Nor must one imagine that the body of the Church, just because it bears the name of Christ, is made up during the days of its earthly pilgrimage only of members conspicuous for their holiness, or that it consists only of those whom God has predestined to eternal happiness. It is owing to the Savior's infinite mercy that place is allowed in His mystical body here below for those whom, of old, He did not exclude from the banquet. For not every sin, however grave it may be, is such as of its own nature to sever a man from the body of the Church, as does schism or heresy or apostasy. Men may lose charity and divine grace through sin, thus becoming incapable of supernatural merit, and yet not be deprived of all life if they hold fast to faith and Christian hope, and if, illumined from above, they are spurred on by the interior promptings of the Holy Spirit to salutary fear and are moved to prayer and penance for their sins.

The Church which Christ founded by His blood, He strengthened on the day of Pentecost by a special power, given from Heaven. For, having solemnly installed in his exalted office him whom He had already nominated as His Vicar, He had ascended into Heaven; and sitting now at the right hand of the Father He wished to make known and proclaim His Spouse through the visible coming of the Holy Spirit with the sound of a mighty wind and tongues of fire. For just as He Himself when He began to preach was made known by His Eternal Father through the Holy Spirit descending and remaining upon Him in the form of a dove, so likewise, as the Apostles were about to enter upon their ministry of preaching, Christ our Lord sent the Holy Spirit down from Heaven, to touch them with tongues of fire and to point out, as by the finger of God, the supernatural mission and office of the Church.

Christ Is Head of the Body

That this mystical body which is the Church should be called Christ's is proved in the second place by the fact that He must be universally acknowledged as its actual Head. "He," as St. Paul says, "is the head of the body, the Church" (Colossians 1:18). He is the head from whom the whole body, perfectly organized, "groweth and maketh increase unto the edifying of itself."

But our divine Savior governs and guides the society which He founded directly and personally also. For it is He who reigns within the minds and hearts of men, and bends and subjects their wills to His good pleasure, even when they are rebellious. "The heart of the king is in the hand of the Lord; whithersoever he will he shall turn it" (Proverbs 21:1). By this interior guidance He, the "Shepherd and Bishop of our souls," not only watches over individuals but exercises His Providence over the Universal Church, whether by enlightening and giving courage to the Church's rulers for the loyal and effective performance of their respective duties, or by singling out from the body of the Church—especially when times are grave—men and women of conspicuous holiness, who may point the way for the rest of Christendom to the perfecting of His mystical body. Moreover, from Heaven Christ never ceases to look down with especial love on His spotless Spouse so sorely tried in her earthly exile; and when He sees her in danger, saves her from the tempestuous sea either Himself or through the ministry of His angels, or through her whom we invoke as the Help of Christians, or through other heavenly advocates, and in calm and tranquil waters comforts her with the peace "which surpasseth all understanding."

The Pope Is the Visible Vicar of Christ

But we must not think that He rules only in a hidden or extraordinary manner. On the contrary, our Divine Redeemer also governs His mystical body in a visible and normal way through His Vicar on earth. You know, Venerable Brethren, that after He had ruled the "little flock" Himself during His pilgrimage on earth, Christ our Lord, when about to leave this world and return to the Father, entrusted to the Chief of the Apostles the visible government of the entire community He had founded. Since He was all wise He could not leave the body of the Church He had founded as a human society without a visible head. Nor against this may one argue that the primacy of jurisdiction established in the Church gives such a mystical body two heads. For Peter by virtue of his primacy is only Christ's Vicar; so that there is only one chief head of this body, namely Christ, who never ceases Himself to guide the Church invisibly, though at the same time He rules it visibly, through him who is His representative on earth. After His glorious Ascension into Heaven this Church rested not on Him alone, but on Peter too, its visible foundation stone. That Christ and His Vicar constitute one head only is the solemn teaching of Our predecessor of immortal memory, Boniface VIII, in the Apostolic Letter *Unam Sanctam*; and his successors have never ceased to repeat the same.

They, therefore, walk in the path of dangerous error who believe that they can accept Christ as the head of the Church, while not adhering loyally to His Vicar on earth. They have taken away the visible head, broken the visible bonds of unity, and left the mystical body of the Redeemer so obscured and so maimed that those who are seeking the haven of eternal salvation can neither see it nor find it.

The Bishops

What We have thus far said of the Universal Church must be understood also of the individual Christian communities, the dioceses, whether Oriental or Latin, which go to make up the one Catholic Church. For they, too, are ruled by Jesus Christ through the voice of their respective Bishops.

The Church as Mystical Body of Christ

Now We come to that part of Our explanation in which We desire to make clear why the body of Christ, which is the Church, should be called mystical. This appellation, which is used by several early writers of the Church, has the sanction of numerous Pontifical documents. There are several reasons why it should be used; for by it we may distinguish the body of the Church, which is a society whose head and ruler is Christ, from His physical body, which, born of the Virgin Mother of God, now sits at the right hand of the Father and is hidden under the Eucharistic veils; and—something that is of greater importance in view of modern errors—this appellation enables us to distinguish it from any other body, whether in the physical or the moral order.

In a natural body the principle of unity unites the parts in such a manner that each lacks its own individual subsistence; conversely, in the mystical body the mutual union, though intrinsic, links the members by a bond which leaves to each the complete enjoyment of his own personality. Moreover, if we examine the relations existing between the several members and the whole body, in every physical, living body all the different members are ultimately destined to the good of the whole alone; while if we look to its ultimate usefulness, every moral association of men is in the end directed to the advancement of all in general and of each single member in particular; for they are persons. And thus—to return to Our theme—as the Son of the Eternal Father came down from Heaven for the salvation of us all, He likewise established the body of the Church and enriched it with the divine Spirit to ensure that immortal souls should attain eternal happiness according to the words of the Apostle: "All things are yours; and you are Christ's; and Christ is God's." For the Church exists both for the good of the faithful and for the glory of God and of Jesus Christ, whom He sent.

But if we compare a mystical body with a moral body, it is to be noted that the difference between them is not slight; rather, it is very considerable and very important. In the moral body, the principle of union is nothing else than the common end, and the co-operation of all under the guidance of a social authority, for the attainment of that end; whereas in the mystical body of which We are speaking, this collaboration is supplemented by another internal principle, which exists effectively in the whole and in each of its parts, and whose excellence is such that of itself it is vastly superior to whatever bonds of union may be found in a physical or moral body. As We said above, this is something not of the natural but of the supernatural order; indeed, it is something in itself infinite, uncreated: the Spirit of God, who, as St. Thomas, the Angelic Doctor, says, "numerically one and the same, fills and unifies the whole Church."

Hence, in its correct signification, the word "mystical" gives us to understand that the Church, a perfect society of its kind, is not made up of merely moral and juridical elements and principles. She is far superior to all other human societies; she surpasses them as grace surpasses nature, as things immortal are above all those that perish. Such human societies, and in the first place civil society, are by no means to be despised or belittled; but the Church in her entirety is not found within this natural order, any more than the whole of man is encompassed within the organism of our mortal body. Although the juridical principles, on which the Church rests and is established, derive from the divine constitution given to her by Christ and contribute to the attaining of her supernatural end, nevertheless that which lifts the society of Christians far above the whole natural order is the Spirit of our Redeemer who penetrates and fills every part of the Church's being and is active within her until the end of time as the source of every grace and every gift and every miraculous power. Just as our composite mortal body, although it is a marvelous work of the Creator, falls far short of the eminent dignity of our soul, so the social structure of the Christian community, though it proclaims the wisdom of its divine Architect, still remains something inferior when compared to the spiritual gifts which give it beauty and life, and to the divine source whence they flow.

From what We have thus far written and explained, Venerable Brethren, it is clear, We think, how grievously they err who arbitrarily claim that the Church is something hidden and invisible, as also do those who look upon her as a mere human institution possessing a certain disciplinary code and external ritual, but not the power to communicate supernatural life.

For this reason We deplore and condemn the pernicious error of those who dream of a Church of their own imagination, a kind of society that finds its origin and growth in charity, to which, somewhat contemptuously, they oppose another, which they call juridical. But this distinction which they introduce is false: for they fail to understand that the reason which led our divine Redeemer to give to the community of men He founded the constitution of a society, perfect of its kind and containing all the juridical and social elements—namely, that He might perpetuate on earth the saving work of Redemption—was also the reason why He willed it to be enriched with the heavenly gifts of the Paraclete. The Eternal Father indeed willed it to be the "kingdom of the Son of His predilection"; but it was to be a real kingdom, in which all believers should make Him the entire offering of their intellect and will, and humbly and obediently model themselves on Him who for our sake "was made obedient unto death" (Phil. 2:8). There can, then, be no real opposition or conflict between the invisible mission of the Holy Spirit and the juridical commission of Ruler and Teacher received from Christ, since they mutually complement and perfect each other—as do the body and soul in man—and proceed from our one Redeemer who not only said as He breathed on the Apostles, "Receive ye the Holy Spirit" (John 20:22), but also clearly commanded, "As the Father hath sent me, I also send you" (John 20:21); and again, "He that heareth you heareth me" (Luke 10:16).

Sin and Weakness Are Not Excluded

And if at times there appears in the Church something that indicates the weakness of our human nature, it should not be attributed to her juridical constitution, but rather to that regrettable inclination to evil found in each individual, which her divine Founder permits even at times in the most exalted members of His mystical body, for the purpose of testing the virtue of the shepherds no less than of the flocks, and that all may increase the merit of their Christian faith. For, as We said above, Christ did not wish to exclude sinners from His Church; hence if some of her members are suffering from spiritual maladies, that is no reason why we should lessen our love for the Church, but rather a reason why we should increase our devotion to her members. Certainly the loving Mother is spotless in the Sacraments, by which she gives birth to and nourishes her children; in the faith which she has always preserved inviolate; in her sacred laws imposed on all; in the evangelical counsels which she recommends; in those heavenly gifts and extraordinary graces through which, with inexhaustible fecundity, she generates hosts of martyrs, virgins, and confessors. But it cannot be laid to her charge if some members fall, weak or wounded. In their name she prays to God daily: "Forgive us our trespasses"; and with the brave heart of a mother she applies herself at once to the work of nursing them back to spiritual health.

When, therefore, we call the body of Jesus Christ "mystical," the very meaning of the word conveys a solemn warning. It is a warning that echoes in these words of St. Leo: "Recognize, O Christian, your dignity, and being made a sharer of the divine nature do not go back to your former worthlessness along the way of unseemly conduct. Keep in mind of what head and of what body you are a member."†

---

† Encyclical *Mystici Corporis Christi* (June 29, 1943).

The Indestructibility of the Church

The Catholic Church, therefore, is the great visible mystery, because her head on earth, the Vicar of Christ, is visible, her ministers are visible, her life is visible, her worship is visible, her work and activity for the salvation and the perfection of men is visible. Visible, too, is her indestructibility, as it is proved historically, while her past is the token of her future. Hence a great historian, not a Catholic, of the last century, after recognizing, in spite of himself, that the Catholic Church has remained "full of life and of youthful vigor," remarked: "If we think of the tremendous storms it has survived, we find it difficult to conceive how it could perish." But if this indestructibility can be demonstrated by experience, it is, nevertheless, a mystery, because it cannot be explained naturally, but only by the fact, known to us by divine revelation, that Christ, who founded the Church, is with her in every danger until the end of time.‡

The Church, too, had and has her springtime; marvelous like herself. Do not the three great solemnities of Easter, Ascension, and Pentecost, in the season in which nature, awakening to new life, decks itself in greenery and blossom, and labors to produce the gifts of its harvests and fruits, constitute a spiritual spring, which makes nature's spring sweeter, lovelier, and dearer to us? They form, as it were, a sun in which shine three supreme truths, three overwhelming historical facts, three mysteries of unsurpassed splendor in the work of redemption; they are three fundamental and unshakable pillars of the gigantic edifice of the Holy Church. In their light, in their supernatural strength, these truths, equally present in every century of the history of the Church and equally obvious to all the generations of the faithful, illuminate with their historical reality the spring of Christianity, its budding, growth, and bloom even among winds and storms; because Christianity was born a giant, its forehead encircled with the rays of those three truths, which open up the period rightly called heroic: the three centuries from the foundation of the Church up to the peace with the Roman Empire in the year 312 in the time of Constantine.

‡ Address to Lenten Preachers (March 13, 1943).

These three fundamental mysteries, like brilliant rays from that light of the world that is Christ, guide and accompany the young Church, the Bride of Christ, on her way, watching over her first steps and encouraging her to rise, through the dark forest of paganism, and to reach the mountain of her predestined greatness. The first Christians, their minds, with tenacious constancy, absorbed in their faith in rebirth and their own resurrection, their eyes fixed longingly on the glorified figure seated on the right of the Father, and on the heavenly Jerusalem, the eternal, happy dwelling of those who remain faithful up to the end, their souls dominated by the certainty of the supporting presence of the Spirit, promised and sent by Jesus: thus we see them, towering above us with their lofty thought and vigorous action, vying with each other in courage and moral heroism, in the affirmation of the faith, in struggles and suffering, leaving an example which had the power to win victory after victory throughout the centuries and up to the present time; even more so now when, to save and protect the honor and the name of Christian, it is necessary to sustain similar struggles and to face similar dangers. Before such heroes, on whose heads the laurel of the Christian warrior is often entwined with the palm of martyrdom, all uncertainty and hesitancy disappear. Is not the example of their heroic lives, calling us sharply to order, enough to drive darkness from our minds, breathe courage into our hearts, make us hold our heads high once more, reminding us, Christians of today, of our dignity, making us aspire to the lofty greatness, calling to mind the responsibilities which Christianity inspires in those who profess it?

This early Christianity, of whose beginning we are reminded by the approach of the solemnities of Ascension and Pentecost, is distinguished by four spiritual characteristics that are quite unmistakable: (1) Unshaken certainty of victory, based on profound faith. (2) Serene and unlimited readiness for sacrifice and sufferings. (3) Eucharistic ardor springing from the conviction of the social efficaciousness of a Eucharistic thought on all forms of social life. (4) Aspiration toward an ever closer and unbreakable unity of spirit and hierarchy.

This fourfold character of the early life of the Church presents in each of its dominant notes an appeal and at the same time a hope and a promise for Christianity in our days. But the real Christianity of today is not different from primitive Christianity. The youth of the Church is eternal, because the

Church does not grow old, even though changing step according to the conditions of the time, in her journey toward eternity; the centuries she counts are but a day for her, and but a day are the centuries before her. Her youth in the times of the Caesars is the same that speaks to us.[†]

The Church Is Above Nationalism

The Catholic Church is by her very essence above nationalism. This has a double sense, one negative and one positive. The Church is a mother, *Sancta Mater Ecclesia*, a true mother, the mother of all the nations and all the peoples, no less than of all individual men, and just because she is a mother, she does not and cannot belong exclusively to this or that people, or even to one people more than to another, but to all equally. She is a mother, and therefore is not and cannot be a stranger in any place; she lives, or at least by her nature must live, among all peoples. In addition, while the mother, with her husband and children, forms a family, the Church, by virtue of an incomparably closer union, constitutes, more or better than a family, the mystical body of Christ. The Church, therefore, is above nationalism, because she is an invisible and all-embracing whole.

The Church unites all regions and all periods of redeemed humanity, without exceptions.

Securely established on such deep foundations, the Church, placed as she is in the midst of the history of mankind, among the confusion and the havoc of divergent energies and contradictory tendencies, although exposed to all assaults on her indivisible wholeness, is so far from being shaken by them that from her own life of wholeness and unity she irradiates and diffuses ever new healing and unifying powers among lacerated and divided humanity, powers of unifying divine grace, powers of the unifying Spirit, for which all are hungry, truths that prevail always and everywhere, ideals that throw light always and everywhere.

From this it is clear that it was and is a sacrilege against the *totus Christus*, Christ in His integrity, and at the same time a fatal blow against the unity of

† Radio Broadcast (May 13, 1943).

mankind, whenever an attempt has been or is being made to make the Church a prisoner and a slave of this or that particular people, to confine her to the narrow limits of a nation, as also to ban her from a nation. This laceration of the wholeness of the Church has reduced increasingly and continues to reduce the welfare, in the sense of true fullness of life, of the peoples that are victims of it.

But the national and State individualism of the last few centuries was not alone in trying to harm the interests of the Church, to weaken and impede her unified and unifying forces, which once took an essential part in the formation of the unity of Western Europe. An obsolete liberalism set out, without and against the Church, to create unity by means of lay culture and secularized humanism. Here and there, as the fruit of its dissolving action and at the same time as its enemy, totalitarianism supplanted it. In a word, after little more than a century, what was the result of all those efforts without and often against the Church? The decline of wholesome human liberty; compulsory organizations; a world that, for brutality and barbarity, for destruction and ruin, and above all for fatal disunion and lack of security, had never been equaled.

In confused times such as ours, the Church, for her own welfare and for that of humanity, must do her utmost to stress her indivisible and undivided wholeness. Today more than ever she must take up her stand above all nationalism. This spirit must penetrate and pervade her visible head, the Sacred College, all the action of the Holy See which, especially now, is faced with important duties regarding not only the present but even more so the future.

What is in question here is principally a matter of the spirit, of having the right sense of this supranationalism, and of not measuring or determining it according to mathematical proportions or on a rigorous statistical basis regarding the nationality of individual persons. In the long periods of time in which, by the will of Providence, the Italian nation, more than the others, has given the Church her head and many collaborators to the central government of the Holy See, the Church as a whole has always kept intact her supranational character.

Supranational because she embraces with the same love all nations and all peoples, she is also such, as We have already mentioned, because she is nowhere a stranger. She lives and thrives in every country in the world, and every country in the world contributes to her life and her development.

And so in the Church of today we see being accomplished more and more what St. Augustine magnified in his *City of God*; "The Church," he wrote, "calls her citizens from all parts, from all languages she gathers her pilgrim community on earth; she pays no heed to differences in customs, laws, institutions; she neither suppresses nor destroys any of these things, but rather preserves and follows. Even that which is different in the different nations, she directs toward the one and the same end of earthly peace, unless it prevents the veneration of the one supreme and true God."

Like a mighty lighthouse, the Church, in her all-embracing universality, casts her sheaf of light in these dark days through which we are passing.

For Our part, We are eager to make this same house more and more solid, more and more habitable for everyone, without exception. And so We do not want to omit anything that can express visibly that the Church has this supranational quality, the sign of her love for Christ, whom she sees and serves with the richness of her members scattered throughout the whole world.[†]

The Church Is a Mother

The Church, who was sent by the divine Savior to all peoples to lead them to their eternal salvation, does not intend to intervene and to take sides in controversies about purely temporal matters.

She is a mother. Do not ask a mother to take sides for or against one or other of her children. Everybody must find and feel in her that clear-sighted and generous love, that intimate and unchangeable tenderness, that gives her faithful children the strength to walk with a firmer step in the royal road of truth and light, and inspires in those who have gone astray the desire to return to her maternal guidance.[‡]

Any attentive observer who is able to examine and sum up present circumstances, in their concrete reality, necessarily remains struck by the sight of the severe obstacles that obstruct the apostolate of the Church. Like the flow of incandescent lava that yard by yard covers the slope of the volcano, so the

† Allocution to the Sacred College (December 24, 1945).

‡ Allocution to the Sacred College (December 24, 1946).

devastating sea of the spirit of the times advances threateningly and spreads over all fields of life, all classes of society.

Its process and its rhythm, no less than its effects, vary according to the different countries, from a more or less conscious disavowal of the social influence of the Church to systematic mistrust, which in some forms of government takes on the character of open hostility and real persecution.[†]

But the Church cannot withdraw into inactivity in the secrecy of her temples and desert the mission given her by divine Providence to form the complete man, and to collaborate constantly in the constitution of a solid foundation for society. This mission is essential for her. Considered from this point of view, the Church can be called the society of those who, under the supernatural influence of grace, in the perfection of their personal dignity as sons of God and in the harmonious development of all human inclinations and energies, construct the powerful framework of human society.

Thus the principal significance of the Church's supranationalism is to give lasting figure and form to the foundations of human society, above all diversities, beyond the limits of time and space.[‡]

The Papacy

CHRIST has carried out His will to found one Church, indivisible and indestructible, in the promise to Peter, by the institution of the primacy, that is, of the Papacy. The Church, built on Peter and on his successors, and she alone, was to be the Church of Christ, unique and eternal unto the end of time through submission to a personal, visible head.

It was a disposition of divine Providence that Peter chose Rome as his episcopal seat. Here, in the Circus of Nero, as we know from incontestable archaeological evidence, he died as the confessor of Christ; under the central

† Allocution to the Sacred College (December 23, 1950).

‡ Allocution to the new Cardinals (February 20, 1946).

point of the gigantic cupola of St. Peter's was and is his burial place. His successors, the Popes, have continued his mission up to the present.

In the series of Roman Pontiffs there have been many who, like the Prince of Apostles, sealed with their blood their fidelity to Him whose visible representatives they were. Many were great on account of their holiness, their genius, their learning, their authoritative personality. There have been some others whose purely human qualities were less adequate for the requirements of their supreme pastoral office. But the most violent storms that have raged from the time of the Apostle Peter up to our own days have not been able to shake the Church, nor to impair the divine mission of her heads. Every Pope receives it, at the very moment when he accepts his election, directly from Christ, with the powers and the privilege of infallibility granted him by God.

If ever one day (We say this as a mere hypothesis) material Rome were to crumble, if ever this very Vatican Basilica, the symbol of the one invincible Catholic Church, were to bury beneath its ruins the historical treasures, the sacred tombs it encloses, even then the Church would not crumble or crack, Christ's promise to Peter would always remain true, the Papacy, the one and indestructible Church founded on the Pope alive at that moment, would always endure.[†]

Peter's successors, they, too, mortal like all men, pass away. But the primacy of Peter will always exist, with the special assistance promised him, when Jesus charged him with the task of confirming his brothers in the faith. Whatever may be the name, the face, the human origins of any Pope, it is always Peter who lives in him; it is Peter who rules and governs; it is Peter, above all, who teaches and diffuses over the world the light of liberating truth. That caused a great holy orator to say that God has set up in Rome an everlasting Chair: "Peter will live in his successors; Peter will always speak from his Chair."[‡]

As the Vicar of Him who in a decisive hour, before the representative of the highest earthly authority of that time, spoke the great words, "For this was I born and for this came I into the world; that I should give testimony to the truth. Every one that is of the truth, heareth my voice," We feel that our primary duty to Our office, and also to Our times, is to give testimony,

† Address to the Students of Rome (January 30, 1949).

‡ Address to Newlyweds (January 17, 1940).

with apostolic firmness, to the truth: "*testimonium perhibere veritati.*" This duty necessarily includes the exposure and refutation of human errors and faults, which must be known so that it may be possible to cure them and recover from them: you will know the truth and the truth will make you free. In the carrying out of this duty, We will not let Ourselves be influenced by earthly considerations, nor will We hold back because of diffidence and opposition, refusals and incomprehension, nor for fear of being misunderstood and wrongly interpreted. But We will do so always animated by that spirit of paternal love which, while it suffers from the evils that torment the children, points out to them the remedy, that is, We will try to imitate the divine model of the shepherds, the Good Shepherd Jesus, who is at the same time light and love.[†]

Schisms

This divine mandate, which from the first Peter through the long series of Roman Pontiffs has come down to Us, their unworthy successor, embraces, in the confused and torn world of today, an even greater aggregate of sacred responsibilities, and meets with obstacles and opposition which demand of the Church, in her visible head and her members, increased alacrity and vigilance.

Today, in fact, more than ever there is revealed to the eye of every clear-sighted and just observer the sad record of loss which the schisms from the Mother Church have inflicted on Christianity in the course of the centuries. In a stormy, tormented epoch like ours, when humanity is preparing to reap the consequences of a spiritual decadence which has precipitated it into the abyss; when in all the nations voices are raised demanding, for the gigantic work of postwar reorganization, in addition to exterior guarantees, also the indispensable juridical and moral foundations, it will be of essential importance to know what influence the current of ideas and rules of Christian life will be able to exercise on the contents and on the spirit of this future order and against the repeated predominance of false and fatal tendencies.

The Roman Catholic Mother Church, who has remained faithful to the constitution she received from her divine Founder, and who even today stands

† Encyclical *Summi Pontificatus* (December 24, 1939).

firm in the solidity of the rock on which His will constructed her, possesses in the primacy of Peter and his legitimate successors the certainty, guaranteed by the divine promises, of guarding and transmitting complete and inviolate, through centuries and millenniums, until the end of time, the whole sum of truth and grace that is contained in Christ's mission of redemption. And while the Church, in the stimulating and comforting consciousness of this double possession, finds her strength able to conquer all the darkness of error and moral degradation, she pursues her task in the interests not only of Christianity but of the entire world, inspiring sentiments of conciliatory justice and genuine brotherly love in the great controversies, in which, often, blessing and calamity, plentiful harvests and crop failure, are to be found side by side.

But how much stronger and more efficacious the radiation of Christian thought and life would be on the moral foundations of the future plans for peace and social reconstruction if it were not for the vast division and dispersion of religious denominations which in the course of time have split away from the Mother Church! Who today would not recognize what constancy of faith, what a deep force of resistance against antireligious influences, have been lost by this division into numerous groups?

Rationalism

The story of rationalism and naturalism in the last two centuries is eloquent proof, among many others, of this grievous reality. Where the office entrusted to him who is invested with the primacy, *confirma fratres tuos*—strengthen thy brethren—is unable to exercise and carry on its protective and preserving action, the tare of rationalism has penetrated in a thousand different ways, with its swarms of harmful parasites, into the thoughts and minds of many who call themselves Christians, poisoning what had remained in them of the divine seed of revealed truth, causing above all darkness, schism, and increasing abandonment of faith in the divinity of Christ.

The Bond of Caesarea Philippi

From the day of the promise given at Caesarea Philippi, and of its fulfillment on Lake Tiberias, there exists a living bond between Christ and Peter, a bond which, though mysterious, is nonetheless real, a bond knotted in time but having its origin in the eternal counsels of the Almighty. The heavenly Father, who revealed the mystery of the divinity of Christ to Simon, the son of Jona, and thus made him able to answer with an open and ready confession the Redeemer's question, had from all eternity predestined the fisherman of Bethsaida for his unique office; and Christ Himself merely carried out the Father's will when in His promise and in the conferment of the primacy He used words which were to establish forever the uniqueness of the privileged position attributed to Peter.

Those, therefore, who—as was stated (or, rather, repeated) not so long ago by some representatives of religious denominations that profess to be Christians—declare that there is no Vicar of Christ on earth, because Christ Himself has promised to remain with His Church as her Head and Lord until the end of time, besides depriving every episcopal office of its foundation, completely misunderstand the profound meaning of the pontifical primacy, which is not negation, but fulfillment of that promise. For, if it is true that Christ in the fullness of His divine power disposes of the most varied forms of illumination and sanctification, in which He is really with those who confess Him, it is no less certain that He entrusted Peter and his successors with the guidance and the government of the Universal Church and the treasures of truth and grace of His work of redemption. The words of Christ to Peter leave no doubt as to their meaning: this was recognized and believed by both East and West, in times above suspicion, and with admirable harmony. To insist on creating an opposition between Christ as head of the Church and His Vicar, to see in the affirmation of the one the negation of the other, is to introduce confusion into the clearest and most luminous pages of the Gospel, to shut one's eyes to the most ancient and venerable testimony of tradition, and to deprive Christianity of that precious inheritance, a true knowledge and esteem of which may, at a time that is known only to God and by means of the light of grace which He alone can give, arouse in our separated brethren the longing for their ancestral home and the efficacious resolve to return to it.

The Vicar of Christ

When, every year, on the evening before the feast of the Prince of the Apostles, We visit Our Patriarchal Vatican Basilica, to implore, on the tomb of the first Peter, the strength to serve the flock entrusted to Us according to the designs and ends of the eternal High Priest, from the majestic vault of that lofty temple there shimmer before Our eyes in gleaming mosaics the mighty words with which Christ manifested His intention of building the Church on the rock of Peter, and they remind Us of Our imperious duty to preserve intact this incomparable heritage of the divine Redeemer. While We behold shining before Us the "glory" of Bernini, and above the Chair, held up by the gigantic figures of Ambrose and Augustine, of Athanasius and John Chrysostom, We see resplendent and dominating in a blaze of light the symbol of the Holy Ghost, We feel and experience the fullness of the sacred character, of the superhuman mission, that the will of the Lord with the assistance of the Spirit, promised and sent by Him, has conferred on this central point of the Church of the Living God, *columna et firmamentum veritatis*—pillar and support of truth.[†]

The imposing colonnade of Bernini opens wide its arms, in a symbolic gesture, as if to say to the travelers and pilgrims of every language and every nation that this vast temple is ready to receive them all in truth and in love.[‡]

On Prayer

Devotion is a great virtue that safeguards all the others. But its most beautiful and expressive act is prayer, which, for man, who is body and soul, represents the daily food of the soul just as material bread is the daily nourishment of the body.

Prayer is, first of all, collecting one's thoughts before the Lord. To seek out God, to find Him, it is enough to enter into yourselves, morning, night,

† Allocution to the Sacred College, June 2, 1944.

‡ Homily, First Anniversary of Pontificate, March 3, 1940.

or at any moment of the day. If you are joyfully in a state of grace, you will see in the intimacy of your soul with the eyes of faith God ever present as an immensely kind Father, ready to hear your requests and tell you also what He expects of you; you will find God present as a judge, merciful and ready to forgive; or, better still, as the Father of the prodigal son, who will open to you His arms and heart, if you will only prostrate yourselves penitent, confessing: "Father, I have sinned against Heaven and against Thee." Oh, how many souls have been saved from obstinacy in sin, hardening, and eternal perdition with a brief examination of conscience every evening! How many owe their salvation to daily prayer!

Such an exercise of Christian devotion does not mean transforming the home into a church or oratory; it is a sacred impulse of souls which feel in themselves the strength and life of faith. Even in ancient pagan Rome, the family home used to have a sanctuary and an altar dedicated to the tutelary gods which, especially on festive days, were adorned with garlands of flowers and on which supplications and sacrifices were offered. It was a cult blemished by the error of polytheism; but at its recollection how many Christians should blush with shame, who, with the sign of Baptism on their brows, find neither the space in their rooms to place an image of the real God, nor the time, in the twenty-four hours of the day, to gather around Him the homage of the family!

Nothing furthers trusting prayer as much as the personal experience of efficacious prayers which loving Providence has answered, granting largely and fully that which was requested.

And yet for some, for many who do pray, the divine favors seem to be too slow in coming. What they ask seems to them good, useful, necessary, and beneficient not only for the body but also for their souls and for the souls of those dear to them; they pray with fervor for weeks and months, and yet have not received anything. The health necessary to care for her family has not yet been granted to the mother. The son and the daughter whose conduct endangers their eternal salvation have not yet mended their ways. Material difficulties that oppress parents who struggle to assure their children a piece of bread, instead of abating, become harsher and more menacing.

Under the weight of such thoughts, many look with surprise upon the sacred altars before which prayer is offered and perhaps remain scandalized and perplexed in hearing the Sacred Liturgy incessantly recall and proclaim the promises of the divine Savior: "Whatever you ask in prayer, believing, you will obtain... Ask and it shall be given unto you... He who asks, receives... Whatever you will ask of My Father, in My name, I shall do... In truth, in truth, I say unto you, that whatever you may ask of the Father in My name, He will give it unto you." Could the promises of the Savior have been more explicit, more clear, more solemn? Are not some, perhaps, tempted to see almost a derision in the silence of God to their petitions?

But God neither lies nor can lie; that which He has promised, He will keep; that which He has said, He will make good.†

Our Savior has nowhere promised to make us infallibly happy in this world; He has promised—as we read in the Gospels—to hear us as the father does the child, to whom he does not give, even if asked for it, a stone or a serpent or a scorpion for food, but bread, fish, and eggs, which nourish him and advance him in his living and growing. What Jesus, our Savior, has pledged to grant us infallibly as the fruit of our prayers are not those favors men often ask out of ignorance of what is really necessary for their health, but that "good spirit," that bread of supernatural gifts necessary or useful to our souls; that fish prepared by Him, which, as a future symbol, Christ reborn gave as food to the Apostles on the banks of Lake Tiberias; that egg, food for the little ones of piety and devotion, which men often do not distinguish from the stones most harmful to their spiritual health, offered to them by the tempter, Satan.

Prayer, therefore, should be a petitioning for that which is good for our souls, an incessant petitioning, but also a devout petitioning.

Devout prayer! What is it? It is not a prayer sounding mere words only, while mind and heart and eyes stray in all directions, but rather the prayer of meditation which, before God, is wholly animated by filial confidence, becomes illuminated with live faith, is imbued with love for God and for one's brethren; it is the prayer always unfolding in the grace of God, always meritorious of eternal life, always humble in its intimacy; it is the prayer which, when you kneel before the altars or the images of the Crucified and the Most Holy Virgin in your home, does not know the arrogance of the Pharisee, who vaunts himself better than other men, but, like the poor publican, makes you

† Address to Newlyweds (February 2, 1941, and April 12, 1942).

feel in your own hearts that whatever you may receive is coming to you by the mercy of God.

Prayer is a good which does not humiliate or lower, but rather exalts man and makes him great. The most excellent artists, the masters of visual psychology, have created nothing more soul-stirring than the representation of man in prayer. In the attitude of prayer man reveals his greatest nobility, hence it was strikingly affirmed that "man is great only when he is kneeling."†

The Ten Commandments

CHRIST, as he said, did not come to undo and abolish the Law, but to fulfill it and lead it to perfection; and fulfilled by Him with His doctrine and His teachings are the Ten Commandments, which God proclaimed on Sinai for the people of Israel.

Of God's Commandments in General

The Ten Commandments are a law, given by God Himself, in which are also mirrored the vigor of human reason and of the intelligence of learned men; yet, what manifests itself to whoever examines the religious and moral conditions of the present hour, if not a painful contrast between the highest level of religious formation which today is offered to the people, on the one hand, and, on the other, the negligible profit drawn from it and the diminishing activating force carried into practical life? In earlier periods of Church history, general religious teaching was, as a rule, far simpler; but the entire process of human life was dominated and, through numerous sacred customs, imbued with the fear of God and the incontrovertible obligation to keep His Commandments.

From the middle of the last century, not only has Catholic science, with admirable daring, expanded more and more, but especially the ecclesiastical

† Address to General Audience (July 2, 1941).

ministry itself has illuminated and expounded Catholic faith in its every aspect, amply and imposingly, and furnished moral norms for the most varying conditions of life, both for the individual and for communities, striving in every way to bring the wealth of spiritual light to the souls of men. But when one asks whether among Catholic people the level of religious instruction and of moral conduct has equally risen, the answer, unfortunately, cannot be affirmative. In lamentable contrast with that high doctrinal development, the efficacy and the force of the religious impulse have been decreasing and waning.

We do not deny—in fact, it is clearly apparent—that there is no want of Catholics of exemplary faithfulness to God's Commandments, nor are Christian heroism and sanctity wanting. In this respect, our times do not yield to preceding periods and we do not fear to say that in some aspects they surpass them. But take a look at public life and you will find, alas, that it has become to a large extent de-Christianized, while contempt of and estrangement from the Christian way of life have become widely diffused. An overwhelming antireligious current is opposed to the believers who want to form their whole personal, family, and public life according to the law of God; they meet with grave difficulties and impediments in trying to make their convictions known and appreciated; hence, not a few succumb or become slack in the practice of religion. To breathe in the corrupt atmosphere of great modern cities and live a Christian life without absorbing their poison, one needs a profound spirit of faith and the strength and resistance of the martyrs.

The Guilt of Sin

A fact which always repeats itself in the history of the Church is that when faith and Christian morals clash with strong adverse currents of error or vitiated appetites, attempts are made to overcome the difficulties with some sort of easy compromise, or otherwise to side-step and elude them.

Even in what is due the Commandments of God an expedient is thought to have been found. In the field of morality, it has been said, there is enmity with God, loss of supernatural life, grave sin in an absolute sense, only when the act for which one has to answer was performed not only with the clear consciousness that it infringes the Commandment of God, but also with the express intention of thereby offending the Lord, of destroying union with Him, of denying Him love. If this intention is lacking, that is, if man on his part did not want to sever friendship with God, the individual act—it is maintained—cannot harm him. To cite an example: the multiform deviations from the Sixth Commandment do not represent a grave fault for the believer if he otherwise wants to keep united with God and to remain His friend, nor do they involve mortal sin. Stupefying solution! Who does not see how in the clear knowledge that a determined human act is against the Commandment of God, it is implied that it cannot be directed to the end of union with Him, precisely because it contains the aversion, that is, the estrangement of the soul, from God and His will (*aversio a Deo fine ultimo*), an aversion which destroys union and friendship with Him, which is, precisely, the hallmark of grave sin? Is it, perhaps, not true what faith and theology teach: that each sin is an offense against God and aims to offend Him, because the intention inherent in grave sin is against the will of God as expressed in the Commandment of His which is violated? When man says "Yes" to the forbidden fruit, he says "No" to the prohibiting God; when he puts himself and his will before the law of God, he estranges himself from God and divine will; aversion to God and the intimate essence of grave sin consist in this.

The malice of any human act originates from its not conforming to its proper rule, which is twofold: one, the more proximate, is human reason itself; the other, supreme rule is the eternal law, which may be likened to the reason of God, whose light is reflected in the human conscience when it shows us how to distinguish between good and evil. The true believer does not ignore that the intention pointing to the object of mortal sin is not separable from the intention which violates divine will and law and severs all friendship with God, who knows well how to recognize the good and bad intentions of human acts and to reward or punish them with His penetrating justice.

There Is Only One Way

There is but one way to achieve the love of God and to be in union and friendship with Him: the observance of His precepts. Words count little; what counts are deeds, and therefore the Redeemer used to say: "Not everyone that says to me, Lord, Lord, shall enter into the Kingdom of Heaven: but he who does the will of my Father, who is in Heaven, he shall enter the Kingdom of Heaven."

Acknowledging God by fulfilling His holy will in all His Commandments and, better still, by unifying our will with His will—that, and that alone, is the way to Heaven. St. Paul proclaimed this axiom of moral life in energetic form: "Beware of erring: neither fornicators, nor idolators, nor adulterers, nor the effeminate, nor those who sin against nature, nor thieves, nor the avaricious, nor drunkards, nor evildoers, nor the rapacious, shall be heirs to the Kingdom of God."

The Apostle of the Gentiles had in mind not only the defection from God by the formal negation of faith or formal hate of Him, but also every grave lesion of moral virtue, and His word concerned not only the habit of sinning but also all the individual acts against morals and justice, which are mortal sins and bring with them eternal damnation. To give precisely to the religious man what amounts to a document of immunity from guilt in whatever he might do against the Commandments of God, can surely not be considered to be the redemption from moral misery, whose elimination is today the task of the Church.

Neo-Paganism

Today paganism seems reborn, and many have already exalted it in prose works and poems in opposition to Christianity; but the Church, from her appearance in the world, with the teachings of the Gospel and with the heroic virtue of her Apostles and her believers, took a stand against every sophism and every underhanded or open persecution by paganism. Her struggle always took the form of a frontal attack, opposing to pagan error the illuminated strength of Christian precepts and virtues. Not only the Epistles of St. Paul give a very clear testimony to the loftiness of the moral obligations imposed by the religion of Christ and to the struggle the faithful had to endure to observe them; but also, at the end of the apostolic period, the Letters of the Apocalypse to the seven churches are a no less manifest expression, with their continuous refrain: "*Vincenti... Qui vicerit.*" "To the victor I shall give to eat of the tree of life, the hidden manna; and I will confess his name before my Father and before His Angels. The victor shall not be hurt by the second death."

The Moral Law

The fervor of the Christians in the first centuries made them inclined to profess their faith rather too openly than the opposite; so much so that at times their moral rigor surpassed the very limits of the reasonable measure demanded by the spirit of the Gospel. With great severity the Church Fathers did not hesitate to combat, because of the disorders they caused, the spectacles: gladiatorial contests, the theater, dances, feasts, and pastimes which seemed only natural amusements to pagan society. It is no wonder that faith should radically change and improve the habits of those who came in contact with it.

If, then, today the cry is so often raised: Return to early Christianity! a good beginning toward its realization is the amending and reform of morals; let that cry not be a vain noise but a serious and effective return, such as the exigencies of moral practice and life nowadays so urgently demand.

Christ did not find heroism in everyone; whoever showed but a trace of good will, to him He tendered His hand and inspired him with courage; at the same time, however, He did not refrain from making the highest demands: "If any man will come after Me, let him deny himself and take up his cross daily, and follow Me." "Be you therefore perfect, as also your heavenly Father is perfect." To lead man to such lofty goals, the Church aids everyone, always with the intention of bringing ever closer to the perfection of the heavenly Father all who believe in Christ and practice His teachings and commands.

The Church is on the mount, visible to all, "Mother of the Saints, image of the Supreme City," even if it is evident that the de-Christianization around her has gained and is gaining ground.

The Church stands firmly on her foundation, unshaken by the defections and the persecutions, because she is the force of God and of Christ. It has been said that, if there were no God, He would have to be invented: without a God who traces for man the distinction and limits of good and evil, no moral law would light the way to reason on this earth. Wherever faith in a personal God is dominant, moral order, determined by the Ten Commandments, remains strong; otherwise, sooner or later, it crumbles miserably.

Of God's Commandments in Particular

If now we consider the Commandments of God individually, it may well be said that each one of them has become a cry of warning, pointing out grave moral perils. The past, too, has witnessed serious disorders: who could deny it? But several of the pillars which supported the ethical order, first among them faith in God, authority of the parents and of constituted public power, always remained solid and intact. Today, the whole edifice of morals is undermined, threatened, upset. A characteristic sign of such decadence is that, with the waning of belief in God and with the simultaneous exaggeration and abuse not infrequently exercised by public power, both the concrete forms and the very principle of authority are becoming "stumbling blocks" and being rejected.

We believe, nonetheless, that to improve and heal this state of affairs two remedies would be especially helpful. In the first place, let authority be returned to parents, with all its rights, even where they might have been restricted or absorbed, as, for example, in the fields of teaching and education. Then, let all those who have public authority, all the ruling classes, including the employers and the educators of youth, themselves set the example of righteous living, and let them exercise the moral authority inherent in their office in keeping with the tenets of justice and love. Before such a model of probity the world would be filled with admiration, seeing what prodigies of public tranquillity and trust might result.

In the field of reciprocal loyalty and veracity there reigns and expands a contaminated atmosphere in which persons of good faith find it difficult to breathe. Who would have thought that following the proud peak of civilization and culture which has been the boast of preceding generations, respect for law would encounter perils, trials, and violations such as only the darkest periods of history have known? But even in such matters the key to every solution is given by faith in a personal God, who is fount of justice and has reserved to Himself the right over life and death. Nothing else but this faith can confer the moral force to observe the proper limits in the face of all insidious temptations to overstep them; keeping in mind that, excepting in cases of legitimate defense, of just war fought with just means, and of capital punishment inflicted by the public authority for well-determined and proven gravest crimes, human life is intangible.

On the Commandments called "of the first table," which concern God, We deem opportune two observations. The first concerns the meaning itself of the worship to be rendered to God, a meaning which in the last hundred years has become obscured even among the faithful. If, in fact, it happens in every historical period that in the sanctuary of personal religious life men seek and try to advance their own interests, this is seen to be the case in boundless measure under the influence of the proud and vain culture which dominates the modern generations. They have wanted to reduce the relationship between God and man to the help of God in material and earthly needs; for the rest man wanted to help himself, as if he no longer needed divine support. The worship of God became a concept of usefulness. From the sphere of the spirit, religion fell to that of matter. Religious practice was reduced to seeking favors in Heaven for the needs on earth, almost keeping accounts with God: faith would waver if the help did not correspond to the desire. That religion and faith, above anything else, signify adoration and service of God; that there are Commandments of God which are always binding, in all places and in every circumstance; that, for the Christian, future life should dominate the one on earth; these concepts and these truths, which support and guide the intellect and the will of the believer, had become estranged from the thought and sentiments of the human spirit.

What remedy should one oppose to such failings? It is imperative that the great truths and the great concepts of faith be brought back, as life and reality, to all classes of people, to the upper classes even more than to those disinherited and tried by the want and misery in this world. This should at present be the foremost task of religious education; it is not only required but facilitated, since it is obvious that all the ills and misfortunes humanity now suffers through the decadence of morals and justice are the painful correction of the false concept of God and of religion, which have perverted religious practice.

It has been said that the prodigy of the present years are the millions of faithful who honor God and serve Him, subject to His Commandments, even though they have come to find themselves in indescribable want. Certainly there are such devout and fearless Christians, the glory of the Church.

The Sanctification of Feast Days

The worship of God, which in the course of human life should begin and end each day, imposes special duties for the sanctification of the feasts; and here applies Our second observation. One certainly cannot blame the Church with wanting to apply the Sunday precept with excessive harshness, she who determines and regulates it with that *benignitas et humanitas* of which her divine Founder gave her example. But against the profanation and the secularization of the day of the Lord, which with increasing speed is divested of its sacred character, and thereby estranges men from God, the Church, custodian of divine law, must oppose herself and react with holy firmness.

The Church must resist the absorption and distraction stemming from excessive sports, so that there is no longer time for prayer, for meditation, and for rest; the members of the family are necessarily separated one from the other; the children are alienated from their homes and away from the vigilance of their parents. Resist these pleasures without fear, since, like the immoral movies, they turn Sunday into a day of sin. Finally, man needs Sunday rest and recreation which, above everything else, is to the advantage of religious elevation, spiritual renewal, and the harmonious development of family life.

The Sixth Commandment

God, the name of God, and the worship of God constitute the "first table"; mankind, the duties and rights of human life, appear in the "second table," which, together with the first, forms the Decalogue almost in the way that love of God and love of neighbor unite to make a single love which from God flows to mankind. More numerous are the precepts contained in this "second table," and they call for many observations. But how could We omit recalling the words: *Non moechaberis*—Thou shalt not commit adultery? Is it saying too much if We regret that concerning this Commandment the very countries who boast a higher civilization present a spectacle of the most profound moral devastation? We know well how much economic and social reforms can contribute to the salvation of marriage and of the family; but such salvation, in the final analysis, remains a religious duty and a task whose curative process must start at the roots. The entire conception of the field of life which is contained in the Sixth Commandment is infected by what might be called "movie marriages," which are nothing else but an irreverent and shameless show of marriage conflicts and of conjugal unfaithfulness. The movies present marriage freed from any moral bond, as a setting and source of sensual pleasure only and not as the work of God, a holy institution, a natural office and candid bliss, in which the spiritual element always stands superior and dominates, a school and at the same time a triumph of a love faithful unto death, to the gates of eternity. Is it not, indeed, a duty of the care of souls to revive such a Christian vision of marriage among the faithful?

It is necessary that conjugal life should again be clothed and surrounded by that respect with which sane and incorrupt nature and revelation adorn it from the very beginning: respect for the forces which God has wondrously infused in nature to evoke new life, to build the family for the preservation of the human race. The education of youth to chastity of thought and affections, to continence before marriage, is not the final goal to which Christian pedagogy tends and aims, but it demonstrates the efficacy of its methods in preparing the spirit for the dangers which beset life. The youth who faces up to and victoriously engages in the struggle for purity will also observe the other Commandments of God and will be able to form a family according to the designs of the Creator. How, on the other hand, can chastity and conjugal faithfulness be expected or hoped for in a youth who could never dominate himself and rule his passions, hold bad invitations and bad examples in contempt, and who has permitted himself every moral disorder before marriage?

If the pastor of souls—as he has a sacred obligation before God and the Church—wants to obtain victory against the two cancers of the family, the abuse of marriage and the violation of conjugal fidelity, he must form and instruct with the light of faith a whole generation which from the early years has learned to think in a holy manner, to live in chastity, and to dominate itself.

To have holy thoughts, above all, about women. The "movie marriage" has here perhaps produced its most disastrous effects. It has deprived man of the respect for woman, and then deprived woman of self-respect. May education and the care of souls lead the minds and hearts back to the ancient and pure ideal of woman, pointing out to them the Immaculate Virgin and Mother of God, Mary, whose tender and trusting veneration has been at all times the preservation and salvation of feminine honor![†]

Erroneous Trends in Modern Theology

FROM the first dawn of rational speculation, since man began to reflect about the external universe and his inner world, the philosopher has never remained satisfied with observing the visible surface of things, which fall immediately under our experience, but has always tried to break through the outer shell, to penetrate to their soul, to seize the essence, to guess their nature and intimate constitution, until he is able to form an abstract conception of them from the contingent details, and thus give them a spiritual existence in his thought. In this way, philosophy, while spiritualizing and ennobling the real, at the same time discovers all the rational elements that are hidden in the real itself, unknown and inaccessible to the apprehension of the senses, in order to dwell on the object which is more proper to the mind, ready to embrace it in a wide, comprehensive vision.

And not only does it strip all things, so to speak, of their material concreteness, but it also floods them with the light of its universality. Just as the human mind is not satisfied with appearances, does not stop at phenomena, so it is not content with a fragmentary, disjointed contemplation of the parts of the universe, until it sees the connections, finds the causes and effects, and traces the principles that rule them, connect them up, subordinate and co-ordinate them into a complete picture of harmonious unity. No one dreams of questioning or doubting the value of analysis, to which modern progress owes so much. But

† Allocution to Lenten Preachers (February 23, 1944).

is it not perhaps true that the necessity of the present time is synthesis? Is not the danger already felt that present-day science, in so far as it is and must be the generator and the guardian of civilization, may decline and become lost in particularism, restrictivism, and the absolute prevalence of specialization?

The restlessness, the anxiety of man can be distracted for only a moment by the sight and the study of learned, ingenious constructions; diversion of an instant, like a dream in restless sleep, if the construction, however skillful and apparently well balanced, is not founded on rock. Until he gets a final and satisfactory answer to the questions: What is the meaning of life, the meaning of pain, the meaning of death, he will continue to have the impression, which is unfortunately only too well founded, that he lacks solid ground under his feet. But what answer can philosophy give, if it itself is not based on the absolute, on a personal God, the beginning and the end of all things?

A purely deterministic and materialistic explanation of being and of history, irreconcilable with the most elementary truths of psychology, morality, and history, could not satisfy man nor give him happiness and peace.†

Exacting Truths

The dissensions and errors of man, in religion and morality, have always been the origin and the cause of great sorrow for all well-meaning people, and above all, for the sincere and faithful sons of the Church. This is especially the case today, when we see the very principles of Christian culture being violated on every side.

It is not really astonishing that, outside the fold of Christ, these disagreements and errors have always existed. In fact, although human reason, strictly speaking, with its own strength and natural light, can indeed arrive at the knowledge, real and certain, of one personal God, who supports and rules the world with His Providence, and also at the knowledge of the natural law, imprinted by the Creator on our souls, yet there are many obstacles that prevent our reason from using this natural power efficaciously and fruitfully. For the

† Address to the Congress of Philosophy (November 29, 1946).

truths that concern God and the relationship between men and God completely transcend the order of the things of the senses; and when they are put into practice in our lives, they call for sacrifice and abnegation.

In arriving at such truths, the human intellect meets with obstacles both because of the senses and of the imagination, and on account of evil passions due to original sin. And so it happens that men in these matters gladly persuade themselves that what they do not wish to be true is false, or at least doubtful. For these reasons it has to be said that divine revelation is morally necessary so that religious and moral truths which are not unattainable in themselves may be known by everybody, in the present conditions of mankind, with ease, absolute certainty, and without any error.

Monism, Dialectical Materialism, Existentialism

The human mind may even sometimes find difficulty in coming to an assured judgment of the credibility of the Catholic faith, although God has given so many astonishing outward signs by means of which the divine origin of the Christian religion can be proved with absolute certainty even with only the natural light of reason. For man, either because he is guided by prejudices or because instigated by passions and ill will, is not only capable of denying the obvious evidence of these outward signs, but also of resisting the inspirations that God sends to our souls.

Anyone observing the world of today, that is outside the fold of Christ, will easily be able to see the principal paths which the learned have taken. Some, in fact, without prudence and discernment, admit and set up as the origin of everything the evolutionist system, although it is not absolutely proved even in the field of natural sciences, and boldly adopt the monistic and pantheistic hypothesis of the universe being subject to continual evolution. The champions of Communism readily use this hypothesis in order to defend and propagate their dialectic materialism and banish from all minds every notion of God.

The false statements of this evolutionism, by which everything that is absolute, certain, and unchangeable is repudiated, have prepared the way for the aberrations of a new philosophy which, competing with idealism, immanentism, and pragmatism, has taken the name of existentialism, because, repudiating the immutable essence of things, it deals only with the "existence" of single individuals.

Added to this there is a false "historicism" which takes into account only events of human life and destroys the foundations of any absolute truth and law both in the field of philosophy and in that of Christian dogmas.

In such confusion of opinions, We are somewhat consoled to see those who had once been educated in rationalistic principles not infrequently return today to the sources of revealed truth, and recognize and profess the word of God, preserved in the Holy Scriptures, as the foundation of theology. At the same time, however, We regret the fact that not a few of these people, the more firmly they cling to the word of God, the more they debase the value of human reason, and the more they exalt the authority of God the Revealer, the more bitterly they despise the Magisterium of the Church, set up by Christ our Lord to guard and interpret the truths revealed by God. This contempt is not only in open contradiction with the Holy Scriptures, but is shown to be false even by experience itself. For frequently these same people complain publicly about the discord that reigns among them in the field of dogmas, and thus, unintentionally, they recognize the necessity of a living teaching authority.

Now these tendencies, which more or less stray from the straight and narrow path, cannot be ignored or overlooked by Catholic philosophers and theologians, whose duty it is to defend divine and human truths and to implant them in the minds of men. On the contrary, they must become familiar with these opinions, both because illnesses cannot be treated unless they are first well known, and because sometimes a grain of truth is hidden in the false statements, and, finally, because these errors stimulate our minds to examine with more diligence certain truths of both philosophy and theology.

Now, if our students of philosophy and theology sought only to gather the fruits We have mentioned from these doctrines, examining them with caution, there would be no reason for the teaching authority of the Church to intervene. But although We are aware that, in general, Catholic teachers and scholars avoid such errors, yet it is known that there exist even today, as in the times of the Apostles, people who, too keen on novelty and afraid of being considered ignorant of the discoveries made by science in this age of progress, try to elude the guidance of the sacred teaching authority and are therefore in danger of unconsciously departing from the revealed truths and leading others astray, too.

Another danger should be noted, which is all the more serious in that it is more hidden under an appearance of virtue. Many people, deploring the discord and confusion prevalent in human minds, are fired by imprudent zeal and stimulated by a strong desire to overthrow the barriers that divide the good and the honest among themselves; therefore they embrace a kind of "irenism"; and, overstepping the questions that divide men, not only do they try to drive back, with joined forces, the attacks of atheism, but also to reconcile opposite positions in the field of dogma itself. And, just as once there were those who wondered whether the traditional apologetics of the Church were more of a hindrance than a help in winning souls for Christ, so today we find those who dare to reach the point of asking in all seriousness whether theology and its methods, as they are in use in schools with the approval of ecclesiastical authority, should not only be improved, but also completely reformed, in order that the Kingdom of Christ may be propagated more efficaciously throughout the world, among men of any culture or of any religious opinions whatever.

If they had no other intention than that of making, with some innovations, ecclesiastical science and its method more adapted to present conditions and necessities, there would be little cause for fear; but some of them, carried away by an imprudent "irenism," seem to consider as an obstacle to the re-establishment of fraternal unity all that is founded on the very laws and principles given by Christ and on the institutions founded by Him, or what constitutes the defense and the support of the integrity of the faith. If these crumble, unity will, indeed, be reached, but only in common ruin.

These opinions, whether springing from a deplorable desire for novelty or from praiseworthy motives, are not always proposed with the same graduation, the same clarity, or in the same terms, and their supporters are not always in agreement among themselves; in fact, what is taught today more or less hiddenly and with restrictions and distinctions, tomorrow is proposed publicly by others, more audaciously and without any limitations, scandalizing many, especially the young clergy, and to the detriment of ecclesiastical authority. As greater prudence is observed in printed publications, these subjects are dealt with more freely in pamphlets distributed in private, in typed papers, and at meetings. These opinions are spread not only among the members of the secular and regular clergy, in seminaries and religious institutes, but also among laymen, especially among those engaged in bringing up and educating youth.

As for theology, some of them intend to reduce as much as possible the meaning of the dogmas; to free the dogma itself from the mode of expression the Church has used for so long, and from the philosophical concepts held by Catholic scholars, to return, in explaining the Catholic doctrine, to the expressions used by the Holy Scriptures and by the Holy Fathers. They hope in this way that the dogma, stripped of the elements that are extrinsic, as they say, to divine revelation, may be compared profitably with the dogmatic opinions of those who are separated from the Church, and that in this way it will be possible gradually to arrive at the assimilation of Catholic dogma with the opinions of the dissidents. In addition, by reducing the Catholic doctrine to such conditions, they think they are opening up the way to the possibility, thus satisfying present-day necessities, of expressing the dogmas with the categories of modern philosophy, whether it be immanentism, idealism, existentialism, or any other system. And therefore some of them, the more audacious, maintain that this can and must be done, because the mysteries of the faith, they affirm, can never be expressed with concepts that are absolutely true, but only with concepts that are approximate and continually changing, by which truth is manifested up to a certain point, but at the same time necessarily distorted. Therefore, they consider it not absurd, but absolutely necessary, for theology, as for the various philosophical systems, which in the course of time it uses as instruments, to substitute new concepts for the old; so that it may expound in a human way the same divine truths, using different approaches, that from certain points of view are also opposite, but—as they say—equivalent. They add, too, that the history of the dogmas consists in expounding the various forms which revealed truth has successively assumed, according to the different doctrines and the different opinions that have arisen in the course of the centuries.

Scholastic Concepts and the Teaching Authority of the Church

From what We have said, it is clear that these tendencies not only lead to relativism in dogma, but in fact already contain it; this relativism, furthermore, is much encouraged by the contempt for traditional doctrine and for the terms in which it is expressed. Everybody knows that the expressions of these concepts, used both in the schools and by the teaching authority of the Church, can be improved and perfected; it is, besides, well known that the Church has not always been constant in the use of those same words. It is also evident that the Church cannot be linked with any ephemeral philosophical system; but those ideas and those terms which, with general consent, were composed in the course of several centuries by Catholic scholars to arrive at some sort of knowledge and understanding of the dogma, certainly cannot be based upon such perishable foundations. No, they are based on principles and ideas deduced from a real knowledge of creation; and in deducing them, the human mind was illuminated by revealed truth, as by a star, through the Church. It is, therefore, not surprising if some of these ideas have not only been used in Ecumenical Councils but have also been so solemnly sanctioned that it is not permissible for us to depart from them.

For these reasons, it is extremely imprudent to neglect or reject or deprive of their value the concepts and expressions which people of no common intellect and sanctity, under the vigilance of the sacred teaching authority and not without illumination and guidance from the Holy Spirit, have found and perfected time and again throughout the centuries to express more and more accurately the truths of the faith, and to substitute for these the hypothetical notions and the fluctuating, vague expressions of the new philosophy, which, like the grass in the fields, are here today and withered tomorrow; this would be to make dogma itself like a reed shaken in the wind. Contempt for the words and ideas used by scholastic theologians, in itself, leads to the weakening of speculative theology, which some consider to be devoid of true certainty in so far as it is based on theological reasons.

Unfortunately, these lovers of novelty pass easily from contempt of scholastic theology to indifference and lack of esteem for the authority of the Church itself, which has given such noteworthy approval to that theology. This authority is made to appear by them as an obstacle to progress and a hindrance to science; it is considered by some non-Catholics as an unjust restraint, whereby learned theologians are prevented from giving new life to their science. And although for any theologian this sacred authority should in matters of faith and morals be the immediate and universal rule of truth (inasmuch as Christ our Lord entrusted to it the deposit of the faith—that is, Holy Scriptures and divine tradition—to be guarded, defended, and interpreted), yet sometimes no heed is taken, exactly as if it did not exist, of the duty incumbent on the faithful to avoid those errors which to a greater or lesser extent approach heresy, and therefore "to observe also the constitutions and decrees with which these false opinions are proscribed and prohibited by the Holy See." What is expounded in the Encyclicals of the Sovereign Pontiffs about the character and the constitution of the Church is intentionally and habitually overlooked by some people, with the aim of establishing a vague concept that they say comes from the ancient Fathers, especially Greek. The Pontiffs, in fact—they say—do not intend to pass judgment on questions that are the object of dispute among theologians; it is, therefore, necessary to go back to the primitive sources, and the constitutions and decrees of the teaching authority are to be explained with reference to the writings of the ancients.

When Does the Pope Teach "Ex Cathedra"?

These statements may appear very ingenious; yet they contain an error. It is indeed true that generally the Pontiffs leave theologians free in those questions which, in various ways, are a matter of discussion among the most well-known scholars; but history teaches that several questions which before were open to free discussion later could no longer be discussed.

Nor should it be thought that the teachings of the Encyclicals do not require, in themselves, full assent, on the pretext that the Pontiffs do not exercise here the power of their supreme authority.

In fact, these teachings come from the ordinary authority, to which can also be applied the words: "He that heareth you, heareth me"; and what is more, anything that is proposed and inculcated in the Encyclicals is already, for other reasons, the patrimony of the Catholic doctrine. If, then, the Sovereign Pontiffs, especially in their decrees, pass a judgment on a matter which up till then was open to dispute, it is obvious to everyone that this question, according to the intention and the will of the Pontiffs themselves, can no longer be the object of free discussion among theologians.

It is also true that theologians must always go back to the sources of divine revelation; it is, in fact, their duty to indicate how the teachings of the living authority "are found either explicitly or implicitly" in the Holy Scriptures and in divine tradition. It should be added, also, that both these founts of the revelation contain such and so many treasures of truth as to be, in fact, inexhaustible. For this reason, the sacred sciences take on new youth with the study of the sacred sources; while, on the contrary, as we know from experience, speculation that neglects research into the sacred deposit becomes sterile. For this very reason, theology, even positive theology, cannot be likened to a mere historical science. For God has given His Church, together with these sacred founts, the living authority, also to illustrate and develop those truths which are contained only obscurely and, as it were, implicitly in the deposit of the faith. And the divine Redeemer did not entrust this deposit, for authentic interpretation, either to the individual believer or to the theologians themselves, but only to the authority of the Church. If, then, the Church exercises this office (as has often occurred in the course of the centuries), it is evident that the method which wants to explain things that are clear through things that are obscure is completely false; that, actually, it is necessary for everyone to follow the reverse order. Therefore, Our predecessor, Pius IX, while He taught that it is a noble task of theology to show how a doctrine defined by the Church is contained in the sources, not without serious reason added the following words: "in that same sense in which it has been defined by the Church."

The Interpretation of Holy Scriptures

Let us now return to the new theories about which We spoke before: some of them propose or instill into the mind various opinions that lower the divine authority of the Holy Scriptures. With audacity some of them pervert the meaning of the words of the Vatican Council, wherewith God is defined as the author of the Holy Scriptures; and they renew the opinion, already several times condemned, according to which the authority of Holy Scriptures extends only to those parts concerning God Himself or religion and morality. Actually, they falsely speak of a human meaning of the Bible, under which the divine meaning is hidden; and only the latter, they declare, is infallible.

In the interpretation of the Holy Scriptures they refuse to take into account the analogy of faith and the tradition of the Church; so that the doctrine of the Holy Fathers and of the sacred teaching should be measured with that of the Holy Scriptures, explained, however, by the exegetes in a purely human way and not, rather, the Holy Scriptures explained according to the mind of the Church, which was made guardian and interpreter of the whole deposit of revealed truths by Christ our Lord.

Besides, the literal meaning of the Holy Scriptures and its explanation, worked out, under the vigilance of the Church, by competent exegetes, should, according to their false opinions, give way to a new exegesis, called symbolical and spiritual; and according to this exegesis, the books of the Old Testament, which today in the Church are a closed and hidden wellspring, would finally be open to everybody. In this way—they affirm—all the difficulties which are met by those who hold fast to the literal meaning of the Scriptures would disappear.

It should come as no surprise that such innovations in almost all parts of theology have produced their poisonous fruit. It is questioned whether human reason, without the help of divine revelation and grace, can demonstrate, with arguments taken from created things, the existence of a personal God; it is affirmed that the world had no beginning and that the creation of the world is necessary because it comes from the necessary liberality of divine love; and it is also affirmed that God does not have eternal and infallible foreknowledge of the free actions of man: all opinions contrary to the declarations of the Vatican Council.

The Character of the Mystical Body of Christ

Some others, again, question whether the angels are persons; and if there is an essential difference between matter and spirit. Still others distort the conception of the gratuitousness of the supernatural order, when they maintain that God cannot create intelligent beings without ordaining them and calling them to the vision of bliss. Nor is this enough; for, setting aside the definitions of the Council of Trent, they destroy the true concept of original sin, together with that of sin in general, as being an offense against God, as that also of the satisfaction made for us by Christ. And there are those who maintain that the doctrine of transubstantiation, inasmuch as it is founded on an antiquated conception of substance, must be corrected in order to reduce the real presence of Christ in the Eucharist to symbolism, so that the consecrated species would be no more than efficacious symbols of the spiritual presence of Christ and of His intimate union in the mystical body with the faithful.

Some do not consider themselves bound to the doctrine that We set forth in one of Our Encyclicals and which is based on the founts of revelation, according to which the mystical body of Christ and the Roman Catholic Church are one and the same thing. Some reduce to an empty formula the necessity of belonging to the true Church in order to obtain eternal salvation. Others, again, do not admit the rational character of the signs of credibility of the Christian faith.

It is well known that these errors, and others of the same kind, lurk among some of Our sons, all deceived by imprudent zeal or false science, and We are obliged to repeat, sorrowfully, to these sons very well-known truths and manifest errors, pointing out to them, anxiously, the dangers of error.

Human Reason in Church Doctrine

Everyone knows how highly the Church values human reason, which has the task of demonstrating with certainty the existence of a single personal God, of demonstrating invincibly by means of the divine signs the foundations of the Christian faith itself; and of showing in the proper light the law that the Creator has imprinted on the souls of men; and, finally, the task of arriving at a limited, but very useful, knowledge of mysteries.

But this task can be carried out properly and with ease only if reason has been duly cultivated; if, that is, it is nourished by that healthy philosophy which is, as it were, a patrimony inherited from preceding Christian ages and possesses a higher authority, since the authority of the Church herself has put alongside revealed truth its principles and main assertions, disclosed and established slowly throughout the ages by men of great genius. This philosophy, confirmed and commonly recognized by the Church, defends the real value of human knowledge, the unshakable principles of metaphysics—that is, of sufficient reason, of causality and finality; and, finally, maintains that it is possible to reach certain and unchangeable truth.

In this philosophy there are certainly several things that do not concern faith and morals, either directly or indirectly, and which, therefore, the Church leaves to be discussed freely by experts in the subject; but there is not the same liberty with regard to several others, especially with regard to the principles and principal assertions We have already spoken about. Even in these essential questions We can give philosophy more suitable, richer vestments; philosophy itself can be strengthened by the use of more efficacious expressions, by eliminating certain scholastic methods that are less suitable; it can also be enriched—but prudently—with the addition of certain elements that are the fruit of the progressive work of the human mind; but it must never be subverted or contaminated with false principles, nor regarded as an important monument, yes, but only archaeological. For truth and every philosophical manifestation of it cannot be subject to daily changes, especially when it is a question of the principles of human reason, well known in themselves, or of those assertions that are based both on the wisdom of centuries and also on the foundations of divine revelation. Whatever truth the human mind discovers, after sincere searching, cannot be in contradiction with already known truths; for God, supreme Truth, has created and supports the human intellect not in order that it may daily find new truths which contradict those already acquired, but that, when the errors which may have crept in have been eliminated, truth may be added to truth in the same order and with the same consistency with which we see the very nature of things constituted, on which truth draws. For this reason the Christian, whether he be a philosopher or a theologian, does not embrace hurriedly and lightly all the novelties that are daily excogitated, but examines them with the greatest care and weighs them attentively in order not to lose or corrupt the truth that has already been acquired, which would endanger and harm faith itself.

The Teachings of Thomas Aquinas

If what has been explained above is carefully considered, it will be easy to understand the reason why the Church insists on future priests' being instructed in the philosophical sciences "according to the method, the doctrine, and the principles of the Angelic Doctor," since, as the experience of several centuries has clearly shown, St. Thomas's method is remarkable for its outstanding superiority both in training pupils and in searching for the truth; then, too, his doctrine is in harmony with divine revelation and is very efficacious in protecting the foundations of the faith and also in gathering usefully and safely the fruits of wholesome progress.

It is, therefore, highly deplorable that today the philosophy confirmed and admitted by the Church should be the object of contempt by some people who imprudently declare it to be old-fashioned in form and rationalistic as regards the process of thought. They say that our philosophy erroneously defends the opinion that it is possible to present a metaphysics that is true absolutely; while, on the contrary, they maintain that truths, especially transcendental truths, cannot be more fittingly expressed than by means of diverse doctrines which complement one another, although they may in some respects be contradictory. And so scholastic philosophy, with its lucid exposition and solution of questions, with its careful determination of concepts and its clear distinctions, may be useful—they admit—as a preparation for the study of scholastic theology, which was so well suited to the mentality of medieval man; but it cannot give us—they add—a method and a philosophical orientation that correspond to the needs of our modern culture. They put forward, also, the objection that perennial philosophy is only the philosophy of immutable essences, while modern mentality is interested in the "existence of single individuals and of life that is always in the process of change." But while they despise this philosophy, they exalt the others, both ancient and modern, of Oriental and of Western peoples, so that they seem to be insinuating that all philosophies or opinions, with the addition, if necessary, of some corrections or some completion, can be reconciled with Catholic dogma. But no Catholic can doubt how false all that is, especially when it is a question of systems such as immanentism, idealism, materialism, both historical and dialectic, or even existentialism, when it professes atheism or when it denies the value of reasoning in the field of metaphysics.

Finally, they formulate this reproach to the philosophy of our schools: that in the process of thought it pays attention only to the intellect, and neglects the function of the will and of feeling. This is not true. For Christian philosophy has never denied the utility and the efficaciousness of the readiness of the soul to get to know and to embrace religious and moral truths; on the contrary, it has always taught that the lack of such readiness may be the cause whereby the intellect, under the influence of the passions and malice, may be obscured to the extent of not being able to see rightly. Moreover, the general doctor, St. Thomas, is of the opinion that the intellect may be able in some way to perceive the higher goods of the moral order, both natural and supernatural, in so far as it experiences within itself a certain "fellowship," whether natural or the fruit of grace, with these goods; it is clear of what help this knowledge, however obscure, may be to reason in its searchings. But it is one thing to recognize the power of the will and disposition of the soul to help reason to reach a more certain and stronger knowledge of moral truths, and it is another to maintain, as these innovators do, that the will and feeling have a certain intuitive power and that man, not being able to discern with certainty by his reason what he should embrace as being true, turns to his will which permits him to make a free resolution and choice among opposite opinions. This shows a confusion between knowledge and an act of will.

The Decisions of Leo XIII and Pius X

It is not astonishing that, with these new opinions, the two philosophical disciplines, which, by their nature, are closely linked with the teachings of the faith, that is, theodicy and ethics, are endangered. These people are of the opinion that the function of these two is not that of demonstrating with certainty some truth about God or any other transcendent being, but rather that of showing how perfectly coherent with the necessities of life are the truths that faith teaches about God, a personal Being, and about His precepts, and that, therefore, they must be accepted by everybody to avoid desperation and to obtain eternal salvation. All these affirmations and opinions are openly contrary to the decisions of Our predecessors Leo XIII and Pius X, and are irreconcilable with the decrees of the Vatican Council.

It would be unnecessary to deplore these aberrations if everyone, also in the philosophical field, were obedient, with due reverence, to the teaching authority of the Church, which, by divine institution, has the mission not only of guarding and interpreting the deposit of revelation, but also of watching over the philosophical sciences themselves in order that Catholic dogmas should not be harmed by false opinions.

Evolution and Genesis

We still have to speak about those questions which, although belonging to the positive sciences, are more or less connected with the truths of the Christian faith. Not a few people, in fact, urgently request that the Catholic religion should take those sciences into greater account. This is certainly a praiseworthy thing, when it is a question of facts that are really proved; but we must move with caution when it is, rather, a question of hypotheses, although with some scientific foundation, which concern the doctrine contained in the Holy Scriptures or also in tradition. If these hypotheses are, directly or indirectly, in contradiction with revealed doctrine, then they can in no way be admitted.

For these reasons the teaching authority of the Church does not forbid that, in conformity with the present state of science and theology, the doctrine of evolution should be examined and discussed by experts in both fields, in so far as it deals with research on the origin of the human body, which it states to come from pre-existent organic matter (the Catholic faith obliges us to believe that souls were created directly by God). But this must be done in such a way that the arguments of the two opinions, that is, the one favorable and the other contrary to evolution, should be weighed and judged with all necessary seriousness, moderation, and restraint, and on condition that they are all ready to submit to the judgment of the Church, to which Christ has entrusted the office of interpreting authentically the Holy Scriptures and of defending the dogmas of the faith. Some, however, overstep the limits of this freedom of discussion, acting as if it were already proved, beyond all doubt, that the human body originated in pre-existent organic matter, on the basis of initial data collected up to now, and of arguments based on these indications; that is, as if there were nothing in the sources of divine revelation that called for the greatest moderation and caution in this matter.

But as regards the other hypothesis, that is, so-called polygenism, the sons of the Church do not enjoy the same freedom. For the faithful cannot embrace this opinion which states that after Adam there existed here on earth real men who were not descended, by natural generation, from him, the forefather of all men; or else that Adam represents groups of many forefathers; now, these statements cannot be reconciled with what the founts of revelation and the decrees of the authority of the Church teach us about original sin, which comes from a sin really committed by Adam individually and personally, and which, transmitted to everyone through the generations, is an inherent property in each man.

As in the biological and anthropological sciences, so also in the historical sciences there are people who audaciously overstep the limits and the precautions set up by the Church. Particularly deplorable is a certain system of interpreting the historical books of the Old Testament too freely; the upholders of this system, to defend their ideas, wrongly refer to the letter that was sent not long ago to the Archbishop of Paris by the Pontifical Commission for Biblical Studies. This letter, in fact, points out that the first eleven chapters of Genesis, although they do not correspond to the historical method used by the best Greek and Latin authors or by experts of our own time, do, however, belong to the historical category in a real sense, which must be studied in more detail and determined by the exegetes; the same chapters—the letter further points out—with simple and metaphorical expressions, suited to the mentality of a barely civilized people, give an account of the principal truths that are fundamental for our salvation, and also a popular narration of the origin of humanity and of the elect people.

If the ancient authors of the Sacred Scriptures have taken something from popular accounts (which can be admitted), it must never be forgotten that they did so with the help of divine inspiration, which preserved them from all error in the choice and judgment of these documents. Therefore, the popular narrations inserted in the Holy Scriptures cannot be put on the same plane as mythology and the like, which are the fruit of lively imagination rather than of that love of truth and simplicity which are so outstanding in the Sacred Books, and also in the Old Testament, that we must affirm that our authors are obviously superior to the ancient profane writers.

The Obligation of Bishops

We know, indeed, that the majority of Catholic scholars, the fruit of whose studies is harvested by the universities, the seminaries, and the religious colleges, are far from those errors which, openly or secretly, are being spread today, either on account of the craze for novelty or also because of immoderate apostolic zeal. But We know, too, that these new opinions may take hold of imprudent persons; therefore, We prefer to prescribe a remedy at the outset, rather than wait to administer the medicine when the illness is already advanced. For this reason, after mature reflection and consideration before God, in order not to fail in Our sacred duty, We order Bishops and the Superiors General of religious Orders and Congregations to take every precaution to prevent such opinions from being voiced in schools or in meetings and lectures, or in writings of any kind, or from being taught, in any way, to clergymen or to the faithful.

Teachers of ecclesiastical institutes should know that they cannot, with a safe conscience, exercise the office of teaching that has been entrusted to them unless they accept religiously the rules We have set up, and observe them exactly in the teaching of their subjects. They should also infuse into the minds and souls of their students that dutiful reverence and obedience which they, in their assiduous work, must profess toward the teaching authority of the Church.

Let them try with all their strength and passion to contribute to the progess of the sciences they teach; but let them be careful not to overstep the boundary set by Us for the defense of the faith and Catholic doctrine. Let them examine scrupulously, but with all due prudence and caution, the new questions which modern culture and progress have brought to the foreground. Finally, let them not believe, through false "irenism," that it is possible to bring about the happy return into the bosom of the Church of dissidents and those in error, without teaching to everybody, sincerely, the whole truth in force in the Church, without any corruption or elimination.[†]

† Encyclical *Humani generis* (August 12, 1950).

Atheism

THE modern age, adding new mistakes to the doctrinal deviations of the past, has carried them to extremes, from which nothing but bewilderment and ruin could follow. And first of all, it is certain that the deep and ultimate root of the ills which we deplore in modern society is the denial and rejection of a universal norm of morality, both in individual and social life and in international relationships; that is, the disavowal, so widespread in our times, and the neglect of even the natural law which has its foundation in God, the almighty Creator and Father of all, supreme and absolute legislator, omniscient and just avenger of human actions. When God is denied, every foundation of morality is also shaken and there is a smothering, or at least a great weakening, of the voice of nature which teaches even the untaught, and peoples that have not yet reached civilization, what is good and what is bad, what is lawful and what is unlawful, and makes man feel responsible for his actions before a Supreme Judge.

Now, denial of the fundamental basis of morality had its first root in Europe in a departure from that doctrine of Christ of which the Chair of Peter is the depositary and the teacher; a doctrine that at one time had given spiritual cohesion to Europe, which, educated, ennobled, and refined by the Cross, had achieved such a degree of civil progress as to become the teacher of other peoples and other continents. Instead, detaching themselves from the infallible guardianship of the Church, not a few seceding brethren have gone so far as to subvert the central dogma of Christendom, the divinity of the Savior, thus quickening the process of spiritual dissolution.

Many perhaps, in departing from the doctrine of Christ, were not fully aware that they were being deceived by the mirage of glittering phrases that proclaimed such detachment to be a liberation from the bondage in which they were said to have been held before; nor did they foresee the bitter consequences of the sad barter between the truth that frees and the error that enslaves; nor did they think that, giving up the infinitely wise and fatherly law of God and the unifying and elevating doctrine of the love of Christ, they were giving themselves up to the will of pitiful, changeable human wisdom; they spoke of progress, when they were going backward; of elevation, when they

† Encyclical *Summi Pontificatus* (October 20, 1939).

were degrading themselves; of an ascent to maturity, when they were falling into bondage; they did not perceive the vanity of any human effort to substitute for the law of Christ some other thing that could equal it.

Faith in God and in Jesus Christ once weakened, and the light of moral principles once darkened in souls, there was discarded the only irreplaceable foundation of stability and tranquillity, of that internal and external order, private and public, which alone can generate and safeguard the prosperity of States.†

In the giddiness of material progress, in the victories of human ingenuity over the secrets of nature and over the forces of the elements of the earth, the seas, and the sky, in the anxious competition to surpass the summits reached by others, in the arenas of daring research, in the conquests and in the pride of science, of industry, of laboratories, of factories, in the greed for money and for pleasure, in the tense effort toward a supreme power more feared than contended for, more envied than equaled, in the turmoil of all this modern life, where can the naturally Christian soul of man find peace? Perhaps in finding contentment in itself? Perhaps in boasting to be king of the universe, enveloped by the fog of illusion which confuses matter with the spirit, the human with the divine, the momentary with the eternal? No; intoxicating dreams do not calm the storm in a soul and conscience put into turmoil by the impetus of the mind which stands above matter and, aware of its unrejectable immortal destiny, steps over toward the infinite and toward immense desires. Approach those souls and question them. They will answer you in the language of a child, not of a man. They did not have a mother who, when they were children, would speak of the Father in Heaven; they grew up between walls without a Cross, in homes where religion was not mentioned, in fields far away from an altar and from a steeple; they read books from which the names of God and Christ are absent; they heard priests and monks and nuns vituperated; they went from the countryside, from the city, from their homes, to the factory, to the shop, to the halls of knowledge, to every art and work, without entering a church, without knowing the parish priest, without a good thought put in their hearts.‡

Too well known are the dangers and incentives, spiritual and moral, that now more than ever threaten the Christian principles of faith and life...

‡ Address to the Leaders of Catholic Action (May 3, 1951).

Pulled into the giddy and impassioned whirl of happenings, too often the mind runs the risk of having its faculty and readiness to judge events according to the pure and unshakable rules of divine law dulled and weakened. And yet the Christian, strong in his faith, intrepid in his duty, if he must find himself prepared to participate in the events, the duties, and the sacrifices of the day, must be no less ready to reject the errors of his times; in such a manner that, the more he perceives the gathering of the darkness of unbelief and malice, the more brave and ready should he show himself in making resplendent the light of Christ, a guide to the erring, leading and escorting them home to the spiritual heritage which so many have forgotten or abandoned. Inaccessible to the blandishments of others, he will keep to the path without going astray in the night of earthly darkness. He will lift his eyes to the stars in the Heaven of eternity, the consoling goal and reward of his hope. The harder and heavier the sacrifices demanded of mankind, the more vigorous and active will be the force of the divine precept of love in his soul, and the longing and eagerness to make it the guide of his intentions and actions. And if the proud spirit of an atheistic materialism will ask him the question: "*Ubi est spes tua?*—Where is your hope?" then, fearing neither the present nor the future, he will answer with the righteous of the Old Covenant: "*Nolite ita loqui; quoniam filii sanctorum sumus, et vitam illam expectamus, quam Deus daturus est his, qui fidem suam nunquam mutant ab eo*—Speak not so: For we are the children of saints, and look for that life which God will give to those that never change their faith from Him."†

The Holy Scriptures

The Present Status of Biblical Studies

There is no one who does not see that the conditions of Biblical studies and their subsidiary sciences have greatly changed within the last fifty years. When

† Address to the Sacred College (June 2, 1940).

Our predecessor published the Encyclical *Providentissimus Deus*, only a few sites in Palestine had begun to be explored by excavations related to the Bible. Now, however, this kind of investigation is much more frequent and, since more precise methods and technical skill have been developed in the course of actual experience, it gives us information at once more abundant and more accurate. How much light has been derived from these explorations for the more correct and fuller understanding of the Holy Scriptures is known to all experts, as well as to all those who devote themselves to Biblical studies. The value of these excavations is enhanced by the repeated discovery of written documents, which considerably increase our knowledge of the languages, letters, events, customs, and forms of worship of most ancient times.

The Discovery of Papyri

Of no less importance is the discovery and investigation, so frequent in our times, of papyri which have contributed so much to the knowledge of letters and institutions, both public and private, especially of the time of Our Savior. Moreover, ancient codices of the Holy Scriptures have been found, and edited with discerning thoroughness; the exegesis of the Fathers of the Church has been more widely and thoroughly examined; in sum, the manner of speaking, narrating, and writing in use among the ancients is illuminated by innumerable examples. All these advantages which, not without a special design of divine Providence, our age has acquired, are as it were an invitation and inducement to interpreters of the Holy Scriptures to make diligent use of this light, so abundantly given, to penetrate more deeply, explain more clearly, and expound more lucidly the Word of God.

Study of Biblical Languages

The Church Fathers, especially St. Augustine, had already recommended to the Catholic exegete, who undertook the investigation and explanation of the Sacred Scriptures, the study of the ancient languages and recourse to the original texts. However, such was the state of letters in those times that not many—and these few but imperfectly—knew the Hebrew language. In the Middle Ages, when scholastic theology was at the height of its vigor, the knowledge of even the Greek language had long since become so rare in the West that even the greatest Doctors of that time, in their exposition of the Holy Scriptures, had recourse only to the Latin version, known as the Vulgate. In this our time, however, not only is the Greek language, restored to new life since the Renaissance, familiar to almost all students of antiquity and letters, but the knowledge of Hebrew also and of other Oriental languages has spread far and wide among scholars. Moreover, there are now such abundant aids to the study of these languages that the Biblical scholar who by neglecting them would deprive himself of access to the original texts could not escape the stigma of levity and sloth.

Importance of Textual Criticism

The great importance which should be attached to textual criticism was aptly pointed out by Augustine, when, among the precepts for the study of the Holy Scriptures, he recommended above all work with a correct text. "The correction of the codices," says this enlightened Doctor of the Church, "should first of all engage the attention of those who wish to know the Sacred Scriptures so that the incorrect may give place to the correct." In the present day indeed this art, which is called textual criticism and which is used with great and praiseworthy results in the editions of profane writings, is also quite rightly employed in the case of the Holy Scriptures, because of that very reverence which is due to the Word of God. For its very purpose is to ensure that the sacred text be restored as perfectly as possible, be purified from the corruptions due to the carelessness of the copyists, and be freed, as far as possible, from interpolations and omissions, from the interchange and repetition of words, and from all other kinds of mistakes, which are wont to make their way gradually into writings handed down through many centuries. It is scarcely necessary to point out that this type of criticism—which some fifty years ago was applied by some quite arbitrarily and often in such a way that one might say that they tended to introduce into the sacred text their own preconceived ideas—today has rules so firmly established and secure that it has become a most valuable aid to the purer and more accurate editing of the sacred text and that any abuse can easily be discovered.

The "Literal" Meaning

Thoroughly prepared by the knowledge of the ancient languages and by the aids afforded by textual criticism, let the Catholic exegete undertake the greatest task of all those imposed on him, namely that of discovering and expounding the genuine meaning of the Sacred Books. In the performance of this task let the interpreters bear in mind that their foremost endeavor should be to discern and define clearly what has been called the "literal" sense of the Biblical words. Aided by the context and by comparison with similar passages, let them therefore, by means of their knowledge of languages, search out with all diligence the literal meaning of the words; all these aids, indeed, are also used in the study of profane writers, so that the mind of the author may be made abundantly clear. The commentators of the Holy Scriptures, mindful of the fact that here they deal with a divinely inspired text, the care and interpretation of which have been confided to the Church by God Himself, should no less carefully take into account the explanations and declarations of the teaching authority of the Church, as the interpretations given by the Holy Fathers, and also "the analogy of faith," as Leo XIII most wisely observed in the Encyclical *Providentissimus Deus.* With special zeal they should apply themselves not only to expounding exclusively those matters which belong to the historical, archaeological, philological, and other auxiliary sciences—as, to Our regret, is done in certain commentaries—but, having duly referred to these, in so far as they may aid the exegesis, they should set forth in particular the theological doctrine concerning faith and morals of the individual books or texts, so that their exposition may not only aid the professors of theology in their expositions and proofs of the dogmas of faith but also be of assistance to priests in their presentation of Christian doctrine to the people, and so finally may help all the faithful to lead a life that is holy and worthy of a Christian.

The Spiritual Meaning

An exposition of this kind, which is in the main theological, would serve to silence those who assert that they rarely if ever find anything in Biblical commentaries to raise their hearts to God, to nourish their souls, or to promote their interior life, and who recommend as only recourse a certain spiritual and, as they say, mystical interpretation. How little justified this assertion is appears from the experience of many who, assiduously considering and meditating the word of God, advanced in perfection and were moved to an intense love for God; and this same truth is clearly proved by the constant tradition of the Church and the precepts of the greatest Doctors. Doubtless not all spiritual sense is excluded from Sacred Scripture. For what was said and done in the Old Testament was ordained and disposed by God with such consummate wisdom that things past prefigured spiritually those that were to come under the new dispensation of grace. Wherefore the exegete, just as he must search out and expound the literal meaning of the words as they were intended and expressed by the sacred writer, so also must do for the spiritual sense, provided it is clearly intended by God. For God alone could have known this spiritual meaning and have revealed it to us. Now, our divine Savior Himself points out to us and teaches us this same sense in the Holy Gospel; the Apostles also, following the example of the Master, profess it in their spoken and written words; the unchanging tradition of the Church approves it; finally, the most ancient usage of the liturgy proclaims it, wherever the well-known principle may be rightly applied: "The rule of prayer is the rule of faith."

Let Catholic exegetes then disclose and expound this spiritual significance, intended and ordained by God, with that care which the dignity of the divine word demands; but let them scrupulously refrain from proposing as the genuine meaning of Sacred Scripture other figurative interpretations. It may indeed be useful, especially in preaching, to illustrate and present the matters of faith and morals by a broader use of the Sacred Text in the figurative sense, provided this be done with moderation and restraint; it should, however, never be forgotten that this use of the Sacred Scripture is, as it were, extrinsic to it and accidental, and that, especially in these days, it is not free from danger, since the faithful, in particular those who are well informed in the sciences sacred and profane, wish to know what God has told us in the

Holy Scriptures rather than what an ingenious orator or writer may suggest by a clever use of the words of Scripture.

Interpretation of Sacred Scripture

We may rightly and deservedly hope that our times also will contribute something toward the deeper and more accurate interpretation of Sacred Scripture. For not a few things, especially in matters pertaining to history, were hardly touched upon or not fully explained by the commentators of past ages, since they lacked almost all the information required for a more explicit exposition. How difficult, and indeed well-nigh unintelligible, certain passages were even for the Church Fathers is shown, among other things, by the oft-repeated efforts of many of them to explain the first chapters of Genesis; likewise by the reiterated attempts of St. Jerome to translate the Psalms in such a manner that the literal sense, that which is expressed by the words themselves, might be clearly revealed. In other books or texts, one has only recently become aware of difficulties of interpretation, as a more profound knowledge of antiquity has given rise to new questions, which permit deeper insight into the points at issue. It is therefore quite wrong to pretend, as do some persons not fully informed of the status of Biblical studies, that nothing remains to be added by the Catholic exegete of our time to what Christian antiquity has produced; since, on the contrary, these our times have brought to light a great many things which call for fresh investigation and new examination, and which stimulate not a little the practical zeal of the present-day interpreter…

The Use of the Bible in the Care of Souls

Whosoever considers the immense labors undertaken by Catholic exegetes during well-nigh two thousand years, so that the word of God, imparted to men through Holy Scripture, might daily be more deeply and fully understood and more intensely loved, will easily be convinced that it is the serious duty of the faithful, and especially of priests, to make free and holy use of this treasure, accumulated throughout so many centuries by the greatest intellects.

For the Sacred Books were not given to men by God to satisfy their curiosity or to provide them with material for study and research, but, as the Apostle observes, in order that these Divine Words might "instruct in justice, by the faith which is in Christ Jesus," and "that the man of God may be perfect, equipped for every good work."

Let priests, therefore, who are bound by their office to care for the eternal salvation of the faithful, after they have themselves by diligent study perused the sacred pages and made them their own in prayer and meditation, assiduously distribute the heavenly treasures of the Divine Word in sermons, homilies, and exhortations; let them confirm Christian doctrine by sentences from the Sacred Books and illustrate it by outstanding examples from sacred history and in particular from the Gospel of Christ our Lord; and—avoiding with the greatest care those purely arbitrary and far-fetched adaptations which are not a use but rather an abuse of the Divine Word—let them set forth all this with such eloquence, lucidity, and clearness that the faithful may not only be moved and inspired to reform their lives, but may also conceive in their hearts the greatest veneration for Sacred Scripture. This veneration the Bishops should endeavor daily to increase and perfect among the faithful committed to their care, encouraging all those initiatives by which men, filled with apostolic zeal, laudably strive to excite and foster among Catholics a greater knowledge of and love for the Sacred Books. Let them favor, therefore, and lend help to those devout associations whose aim it is to distribute copies of the Sacred Scriptures, especially of the Gospels, among the faithful, and see to it that they are daily read in Christian families with piety and devotion.[†]

To Priests

We priests are ambassadors of Christ in the world, as it were, God exhorting men through our mouths. To this high conception of priesthood proposed to us by the Apostle of the Gentiles, let us raise up, beloved Sons, our eyes, our

† Encyclical *Divino afflante spiritu* (September 30, 1943).

aspirations, and our purposes; and through our active zeal let us exalt and render venerable in the midst of the Christian people our noble rank of mediators and ambassadors of Christ. But in the sacred hierarchy, who else is nearer to the people than the parish priest, whose mission is characterized and defined by three words: apostle, father, shepherd?

Office and Obligation of the Parish Priest

In every parish priest there is an apostle; but, above all, he who carries on his work in a big city should feel within him the flame of the apostolic and missionary spirit and of the conquering zeal of a St. Paul. If you consider our modern times with their political and religious upheavals, with their variety of philosophic and scientific aberrations in instruction and education, you will soon see that the ancient spiritual conditions of society have changed to a point that not even here, in this our Rome, can one speak of a truly Catholic ground because, besides those who have remained firm in their faith—and they are splendid legions—there is no lack in every parish of a set of people who, grown indifferent to and estranged from the Church, constitute a missionary territory to be reconquered for Christ.

Pastoral Care

The parish priest is shepherd and father, shepherd of souls and spiritual father. We must always bear in mind, beloved Sons, that the action of the Church, turned entirely toward the Kingdom of God which is not of the world, if it is not to be sterile but rather vivifying, healthy, and effective, must be directed to the end that men may live and the in the grace of God. To instruct the faithful in Christian thought, to renew men in the following and imitation of Christ, to smooth the way, though always narrow, to the Kingdom of Heaven and render the city truly Christian; such is the mission of the priest, as teacher, father, and shepherd of his parish.

In the fulfillment of these duties, do not allow your zeal to be directed or fettered by your administrative work. Perhaps not a few of you are obliged to carry on a daily struggle, in order not to be weighed down by administrative worries and to find the means and time indispensable for the care of souls. Now, if organization and administration are without doubt valuable means of the apostolate, they must nevertheless be adapted and subordinated to the spiritual ministry and to the veritable and proper office of active pastorship.

By the divine counsel, also the priest, like every Bishop is "*ex hominibus assumptus, pro hominibus constituitur in iis quae sunt ad Deum, ut offerat dona et sacrificia pro peccatis*—taken from among men, ordained for men in the things that appertain to God, that he may offer up gifts and sacrifices for sins"; and so his sacred character as intermediary between God and men reveals itself, unfolds itself, rises and fully sublimates itself surrounded and enveloped by the supreme light of its mystery in the sacrifice of the Holy Mass and in the administration of the Sacraments. At the altar, at the baptismal font, in the tribunal of penance, at the Eucharistic table, at the marriage blessing, at the sickbed, in the agony of the dying, among children eager for the future and the road of life, in the families and the schools, in hospitals, in the pulpit and in assemblies, the priest is the servant, the most effectual instrument of the power, the love, the pardon, the redemption lavished by God upon fallen man...

Take care, therefore, that your dignity always shine before your people, and that they know and understand with a lively faith the meaning and value of the Holy Sacrifice and the Sacraments which you administer, so that they may with lively and personal participation follow the sacred ceremonies and all the ineffable beauties of the holy liturgy.

Administering the Sacraments

After the Holy Sacrifice, your most serious and important act is the administering of the Sacrament of Penance, which has been called the plank of salvation after shipwreck. Be ready and generous in offering that plank to those sailing the tempestuous sea of life. Persist in this with special zeal and perfect self-devotion; sit in that divine tribunal of accusation, repentance, and pardon, as judges who nurture in their breasts the heart of a father, a friend, a physician, and a teacher. And if the essential aim of this Sacrament is to reconcile man with God, do not lose sight of the fact that, in the achievement of such a lofty purpose, a powerful aid is that spiritual direction which draws souls close to the paternal voice of the priest, to pour out to him their afflictions, their troubles, and their doubts, and makes them listen trustfully to his advice and admonishments. The Christian people feel an urgent need for confessors who, through virtue and theological and ascetic training, through maturity and calm judgment, are capable of giving enlightened and reliable rules for a good life, in a simple and clear manner and with tact and benevolence.

Preaching

What We have said up till now concerns particularly the devout and watchful minister of the parish. In addition to this, it is his strict duty to announce the word of God, essential duty of the apostle to whom is entrusted the *verbum reconciliationis*—the word of reconciliation. "*Vae enim mihi, si non evangelizavero*—For woe is unto me if I preach not the Gospel." Because *"Fides ex auditu, auditus autem per verbum Christi... Quomodo credent ei, quem non audierunt? Quomodo autem audient sine praedicante?*—Faith then cometh by hearing; and hearing by the word of Christ... How shall they believe him whom they have not heard? And how shall they hear, without a preacher?" As the intellect gives light to the will, so truth is the lamp of good action. The word is the vehicle of truth and unhappily also of error, which knocks at the door of the intellect and the will. You understand why the admonishments of the Apostle link faith and hearing, hearing and preacher, and why, to cure the blindness of the world by the knowledge of God, speaking from the shining wisdom of the universe, "*placuit Deo per stultitiam praedicationis salvos facere credentes*—it pleased God, by the foolishness of our preaching, to save them that believe." This is sublime folly: for the folly of God is wiser than men and the "shame of Golgotha" is the glory of Christ. Like the admonishments of the Apostle, these truths are also fitted to our times, in which religious ignorance is profound and fraught with dangers...

With adults and those who are mature, be, in imitation of the Apostle Paul, Fathers and Doctors of perfection; with children and the young, make yourselves little, like mothers. Think not that with children and the ignorant you humiliate yourselves.

Catechizing

Equal in value to preaching is catechizing, the instruction of the young and the instruction of adults. In this office, the clergy of the parish can certainly count on the support of Catholic lay people; and to all those who collaborate in such a holy work, We are happy to send with fatherly feeling Our deep thanks and the Apostolic Blessing. Do not forget that the sacred canons regard this important mission as the first and natural care of him who has been given the cure of souls. The zeal of the priest and his ability will be a stimulus and example to his lay fellow workers; and the catechism hour will offer the parish priest a propitious occasion for meeting the younger generation of the parish. Whenever possible, do not neglect the opportunity of personally preparing the children for their first confession and communion; this is the first secret meeting of you and Christ, the divine Friend of children, with candid souls that approach you and the altar, and open up, like spring flowers in the first rays of the sun. They will keep this memory throughout the whole fluctuating course of their lives.

Lastly, We do not wish to pass over a characteristic feature of the picture of the Good Shepherd, who was not only the true Light which illuminates every man coming into the world, He the truth, He the way, He the life. He also lavished His healing virtue on bodies and every human misery, *bene faciendo et sanando omnes*—doing good to all and healing all, and leaving to His Apostles and His Church the mandate of compassionate love for the poor, the suffering, the derelict, because life here below is a flux and reflux of good and evil, of tears and joy, of needs and assistance, of falls and risings, of struggles and victories. But the love for brothers all redeemed by Christ is the mysterious balm for every sorrow and misery.[†]

Rights and Duties of the Priest in Questions Regarding Public Life

It is the right and at the same time the essential duty of the Church, to instruct the faithful in word and writing, from the pulpit or in the other customary

† Address to Parish Priests and Lenten Preachers (September 6, 1940).

forms, in regard to everything that concerns faith and morals or is irreconcilable with her own doctrine and therefore inadmissible for Catholics, be it a question of philosophical or religious systems, or of the ends intended by their fosterers, or of their moral conceptions concerning the life of either individuals or the community.

The exercise of the right to vote is an act of serious moral responsibility, at least when it is a question of electing those who are called to give the country its constitution and laws, particularly those concerning, for example, the sanctification of holidays of obligation, matrimony, the family, the school, and settlement according to justice and equity of the multifarious social conditions. It is therefore for the Church to explain to the faithful the moral duties which derive from that electoral right.

The Catholic priest cannot simply be put on the same level as public officials or those invested with public authority or military or civil functions. Those are employees or representatives of the State, on which (without prejudice to the divine law) they are dependent and the legitimate interests of which they care for; the State, therefore, may issue orders pertaining to their conduct, even in political questions. The priest, on the other hand, is a minister of the Church and has a mission, which, as We have already pointed out, extends to the whole range of the religious and moral duties of the faithful. In the fulfillment of his mission he may therefore be obliged to give advice or instructions regarding public life also. Now it is evident that the possible abuses of such a mission cannot simply be left to the judgment of the civil power; otherwise, the shepherds of souls would be exposed to hindrance and vexations provoked by groups ill-disposed toward the Church, under the facile pretext of wanting to separate the clergy from politics. It must not be forgotten that, precisely under the pretext of wanting to oppose so-called "political Catholicism," National Socialism, which in reality only aimed at the destruction of the Church, moved against the latter all the apparatus of persecution, vexation, police espionage, against which Churchmen had to defend themselves and carry on a courageous struggle, even from the pulpit, with a heroism that today is admired throughout the world.[‡]

‡ Allocution to the Sacred College (March 16, 1946).

The Lay Apostolate

It is often said that the Church, in the last four centuries, has been exclusively "clerical" in order to react to the crisis which in the sixteenth century called for the abolition, pure and simple, of the hierarchy. And on such a premise it is insinuated that it is time she expand her cadres.

Such a judgment is far removed from reality, for it is precisely from the time of the Council of Trent that the laity has begun to organize itself and progress in apostolic activity. This is easily ascertainable; it is enough to recall, among many, two evident historical facts: the Marian Congregations of men actively exercising the lay apostolate in all the sectors of public life, and the progressive participation of women in the modern apostolate. And it is opportune to remember, in this connection, two great figures of Catholic history: that of Mary Ward, the incomparable woman whom Catholic England, in the darkest and bloodiest hours, gave to the Church; and St. Vincent de Paul, without doubt one of the greatest founders and promoters of the works of Catholic charity.

Nor should one fail to recognize the beneficial influence in the Catholic world, of the union which, up to the time of the French Revolution, linked in reciprocal relationship the two authorities established by God: Church and State. The closeness of their relationship on the common ground of public life created a general atmosphere of Christian spirit which, in large part, dispensed both priests and laymen from the onerous duty which they have to shoulder today in order to assure the defense and the practical realization of faith.

Development of the Separation of Church and State

At the end of the eighteenth century a new factor comes into play: on the one hand, the Constitution of the United States of America, which developed with extraordinary speed and where the Church was very soon to grow considerably in strength and vigor; on the other, the French Revolution, which, with its consequences in Europe and beyond the oceans, ended up in separating the Church from the State. Though not taking place everywhere at the same time and in the same way, this rupture had everywhere the logical result of compelling the Church to provide with her own means for the continuation of her activity, the fulfillment of her mandate, and the defense of her rights and her freedom. It was the origin of the so-called Catholic movements which, guided by priests and laymen, strong in their cohesion and sincere loyalty, led the great mass of believers to struggle and victory. Is this not, indeed, an initiation and an introduction of laymen into the apostolate?

The Mass of the Lukewarm

There is also, it is true, a mass of lukewarm, irresolute, and unstable persons, for whom religion may still be of some meaning, but a very vague one which has not the slightest influence on life. This amorphous mass, as experience teaches, can find itself suddenly, from one day to the next, faced with the need of making a decision.

As for the Church, she has a triple mission to accomplish for all: to make fervent believers adequate to the exigencies of these times; to introduce into the safe, healthy intimacy of the home those who are hesitating on the doorstep; to bring back to the fold those who have strayed from religion and who cannot be abandoned to their pitiful fate. A splendid task for the Church, but made extremely difficult by the fact that, even if on the whole she has greatly propagated herself, her clergy has not increased correspondingly. Now the clergy must dedicate itself, first of all, to the exercise of the ministry proper to the priest, wherein no one can substitute for him. The contribution of the laity to the apostolate is therefore an indispensable necessity.

All the faithful, without exception, are members of the mystical body of Jesus Christ. It follows that the law of nature, and even more strongly the law of Christ, obliges them to give a good example of a truly Christian life: "*Christi bonus odor sumus Deo in iis qui salvi fiunt et in iis qui pereunt*—For we are the good odor of Christ unto God, in them who are saved and in them who perish." All are therefore held, and today quite especially, to think, in prayer and sacrifice, not only of their own private needs, but also about the great intentions of the Kingdom of God in the world, according to the spirit of the "Our Father" taught to us by Jesus Christ Himself.

Not Everyone Is Called to the Apostolate

Can it be said that all are equally called to the apostolate in the strict sense of the word? God has not given everyone either the possibility or the aptitudes. One cannot demand that the bride dedicate herself to these works; or the mother who educates her children in the Christian manner and, in addition, must work to help her husband support the family. Not all, then, are called upon to be apostles.

It is certainly difficult to set the bounds of the field of action of the lay apostolate, properly called. Should one, for example, include the education given by a mother to her family, or by educators and teachers filled with holy zeal in the practice of their pedagogic profession; or the conduct of a reputable and firmly Catholic physician, whose conscience never compromises with natural and divine law, and who exerts all his efforts for the upholding of the Christian dignity of marriage and the protection of the sacred rights of the progeny; or even the action of a Catholic statesman in favor of a generous housing policy for the underprivileged?

Much would speak for a negative answer, if one considered all this as nothing but the simple fulfillment of professional duties, highly laudable, but in any case obligatory.

We know, however, that this simple fulfillment of a professional duty by millions and millions of conscientious and exemplary faithful is a powerful and irreplaceable factor in the salvation of souls.

Doubtless, the lay apostolate, in its true meaning, is mainly organized in Catholic Action and in other institutions of apostolic activity approved by the Church; but, besides these, there can be and there are lay apostles, men and women, who not only perceive the good to be accomplished, and the possibilities and means of doing it, but who do it out of a desire to bring other souls to truth and grace. We have in mind also a great many excellent laymen who, in the countries where the Church is persecuted as she was in the first centuries of Christianity, substitute to the best of their abilities for imprisoned priests, risking even their lives in order to impart the teachings of Christian doctrine, to instruct on religious living and the correct manner of Catholic thinking, to induce others to frequent the Sacraments, especially that of the Eucharist. All of these laymen you see at work; do not worry about asking to what organization they belong; admire, rather, and recognize gratefully the good they accomplish.

Far from Us any thought of undervaluing organizations or dis-esteeming their significance as a factor in the apostolate; We value them highly, above all in a world where the adversaries of the Church press upon her with the compact mass of their own organizations. But that must not lead us to a petty exclusivity, to what the Apostle used to call "*explorare libertatem*—to spy upon our liberty" (Gal. 2:4).

Subordination and Interpretation

It is evident that the lay apostolate is subordinate to the ecclesiastical hierarchy, which is of divine institution; therefore it cannot be independent of it. To think differently would be to strike at the very foundation wall on which Christ Himself built His Church.

Hence, it would be erroneous to believe that, within the jurisdiction of the diocese, the lay apostolate is placed on a line parallel to the hierarchical apostolate, so that the Bishop himself cannot subordinate the parochial apostolate of the laity to the parish priest. He can indeed, and he can also establish as a general rule that the works of the lay apostolate intended for the parish itself should be placed under the authority of the parish priest. The Bishop has constituted him pastor of the entire parish, and, as such, he is responsible for the salvation of all his flock.

That there may be, on the other hand, extraparochial and even extradiocesan works for the lay apostolate—We prefer to say supraparochial and supradiocesan—according to where the good of the Church requires it, is also true and it is not necessary to repeat it.

If We compare the lay apostolate, or, more exactly, the militant Christian belonging to Catholic Action, to an instrument in the hands of the hierarchy, as is commonly done, We want to express that the ecclesiastical superiors must use him in the way the Creator and Lord makes use of rational beings as instruments, as secondary causes, "with a sweetness full of consideration." They should use their services, then, conscious of their own grave responsibility, encouraging them, suggesting initiatives, accepting gladly those that might be proposed, and, according to the opportuneness, approving them with broad vision. In decisive battles, the happiest initiatives come at times from the front. The history of the Church offers innumerable examples.

The basic requirement in apostolic work is the most cordial understanding between priests and laity. The apostolate of the one is not in competition with that of the other. In truth, We are not too pleased to hear here and there the expression "emancipation of the laity." It has a somewhat jarring note, and is also historically inexact. Were the great leaders, to whom We alluded in speaking of the Catholic movement of the last fifty years, children or minors who had to be emancipated? In the kingdom of grace all are considered adults. And that is what matters.

The appeal to the collaboration of the laity is not due to the weakness or failure of the clergy in the task of the present hour. That there are individual weaknesses belongs to the inevitable wretchedness of human nature, and one meets with them on both sides. But, generally speaking, the priest has eyes as good as those of the laymen to perceive the signs of the times, and he does not have a less sensitive ear to listen to the human heart. The layman is called to the apostolate as a collaborator of the priest, an often precious collaborator, and furthermore necessary because of the small numbers of the clergy, too scarce, We were saying, to be able to accomplish, alone, its proper mission.†

Catholic Action

"Catholic Action"—the very word "action," exact and comprehensive at the same time, indicates the nature of the organization and distinguishes it from other Catholic associations. Not that these, too, do not exercise an action, but their action generally inclines toward a particular and determined object to be attained through an organized and permanent effort, whether they develop their activities in the religious and charitable sphere or in the

† Address to Lay Apostolate (October 14, 1951).

social and economic sphere or in other fields of culture. Thus, these organizations generally take their name from the end they have in view.

"Catholic Action," however, is called by its name because, having a general rather than a particular or specific purpose, it is not a fixed axis around which gravitates the mechanism of any type of organization, but it is rather a meeting place where active Catholics join and organize.

Catholic Action—by a special title—is directly subordinated to the authority of the ecclesiastical hierarchy, whose collaborator it is in the apostolate. In Italian Catholic Action the presidency and the direction of the various diocesan and parochial groups belong to laymen, who, however, are seconded and guided by the ecclesiastical helpers; while in the Marian Congregations, which may also, rightfully, be called Catholic Action, the parish priest is the president. But in order that the assistance given to the women's associations may be really salutary and fruitful, the priests here act with greater reserve, leaving entirely to the care of wise, devout, religious women what the latter can—sometimes even better—do by themselves, restricting their own work to the priestly ministry.

These considerations regarding the organization of Catholic Action prompt Us to add a few general warnings suggested, among other things, by certain erroneous tendencies which have become evident in our times.

First of all, a word on the conception of the apostolate. It does not consist solely in the delivery of the good tidings of the Gospel, but also in leading men to the fount of salvation, though with full respect for their liberty, in converting them and educating the baptized, with serious effort, to become perfect Christians.

Laymen and the Hierarchical Apostolate

It would, moreover, be erroneous to see in Catholic Action—as some have recently asserted—something essentially new, a change in the structure of the Church, a new lay apostolate, working side by side with the Church and not subordinated to her. There has always been in the Church a collaboration of laymen with the hierarchical apostolate, in subordination to the Bishop and those to whom the Bishop has entrusted the responsibility of the care of souls under his authority. Catholic Action has wanted to give that collaboration only a new and timely form and organization for its improved and more efficacious operation.

Although Catholic Action, like the Church herself, is at first organized according to dioceses and parishes, nevertheless this does not prevent its further development beyond and above the restricted limits of the parish. As a matter of fact, it must be recognized that in spite of the great importance of the values and of the fundamental and irreplaceable endeavors of the parish, the rapidly increasing technical and spiritual complexity of modern life may urgently call for a wider extension of Catholic Action. But even so, Catholic Action must always remain a lay apostolate subordinated to the Bishop and his delegates.

The activity of Catholic Action extends to the whole religious and social sphere, that is, as far as the mission and work of the Church reaches. Now, we know very well that the normal growth and strengthening of religious life presupposes a certain measure of healthy economic and social conditions. It is heart-rending for everyone to see how economic distress and social ills make it more difficult to lead a Christian life according to the Commandments of God, and too often exact heroic sacrifices. But one cannot conclude from this that the Church must start by setting aside her religious mission and bring about, first of all, the healing of social distress. If, from the time of the Apostles, the Church has always been prompt in her defense and promotion of justice, in the face of the most serious social abuses, she has fulfilled her mission and, with the sanctification of souls and the conversion of the inward sentiments, she has sought to begin the correction also of social ills and injuries, convinced as she is that religious forces and Christian principles serve, more than any other means, to reach a cure.

The external and well-disciplined organization of Catholic Action does not exclude but, on the contrary, promotes personal perspicacity and the spirit of foresight and individual initiative—according to each person's qualities and capabilities—in permanent contact with the members of Catholic Action in the same locality and circle. Each one holds himself cordially ready whenever the need for some Catholic activity or campaign arises. Through his or her enthusiasm and devotion, each one contributes a disinterested assistance to other unions and associations, which may require co-operation so as to achieve their objectives more completely and surely.

In other words, the mentality of associates who would regard themselves as the inert wheels of a gigantic machine, incapable of moving until they were made to turn by the central force, would not be compatible with the true conception of Catholic Action. Nor would it be admissible to consider those in charge of Catholic Action as operators of an electric power station in front of the control panel, ready only to pull switches in order to regulate or direct the current in the vast system.

Above all, they must exercise a personal moral influence which will be the normal result of the esteem and sympathy which they may arouse and which will give prestige to their suggestions, to their advice, and to the authority of their experience every time there is a question of putting into motion the Catholic forces ready for action.

No Party Politics

There is no need for Us to stress that Catholic Action is not called upon to be a force in the field of party politics. Catholic citizens, as such, may well unite in an association of political activity; they have a perfect right to do so, no less as Christians than as citizens. The presence in its ranks, and the participation of members of Catholic Action—in the above sense and limits—is legitimate and may also be altogether desirable. On the other hand, it would not be permissible for Catholic Action to become an organization of party politics.

By reason of its nature, Catholic Action has not even the mission of being at the head of other associations and of exercising over them an office of quasi authoritative patronage. The fact that it is placed under the immediate direction of the ecclesiastical hierarchy does not bring with it any such consequence.

The specific purpose of Catholic Action consists, as We have said, in the fact that it is the meeting place of those active Catholics who are always ready to collaborate with the apostolate of the Church—apostolate through divine hierarchical institution—which finds its collaborators in the baptized and confirmed, who are supernaturally united to the Church. From this derives a consequence, which at the same time is a paternal warning, not for Catholic Action of any particular country but for Catholic Action of every country at all times. That is, its structure must be adapted in different territories to the particular circumstances of the place; but in one point all its members must be equal: "feel with the Church" in devotion to the cause of the Church, in obedience to those whom the Holy Spirit has appointed Bishops to rule the Church of God, in filial submission to the Supreme Shepherd, to whose care Christ has entrusted His Church.[†]

Five Tasks of Catholic Action

What are today, for the men of Catholic Action, the most important tasks, the main spheres for their activity? We feel We should briefly indicate five especially:

Religious culture. A deep, firm knowledge of the Catholic faith, of its truths, of its mysteries, and of its divine forces. The expression "anemia of religious life" has been coined. It rings like a cry of alarm. That anemia must be attributed—in the first place and in all classes, among the educated as well as among the uneducated—to an often almost complete ignorance of religious matters. This ignorance must be fought, rooted out, and conquered.

Sanctification of feast days of obligation. Sunday must become once again the Lord's Day, the day of the adoration and glorification of God, of the Holy Sacrifice, of prayer, of rest, of recollection and reflection, of happy gatherings in the intimacy of the family. Painful experience has taught us that for not a few, even among those who work hard and honestly all through the week, Sunday has become the day of sin.

Truly, the outcome of this struggle between faith and disbelief will in great part depend on what one or the other of the two fronts will be able to make of Sunday; will it still carry engraved on its brow, clear and shining, the holy name of the Lord, or will this be completely obscured and neglected?

Salvation of the Christian family. The Christian mother must be preserved; Christian education of the young must be preserved, and therefore also the Christian school; it is necessary to preserve the Christian hearth, stronghold of the fear of God, of inviolate faithfulness, of sobriety, of love and peace, where

---

† Address to Leaders of Catholic Action (May 3, 1951).

rules that spirit which pervaded the house of Joseph in Nazareth.

To save the Christian family is precisely the principal mission of the Christian man. Do not forget: on his wishes, no less than on the woman herself, depends the destiny of the mother and of the family.

Social justice. For Catholics, the road to follow in the solution of the social question is clearly indicated by the doctrine of the Church.

A more equitable distribution of wealth is and remains a point in the program of Catholic social doctrine.

Without doubt, the result of the natural trend of things—and this is neither economically nor socially abnormal—is that the goods of the earth, within certain limits, are unequally divided. But the Church is against the accumulation of these goods in the hands of a relatively few extremely rich men, while vast sections of the people are condemned to pauperism and economic conditions unworthy of human beings.

In the same spirit, another moral sentiment must be revived: *loyalty and veracity in human coexistence*, consciousness of responsibility for the common good. It is disquieting to see to what extent loyalty and honesty have disappeared in economic and social life, as a consequence of the incredible disturbances of the war and postwar period. What is made manifest in this field is no longer just an external defect of character but reveals a serious internal malady, a spiritual poisoning which, to a large degree, is also the cause of that religious anemia.

The economic and financial chaos produced by every great cataclysm has stimulated and sharpened greed for gain which drives souls to ambiguous speculations and maneuvering to the detriment of the whole population. We have always blamed and condemned such maneuvering, no matter where it may have its origin, no less than every illicit business, every falsification, and all disobedience of just laws made by the State for the good of the civil community.

It is therefore for the men of Catholic Action to collaborate in the healing of this evil by word and work, above all by their own example, and then also through the most effective possible influence on public opinion.[‡]

‡ Address to Union of Men of Catholic Action (September 7, 1947).

PART FOUR

SOCIETY AND POLITICS

Individual and State

WHERE the dependency of human rights on divine rights is denied, where the highest appeal is to a vague concept of purely earthly authority, where an autonomy founded only on a utilitarian morality is claimed; there human rights themselves justly lose, in their most serious applications, the moral force which is the essential condition for their winning recognition and demanding sacrifices.

It is certainly true that power based on such weak, precarious foundations may sometimes achieve, because of contingent circumstances, material success which astonishes the superficial observer; but there comes a moment when there triumphs that inescapable law which strikes everything that is built on a hidden or open disproportion between the greatness of material and outward success and the weakness of inner values and their moral foundation. This disproportion always exists where public authority fails to recognize or repudiates the sovereignty of the supreme Legislator, who, if He has given power to the rulers, has likewise determined and set its limits.

Civil sovereignty, in fact, was desired by the Creator in order that it might regulate social life according to the prescriptions of an order which is unchangeable in its universal principles, and that it might help the human being, in the temporal order, to attain physical, intellectual, and moral perfection and assist him in reaching his supernatural goal.

It is, therefore, the noble prerogative and mission of the State to control, help, and regulate the private and individual activities of national life, to make them converge harmoniously in the common good, which cannot be determined by arbitrary conceptions, nor draw its standards primarily from the material prosperity of society, but rather from the harmonious development and the natural perfection of man, for which society is destined, as a means, by the Creator.

To consider the State as an end, to which everything should be subordinated and directed, could only do harm to the true and lasting prosperity of nations. And that happens both when this unlimited authority is attributed to the State on behalf of the nation, the people, or even a social class, and when it is claimed by the State, as the absolute master, acting independently from any mandate.

For if the State attributes to itself and regulates private initiatives, these, governed as they are by delicate and complex internal laws, which guarantee and assure the attainment of the aim which they have in view, may suffer, with harm to the common good, by being dissociated from their natural sphere, that is, from responsible private activity.

Even the first and essential cell of society, the family, like its welfare and its growth, would then run the risk of being considered exclusively from the viewpoint of national power, and it would be forgotten that man and the family are by their nature prior to the State, and that the Creator gave them both strength and rights and assigned to them a mission, in keeping with unquestionable natural demands.

One-Sided Education of Youth

The education of the new generations would aim not at a balanced, harmonious development of physical forces and of all the intellectual and moral qualities, but at a unilateral formation of those civic virtues which are considered necessary for the achievement of political success; whereas those virtues which give society the sanction of generosity, humanity, and respect would be less stressed, as though they diminished the pride of the citizen.

We can see with painful clearness the dangers We fear will confront this generation and those to come as a result of the lack of recognition, of the diminution and gradual abolition of the rights of the family. Therefore, We proclaim Ourselves the determined defender of these rights, fully conscious of the duty Our apostolic ministry imposes upon Us.

The Right of Parents

The heavier the material sacrifices the State imposes on individuals and families, the more sacred and inviolate must be to it the rights of consciences. The State can lay claim to property and life, but never to the soul, redeemed by God. The mission assigned by God to parents, of providing for the material and spiritual welfare of their offspring and of giving them a harmonious formation, animated by a true religious spirit, cannot be taken away from them without a grave violation of their rights. This formation must of course also aim at preparing youth to carry out intelligently, conscientiously, and proudly those duties of a generous patriotism which gives to one's earthly fatherland its due measure of love, dedication, and collaboration. But, on the other hand, a formation that would omit or, worse still, purposely neglect to direct the eyes and heart of youth to their supernatural fatherland, would be a wrong done to youth, a wrong to the inalienable obligations and rights of the Christian family, an encroachment for which a remedy must be found also in the interest of the welfare of the people and the State. Such an education might seem to those responsible for it to be a source of additional strength and vigor; in reality it would be just the contrary, as the unhappy consequences would demonstrate. The crime of high treason against the King of kings and the Lord of rulers, perpetrated by an upbringing indifferent or hostile to the Christian spirit, the reversal of the "let the little children come unto Me," would bear the bitterest fruit.

On the other hand, that State which frees the torn, bleeding hearts of Christian fathers and mothers from their worries and re-establishes their rights is only promoting its own internal peace and setting the foundations of a happier future for the country. The souls of the children, given by God to the parents, consecrated in baptism with the regal seal of Christ, are a sacred trust, watched over by the jealous love of God. Christ Himself, who uttered the "let the little children come unto Me," also threatened with terrible punishment, in spite of His goodness and mercy, those who outrage the favorites of His heart. And what greater and more lasting outrage is there than to bring youth up to follow a goal that takes it away from Christ, the way, the truth, and the life, and leads it to open or secret apostasy? This Christ, from whom they want to alienate the young generations, present and future, is He who received from His eternal Father every power in Heaven and on earth. He holds the destiny of States, peoples, and nations in His almighty hand. It is in His power to cut short or to prolong life, growth, prosperity, and greatness. Of all that is on earth only the soul has everlasting life. An educational system that would not respect the sacred place of the Christian family which is under the protection of the holy Law of God, one that sapped its foundations, that barred from youth the way to Christ, to the Savior's springs of life and joy, and that considered apostasy from Christ and from the Church as a symbol of fidelity to the people or to a specific class, would be pronouncing its own condemnation and would in the course of time experience the inescapable truth of the prophet's words: "They that depart from Thee shall be written in sand."[†]

Church and State

The Essential Differences Between the Ecclesiastical and the Civil Judicial Establishments Considered in Their Origin and Their Nature

A rapid superficial glance at judicial laws and practice might lead one to believe that the ecclesiastical and civil procedures present only secondary differences, more or less like those noticeable in the administration of justice in two civilized States of the same juridical family. Even in their immediate objective they seem to coincide: actuation or enforcement, by means of a sentence, of the right established by the law that, in a particular case, is contested or infringed, that is, through a judgment emanating from the competent authority in conformity with the law. The several degrees of judicial instances are similarly to be found in both; in both, procedure shows the same principal elements: a request to bring the case to trial, summons, examination of witnesses,

† Encyclical *Summi Pontificatus* (October 20, 1939).

production of documents, questioning of plaintiff and defendant, conclusion of the trial, sentence, right of appeal.

Despite this, the great external and internal resemblance must not make one forget the great differences existing, firstly, in the origin and nature, secondly, in the object, thirdly, in the purpose.

Totalitarianism, Authoritarianism, Democracy

The judicial power is an essential part, and a necessary function, of the power of the two perfect societies, the ecclesiastical and the civil. For this reason, the question of the origin of judicial power becomes identified with that of the origin of power itself.

But precisely because of this, in addition to the resemblances already mentioned, some have tried to find other, even deeper ones. It is strange to see how some followers of the various modern conceptions concerning civil power have invoked, to confirm and support their opinions, presumed analogies with ecclesiastical power. This is no less true for the so-called "totalitarianism" and "authoritarianism" than for their opposite pole, the modern democracy. But, in reality, those deeper resemblances do not exist in any of the three cases, as will clearly be shown by a brief examination.

It is unquestionable that one of the vital needs of any human community and, therefore, that of the Church and State, is that unity in the diversity of its members should be durably ensured.

Now, "totalitarianism" can in no wise ever satisfy that need, for it gives to the civil power, in content and form, an undue scope in all fields of activity, and thus compresses everyone's own legitimate life—personal, communal, and professional—into a mechanical unit or plurality under the seal of nation, of race, or of class.

In Our Christmas Radio Broadcast of 1942, We particularly emphasized the sad consequences for judicial power of the conception and practice which abolishes the equality of all before the law and leaves judicial decisions at the mercy of a changeable collective instinct.

Furthermore, who could ever think that such erroneous interpretations infringing upon human rights can have determined the origin or influenced the action of the ecclesiastical tribunals? This never has been and never can be, because it is contrary to the very nature of the Church's social power, as we shall see presently.

But that fundamental need is also far from being satisfied by that other conception of civil power which can be indicated by the name of "authoritarianism" because it excludes citizens from any efficacious participation in, or influence on the formation of, the social will. It consequently splits the nations up into two categories, that of dominators and that of the dominated, whose reciprocal relations come to be purely mechanical, under the dominion of force, or, in other words, have a merely biological foundation.

The State: A Community for the Common Good

Who does not see how, in this way, the true nature of the authority of the State becomes profoundly subverted? Both of itself and through the exercise of its functions, this authority should tend to render the State a true community, closely united in its ultimate purpose, which is the common good. But in that system the notion of common good becomes so changing and so clearly shows itself to be, as it were, a deceitful cloak for the unilateral interest of the dominator, that an unbridled legislative "dynamism" precludes all juridical security and therefore suppresses a fundamental element of any true judicial order.

Never could such false dynamism submerge and take away the essential rights recognized as pertaining to individual physical persons and moral bodies in the Church. The nature of ecclesiastical power has nothing in common with that "authoritarianism," which has no point of reference with the hierarchical constitution of the Church.

Still to be examined is the democratic form of civil power, in which some would see a closer resemblance to the ecclesiastical power. Without doubt, where there is a true theoretical and practical democracy, it fulfills that vital requirement of every sound community to which We have referred. But this also happens, or may happen, in analogous conditions in other legitimate forms of government.

Differences Between Church and State

Ecclesiastical power is in fact essentially different from the civil power, and therefore also judicial power in the Church.

The origin of the Church, unlike that of the State, does not pertain to the natural law. The widest and most careful analysis of the human person offers no grounds for thinking that the Church, like civil society, would have had perforce to spring up and develop naturally.

She derives from a positive act of God, beyond and above the social disposition of man, though it is in perfect harmony therewith; therefore, ecclesiastical power—and hence also the corresponding judicial power—was born from the will and the act through which Christ founded His Church. But, once the Church had been constituted as a perfect society by the Redeemer, that did not prevent a good many features of resemblance to the structure of civil society from springing out of her very nature.

In one point, however, this fundamental difference appears with particular evidence. The foundation of the Church as a society was effected, unlike the origin of the State, not from the bottom up but from the top down, which means that Christ, who in His Church achieved on earth the Kingdom of God by Him announced and intended for all men of all times, did not entrust to the community of the faithful the mission of Teacher, Priest, and Shepherd received from His Father for the salvation of the human race but communicated it to a college of Apostles, or messengers, chosen by Himself, so that through their preaching, their sacerdotal ministry, and through the social power of their office they might bring into the Church the multitude of the faithful, in order to sanctify and enlighten them and lead them to the full maturity of followers of Christ.

Consider the words with which He communicated His powers to them: the power to offer up the Sacrifice in memory of Him; the power to remit sins; the promise and giving of the supreme power of the keys to Peter and to his successors personally; and the communication of the power to bind and to loose to all the Apostles. Meditate finally on the words in which, before His ascension, He transmits to these same Apostles the universal mission received from His Father. Is there, perhaps, anything in all this that can give rise to doubts or equivocations? The whole history of the Church, from her beginning up to our own days, does not cease to re-echo those words and to render the same testimony with a clearness and precision which no subtlety could dull or mask. Now, all these words, all these testimonies, proclaim in unison that in the ecclesiastical power the essence, the central point according to the explicit will of Christ, and hence by divine right, is the mission given by Him to the ministers of effecting salvation in the community of the faithful and in all mankind.

Canon 109 of the Code of Canon Law has put this marvelous edifice in a clear light: "*Qui in ecclesiasticam hierarchiam cooptantur, non ex populi vel potestatis saecularis consensu aut vocatione adleguntur; sed in gradibus potestatis ordinis constituuntur sacra ordinatione; in supremu pontificatu, ipsomet iure divino, adimpleta conditione legitimae electionis eiusdemque acceptationis; in reliquis gradibus iurisdictionis, canonica missione*—Admittance into the ecclesiastical hierarchy is not derived from the consent or approval of the people or of secular authorities; rather, the chosen ones enter the sacred hierarchy through consecration; the supreme pontificate is conferred directly by divine law, after fulfillment of the condition of a legal election and acceptance of this election; admittance into the other ranks of ecclesiastical government is achieved through canonical mission."

Responsibilities of the Members of the Ecclesiastical Hierarchy

"*Non ex populi vel potestatis saecularis consensu aut vocatione*—Not from the consensus or vocation of the people or secular authorities": in the course of the centuries the mass of the faithful or the secular power may often have participated in the designation of those on whom were to be conferred ecclesiastical offices—to which, as a matter of fact, including the office of Supreme Pontiff, can be elected the descendant of a noble lineage as well as the son of the humblest workingman's family. In reality, however, the members of the ecclesiastical hierarchy have received, and always do receive, their authority from on high and must answer for the exercise of their mandate solely either immediately to God, to whom alone is subject the Roman Pontiff, or else, in the other degrees, to their hierarchical superiors, but they have no account to render either to the people or to the civil power, excepting, of course, the right of every one of the faithful to present in due form to competent ecclesiastical authority, or even directly to the supreme power of the Church, his petitions and his appeals, especially when the petitioner or appealer is prompted by motives affecting his personal responsibility for his own or other people's spiritual welfare.

From what We have said, there derive principally two conclusions:

(1) In the Church, otherwise than in the State, the primordial subject of power, the supreme judge, the highest instance of appeal, is never the community of the faithful. Therefore, there does not nor can there exist in the Church, as she was founded by Christ, a popular tribunal or a judicial power emanating from the people.

(2) The question of the compass or the greatness of ecclesiastical power presents itself also in a way very different from that pertaining to the State. For the Church, what counts, in the first place, is the express will of Christ, in whose power it was to give her, according to His wisdom and goodness, greater or smaller means and powers, excepting, of course, the minimum necessarily required by her nature and purpose. The power of the Church embraces the whole of man, the inner man and the outer man, in view of the attainment of the supernatural end, inasmuch as he is entirely subject to the law of Christ of which the Church was made custodian and fulfiller by her divine Founder, both in the outward sphere and in the inward sphere, or that of the conscience. Full and perfect power, therefore, though alien to that "totalitarianism" which neither admits nor acknowledges an honest reference to the clear and incontrovertible dictates of one's conscience and does violence to the laws of individual and social living written in the hearts of men. Indeed, the Church aims through her power not at the subjection of the human person but at ensuring its freedom and improvement, redeeming it from the weaknesses, the errors, and the deviations of the spirit and heart which, sooner or later, always end in dishonor and slavery.

The sacred character which ecclesiastical jurisdiction derives from its divine origin and from its belonging to the hierarchical power should inspire you, beloved Sons, with the highest esteem for your office and spur you on to fulfill its austere duties with lively faith, with unalterable rectitude, and with ever watchful zeal. But behind the veil of that austerity, what Splendor is not revealed to eyes that are able to see in the judicial power the majesty of justice, which in all its action tends to make the Church, Christ's Bride, appear "holy and immaculate" before her divine Spouse and before men![†]

The Differences Between the Ecclesiastical and Civil Judicial Establishments, Considered in Their Object

What yesterday for many was the duty of the Church and was demanded of her sometimes even in a disorderly manner, that is, to resist the unjust impositions of totalitarian governments, oppressors of consciences, and to denounce and condemn them before the world (which she never failed to do, freely of her own accord and in fitting manner), is today, for those same men, risen to power, a crime and an illicit interference in the field belonging to civil authority. And those very arguments, which the tyrannical governments of yesterday used to bring against the Church in her struggle in defense of divine rights and the dignity and freedom rightly belonging to man, are now being used by the new dominators to fight her persevering action for the safeguarding of truth and justice. But the Church keeps straight on her road, always intent upon the end for which she was instituted by her divine Founder, namely, to lead men along the supernatural paths of virtue and goodness, to heavenly and eternal happiness: in which manner she also promotes at the same time peaceful and prosperous human coexistence.

This thought naturally brings Us again to speak of the essentially different purpose of the two societies. This difference founded on the purpose excludes, without any doubt, the forced submission and quasi insertion of the Church in the State, contrary to the nature of both, which every totalitarianism tends, at least in the beginning, to achieve. However, it certainly does not gainsay any union at all between the two societies, much less does it come to determine between them a cold and dissociating aura of agnosticism and indifference. If anyone should want to understand in this way the correct doctrine that Church and State are two distinct perfect societies, he would be wrong. He would not be able to explain the multifarious forms of union between the

† Allocution for the Inauguration of the Juridical Year of the S. Romana Rota (October 2, 1945).

two powers that have been fruitful, though in different degree, in the past and present; above all, he would not take into account the fact that the Church and the State have their origin in the same source, God, and that both are entrusted with the care of the same man, of his personal, natural, and supernatural dignity. All this Our glorious predecessor Leo XIII could not, and did not wish to neglect, when, in his Encyclical *Immortale Dei* of November 1, 1885, he clearly delineated, on the basis of their different object, the boundaries of the two societies and pointed out that it more closely and chiefly belongs to the State to take care of the earthly interests of men and to the Church to procure for them heavenly and eternal blessings, inasmuch as man needs security and support both from the State for earthly things and from the Church for those that are eternal.

Do we not perhaps see in this, under certain aspects, some analogy with the relations between the body and the soul? The one and the other act jointly in such a way that the psychological character of a man feels at every moment the effects of his temperament and of his physiological conditions while, vice versa, moral impressions, excitement, and passion are reflected so powerfully on physical sensibility that the soul molds even the features of the face, on which it impresses, as it were, its own image.

Ecclesiastical Judicial Power

There exists, therefore, that difference of object, a difference which exercises a diverse and deep influence on the Church and the State, principally on the supreme power of both societies, and therefore also on their judicial power, which is only a part and a function thereof. Independently of the question whether or not individual ecclesiastical judges are or are not conscious of this, all their judicial activity is, and remains, included in the fullness of life of the Church with its high objective: *caelestia ac sempiterna bona comparare*—to be the mediator for celestial and eternal goods. This *finis operis* (end and purpose) of ecclesiastical judicial power gives it an objective mark and makes of it an institution of the Church as a supernatural society. And, as that mark derives from the ultraterrestrial objective of the Church, ecclesiastical judicial power will never fall into the rigidity and immobility to which purely earthly institutions are easily liable, on account of fear of responsibility, or indolence, or even of misguided efforts to safeguard what is, certainly, a great good: the safety of the law.

This does not mean, however, that in the ecclesiastical judicial establishment there is an area left entirely to the arbitrary discretion of the judge in the treatment of individual cases. These errors of a baneful "vitality" in the law are the sad products of our times in activities to which the Church is a stranger. Untouched by an anti-intellectualism rather widely diffused today, the Church remains firm in the principle: the judge decides in every single case according to the law; a principle which, without favoring excessive "juridical formalism," on the other hand rejects the "subjective discretion" which would come to place the judge no longer under, but above, the law. Clearly to understand the juridical provision according to the meaning of the legislator and rightly to examine individual cases in view of the provision to be applied, this intellectual work is an essential part of concrete judicial activity. Without such a procedure the judge's sentence would be a simple command, and not what the term "positive law" would express, namely, the bringing about, in individual and therefore concrete cases, of order in the world which, as a whole, was created by God's wisdom within an order and for order.

Is not this field of judicial activity indeed rich in life? There is more: ecclesiastical law has in view the common good of the ecclesiastical society and is therefore inseparably linked to the objective of the Church. When, therefore, the judge is applying the law to a particular case, he is co-operating in achieving the fullness of the end which lives in the Church. When, on the other hand, he is faced by doubtful cases, or when legislation leaves him freedom, the bond between the ecclesiastical judicial establishment and the objective of the Church will help him to find and motivate the right decision and to preserve his office from the stain of mere arbitrariness.

In any case, therefore, the relation of ecclesiastical judicial power to the end considered appears as the surest guarantee of the true vitality of its decisions, and while it sets up the ecclesiastical judge in an office willed by God, it inspires him with the high sense of responsibility which is, in the Church too, the indispensable safeguard, superior to any legal ordinance, of security under the law.

By this We do not mean in any way to ignore the practical difficulties which, notwithstanding everything, modern life entails for the ecclesiastical judicial power and which, from several aspects, are even more arduous than those in the civil sphere. Suffice it to consider only certain spiritual goods, in face of which the judicial power of the State feels itself less obligated, or even remains consciously indifferent. Typical are, in this sense, the cases of crimes against the faith or of apostasy, those concerning "liberty of conscience" and "religious tolerance," and also divorce. In these cases the Church, and therefore also the ecclesiastical judge, cannot assume the neutral attitude of States of mixed religious belief and still less that of a world fallen into unbelief and religious indifferentism, but they must let themselves be guided solely by the essential object assigned to the Church by God.

In this way we continually encounter again the profound difference to which the diversity of objective gives rise between the ecclesiastical and civil judicial power. Nothing, of course, prevents the one from availing itself of the results reached by the other, either in theoretical notions or in practical experience; it would nevertheless be a mistake to want to transfer mechanically the elements and norms of the one into the other, and, even more so, to want actually to make them equal. Ecclesiastical judicial power and the ecclesiastical judge do not have to look elsewhere for their ideal but must carry it in themselves; they must always keep before their mind's eye that the Church is a supernatural organism, in which is inherent a divine vital principle which must also move and direct the judicial power and the office of an ecclesiastical judge.

Judges of the Church are, in virtue of their office and by divine will, the Bishops of whom the Apostle says that "they have been constituted by the Holy Spirit to rule God's Church." But to "rule" includes to "judge" as a necessary function. Hence, according to the Apostle, the Holy Spirit calls the Bishops no less to the office of judge than to the government of the Church. From the Holy Spirit, therefore, derives the sacred nature of that office. The faithful of Christ's Church "purchased by Him through His Own blood" are those to whom the judicial activity refers. The law of Christ is fundamentally that according to which sentences are pronounced in the Church. The divine vital principle in the Church moves everyone, and all that which is in her, toward her own end, and hence also the judicial power and the judge: *"caelestia ac sempiterna bona comparare*—to provide celestial and eternal goods."†

† Allocution for the Inauguration of the Juridical Year of the S. Romana Rota (October 29, 1947).

The Social Order

The dial of history today is registering a grave, decisive hour for the whole of humanity.

An ancient world lies shattered in ruins. To see a new world arise soon from those ruins, a world more sane, juridically better organized, and more in harmony with the exigencies of nature: that is the yearning of tortured peoples.

Will the painful, deadly errors of the past perhaps be followed by others no less deplorable, and will the world swing indefinitely from one extreme to the other? Or will the pendulum be arrested, thanks to the action of wise leaders, based on directions and solutions which do not contradict divine law and do not contrast with the human and the Christian conscience?

From the answer to this question depends the fate of Christian civilization in Europe and the world, a civilization which, far from casting prejudice upon the manifold forms peculiar to the characteristics of each people, inserts itself in them and revivifies their highest ethical principles: the moral law inscribed by the Creator in the hearts of men, the natural law deriving from God, the fundamental rights and the intangible dignity of the human person. And in order to bend the will of observing them more effectively, it infused into the individual men, into a whole people, and into the community of nations those superior energies which no human power is capable of conferring.

Christian Civilization, Its Fruits and Blessings

Thus it happens that Christian civilization, without suffocating or weakening the sane elements of the most varied native cultures, harmonizes them in essentials, creating in this manner a wide unity of sentiments and moral norms, most solid foundation of true peace, social justice, and brotherly love among all members of the great human family.

In one of those evolutions full of contradictions, the last century has witnessed, on the one hand, the systematic undermining of the very foundations of Christian civilization and, on the other, its constant spreading among all the peoples. Europe and the other continents still subsist, in different measure, from the vital forces and principles which the inheritance of Christian thought had transmitted to them as in a spiritual blood transfusion.

Some go so far as to forget this precious patrimony, to neglect it, even to repudiate it; but the fact of that hereditary succession remains all the same.

The clear-sightedness, devotion, courage, inventive genius, and the sentiment of fraternal charity of all upright and honest minds will determine in what measure and to what degree it will be given to Christian thought to maintain and support the gigantic task of restoring the social, economic, and international life on a plane which does not contrast with the moral and religious content of Christian civilization.

The Right to Private Property

In his Encyclical *Rerum Novarum* our glorious predecessor Leo XIII enunciated the principle that for every just economic and social order "the right of private property must be set as an unshakable foundation."

If it is true that the Church has always recognized "the natural right of property and the hereditary transmission of one's own belongings," it is, however, no less certain that this private property is in a special way the natural fruit of labor: the product of an intense activity of man, who acquires it thanks to his energetic determination to safeguard and develop, with his own strength, his own existence and that of his family, to create for himself and his own a sphere of just freedom, not only of an economic nature, but also political, cultural, and religious.

The Christian conscience cannot admit as just a social order which either denies, on principle, or renders practically impossible or vain the natural right of possession, both over consumer goods and over the means of production.

But it cannot likewise accept those systems which recognize the right of private property according to a wholly false concept, and are therefore in contrast with the genuine and sane social order.

Capitalism

Therefore, where, for example, "capitalism" is based on such erroneous conceptions and unduly claims for itself an unlimited right on property, without any subordination to the common good, the Church has reproved it as contrary to natural law.

We see, in fact, the ever increasing ranks of workers often faced with those excessive concentrations of economic goods which, frequently hidden under anonymous forms, succeed in evading their social obligations and place the worker in the near impossibility of creating property of his own.

We see medium and small property diminish and lose vigor in social life, compressed and restricted as it is to a defensive struggle ever more harsh and without hope of positive success.

We see, on the one hand, tremendous riches dominate private and public economy and often even civic affairs, and, on the other hand, the vast multitude of those who, deprived of any security, direct or indirect, in their life, lose all interest in the true and high values of the spirit, bar themselves against aspirations toward genuine liberty, cast themselves in the arms of any political party, slaves to whoever promises them, in one way or another, bread and tranquillity. And experience has shown of what tyranny humanity is capable in such conditions, even at the present time.

Private Property and Means of Production

Defending the principle of private property, then, the Church follows a lofty ethical-social aim. She does not intend purely and simply to sustain the present state of affairs, as if she saw therein the expression of divine will, nor to protect, as a matter of principle, the rich and the plutocrat against the poor and destitute. Quite the contrary! From her origins, she has been the guardian of the poor and oppressed against the tyranny of the powerful, and she has always championed the just protests of all classes of workers against every iniquity. But the Church aims rather to act so that the institution of private property may become what it should be, according to the designs of divine Wisdom and the dispositions of nature: an element of social order, a necessary prerequisite to private initiative, a stimulus to labor to the advantage of temporal and transcendental goals of life, and hence of the liberty and dignity of man, created in the image of God, who from the very beginning assigned to him to use as he saw fit the mastery over material things.

Take away from the worker the hope of acquiring something in the way of personal property, and what other natural stimulus could you offer him to incite him to intense labor, saving, and sobriety, when today, not a few men and peoples, having lost everything, have nothing left but the ability to work? Or does one wish to perpetuate a wartime economy for which, in some countries, the public power keeps in hand all means of production, providing everything for everybody, but under the lash of a strong discipline? Or does one want the subjugation to the dictatorship of one political group, which, as the dominating class, will dispose of the means of production, but of bread also, and thereby of the will to work of the single individual?

The Right of the State to Expropriation

The social and economic policy of the future, the directive activity of the State, of the communities and professional institutions, cannot attain their lasting aim, which is the real fecundity of social life and the normal yield of the national economy, if not by respecting and safeguarding the vital function of private property in its personal and social value. When the distribution of property is an obstacle to this end—and this is not necessarily always originated by the extensiveness of private property—the State may, in the common interest, intervene to regulate its use, or even, if it is impossible to arrive at another solution, decree expropriation, giving a fair and equitable indemnity. For the same purpose, the small and medium-sized properties in agriculture, in the arts and trades, in commerce and industry, must be guaranteed and promoted; co-operative unions must assure to them the advantages of a large concern; where the large business concern today manifests itself to be more productive, the possibility must be offered to temper the labor agreement with a company-sharing contract.

Nor let it be said that technical progress is opposed to such a regime and pushes in its irresistible current all activity toward gigantic concerns and organizations, before which a social system founded on the private property of the single individual must perforce collapse. No; technical progress does not determine, as a fatal and necessary fact, economic life. Too often it has bowed docilely before the demands of egotistical calculations avid to increase capital indefinitely; why, then, should it not also bend to the need of maintaining and assuring the private property of all, the cornerstone of the social order? Even technical progress, as a social fact, must not prevail over the general good, but must instead be regulated by and subordinated to it.[†]

Dictatorship and Democracy

In an ever-increasing number of noble minds arises a thought, a constantly clearer and firmer will: a thorough reorganization of the world. Members of governments, the responsible representatives of nations, meet for talks and conferences, with a view to determining the basic rights and duties on which a community of States should be re-established, of tracing the path to a better, securer, worthier future for mankind.

Undoubtedly, the value, applicability, or efficacy of this or that proposal may be discussed; judgment on them may be suspended; but it is still true that the movement is in progress.

Furthermore—and this is perhaps the most important point—peoples have, as it were, reawakened from a long torpor. They have assumed a new, questioning, criticizing, suspicious attitude toward the State and those governing. Taught, as they are, by bitter experience, they oppose with greater impetuosity the monopolization of power by a dictatorial authority which is uncontrollable and intangible; and they ask for a system of government more consistent with the dignity and freedom of citizens.

These restless multitudes, in which the onslaught of war has left the deepest traces, are now filled with the persuasion—vague and confused, perhaps, at first, but now incontrovertible—that, if the possibility of controlling and

† Radio Message to the World (September 1, 1943).

correcting the action of those in power had not been lacking, the world would not have been dragged into the disastrous hurricane of war; and that, to prevent any such catastrophe in the future, efficacious guarantees must be vested in the people itself.

In view of this state of mind, is there any cause for wonder if the democratic tendency is pervading peoples and is widely obtaining the approval and assent of those who aspire to co-operate with greater efficacy in shaping the destiny of individuals and society?

The Church Reproves No Form of Government

It is scarcely necessary to recall that, according to the teaching of the Church, "it is not forbidden to prefer moderate governments of a popular form, without prejudice, however, to the Catholic doctrine concerning the origin and use of public power," and that the "Church reproves none of the different forms of government, provided they be in themselves suitable for securing the welfare of citizens."

If, therefore, We direct Our attention to the problem of democracy, in order to consider what are the canons according to which it must be regulated to deserve to be called a true and sound democracy, suitable to the present time, this plainly indicates that the care and concern of the Church is not so much directed to its structure and external organization—which depend upon each nation's individual aspirations—as to man, as such, who, far from being the object and a passive element of social life, truly is, and must be and remain, its subject, its basis, and its end.

Starting from the premise that democracy, taken in its wider meaning, admits of different forms and can find its realization in a monarchy as well as in a republic, two questions come up for our examination: (1) What features must distinguish men living in a democracy and under a democratic regime? (2) What features must distinguish the men holding public power in democracy?

The Citizen in a Democracy

To express his own opinion concerning the duties and sacrifices which are imposed upon him; not to be forced to obey without having been listened to: these are two of the citizen's rights, which have their expression in democracy, as its name itself indicates. From the solidity, the harmony, and the good fruits of this contact between the citizens and the government of a State, it can be seen whether a democracy is truly sound and balanced, and what is its force of life and development. As regards the measure and nature of the sacrifices asked of all the citizens—in our times when the activities of the State are so extensive and decisive—a democratic form of government appears to many people as a natural postulate imposed by reason itself. But when "more democracy and better democracy" is clamored for, the only meaning of such a demand would be to give the citizen increasingly the opportunities to form his own personal opinion, and to express it, and make it prevail in such ways as are consistent with the common good.

People and the "Masses"

From this flows a first necessary conclusion, with its practical consequence. The State does not contain in itself and does not mechanically gather within a given territory an amorphous agglomeration of individuals. The State is, and must be in reality, the organic and organizing unity of a true people.

People and amorphous multitude or, as one says, the "masses," are two different concepts. A people lives and moves by its own vitality; the mass is inert in itself, and can only be moved from without. A people lives by the fullness of the life of the men composing it, each one of whom—at his own post and in his own way—is a person conscious of his own responsibilities and his own convictions. The mass, on the contrary, waits for an impulsion from without, is an easy toy in the hands of whoever would exploit its instincts or emotionality, ready to follow in turn, today this, tomorrow that flag. Out of the vital exuberance of a true people, life flows out abundantly, richly, in the State and in all its organs, pouring into them, with unceasingly renewed vigor, the consciousness of their own responsibility, the true sense of the common good. The elementary force of the mass, skillfully handled and used, can also be employed by the State; in the ambitious hands of one or several individuals, joined artificially by their selfish tendencies, the State can, with the support of the mass reduced to a mere machine, impose its arbitrary will on the better part of the true people: the common interest is thereby affected grievously and for a long time, and the wound is often exceedingly difficult to heal.

Out of this there clearly flows another conclusion: the mass—such as We have now defined it—is the chief enemy of true democracy and of its ideals of freedom and equality.

In a people worthy of this name, the citizen feels in himself the consciousness of his personality, of his duties and rights, of his own freedom, coupled with respect for the freedom and dignity of others. In a people worthy of this name, all inequalities, issuing not from an arbitrary will but from the very nature of things, inequalities of education, possession, social status—without prejudice, let it be well understood, to justice and mutual charity—are no obstacle to the existence and prevalence of a genuine spirit of true brotherliness. On the contrary, far from affecting civil equality in any way, they confer upon it its legitimate meaning, that is to say that, before the State, each individual has the right honorably to live his own personal life, in the place and in the conditions which have been assigned to him by the designs and dispositions of Providence.

In contrast with this picture of the democratic ideal of liberty and equality in a people which is governed by honest and provident hands, what a spectacle is offered by a democratic State left to the arbitrariness of the mass! Freedom, as a moral duty of the person, is turned into a tyrannical pretension to give free vent to men's impulses and appetites to the detriment of other people. Equality degenerates into a mechanical levelling, into a drab uniformity: the sentiment of true honor, personal commitment, respect for tradition, dignity—in a word, all that gives life its true value—little by little sinks and disappears. And there remain only, on one hand, the deluded victims of an illusory outward show of democracy, naively mistaken for the very spirit of democracy and for freedom and equality; and, on the other, the more or less numerous profiteers who have been able, through financial or organizational manipulation, to secure for themselves a privileged condition and a position of power over others.

Qualities of Officeholders in a Democracy

The democratic State, whether monarchical or republican, must, like any other form of government, be vested with the power to command with real and effectual authority. The absolute order of beings and ends itself, which shows man as an autonomous person, that is to say, the subject of inviolable duties and rights, both origin and end of his social life, embraces also the State as a necessary society vested with authority, without which it could neither exist nor live. If men, availing themselves of personal freedom, should disown any subordination to a higher authority vested with the right of coercion, they would thereby undermine the foundation of their own dignity and freedom, that is to say, the absolute order of beings and ends.

Established on this same basis, the individual, the State, and the public power, with their respective rights, are bound together and connected in such a way that they either stand or fall together.

And inasmuch as the said absolute order, in the light of sound reason, and especially in the light of the Christian faith, can have no other origin than in a personal God, our Creator, it follows that man's dignity is the dignity of God's image, the dignity of the State is the dignity of the moral community willed by God, the dignity of the political authority is the dignity of its participation in God's authority.

No form of government can afford not to take into account this inner and indissoluble connection, democracy least of all. Therefore, if an individual holding office fails to see that connection or more or less neglects it, he shakes his own authority in its very basis. Similarly, if he fails to take such connection sufficiently into account, and does not see in his office the mission to realize the order willed by God, there will be the danger that the egoism born of power or selfish interests may prevail over the essential requirements of political and social ethics, and that the vain semblances of a democracy which is so only in form may serve, as often happens, as a mask for what is in reality least democratic.

Only a clear understanding of the ends assigned by God to every human society, coupled with a deep feeling for the sublime duties of social activity, can enable those in whom power is vested to fulfill their legislative, judicial, or executive obligations with the consciousness of their own responsibilities and with the objectivity, impartiality, loyalty, generosity, and incorruptibility without which it would be very difficult for a democratic government to succeed in securing the respect, confidence, and assent of the best part of the people.

The People's Representatives

A profound sense of the principles of a political and social order, sound and in harmony with the canons of law and justice, assumes particular importance in those who, in any form of democratic government, hold, wholly or in part, the legislative power, as the people's representatives, and inasmuch as the center of gravity of a properly constituted democracy lies in this popular representation, from which the political currents radiate into all fields of public life—for good as well as for evil—the question of the moral character, practical fitness, and intellectual capacity of members of Parliament is, for all peoples under a democratic regime, a question of life or death, of prosperity or decadence, of recovery or perpetual uneasiness. In order to be able to develop fruitful action and to gain esteem and confidence, any legislative body must—as indubitable experiences attest—gather within itself a choice selection of men who are intellectually outstanding and of firm character, and who look upon themselves as the representatives of the whole people and not, instead, as the agents of a group to whose particular interests the true needs and requirements of the common welfare are unfortunately too often sacrificed. A selection of men not restricted to any one profession or condition, but which can be the image of the manifold life of the whole people. A selection of men with solid Christian convictions, just and sure of judgment, of practical, well-balanced disposition, true to themselves in all circumstances; men of clear and sound philosophy, of steadfast and straightforward purposes; men capable, above all, by virtue of the authority emanating from their pure conscience and widely radiating around them, of being guides and leaders, especially at times when pressing necessities overexcite the impressionability of the people, and make it more liable to be misled and to go astray; men who, in transitional periods, which are generally tormented and torn by passion and by differences of opinion and conflicting programs, feel it doubly their duty to inject into the veins of the people and the State, consumed by the fire of a thousand fevers, the spiritual antidote of clear views, thoughtful kindliness, and justice equally favorable to all, together with a straining of wills toward national union and harmony in a spirit of genuine brotherhood.

Peoples whose spiritual and moral temperaments are sufficiently sound and fruitful find in themselves, and can give to the world, the heralds and instruments of democracy who live with such dispositions and know how to put them to practical use. Where, instead, such men are wanting, others come to take their post, to make of political activity the arena of their ambition, a race toward gains for themselves, their caste, or their class, while the pursuit of private interests causes the true commonweal to be lost sight of or endangered.

State Absolutism

A sound democracy, founded upon the unchanging principles of natural law and revealed truths, will be resolutely contrary to that corruption which attributes to State legislation an unbridled and unlimited power, and which renders the democratic regime itself, despite contrary but vain appearances, a system of absolutism, pure and simple.

State absolutism (not to be confused, as such, with an absolute monarchy, with which We are not now concerned) in fact does consist in the erroneous principle that the authority of the State is unlimited, and that, against it—even when it gives free vent to its despotic aims, overstepping the boundaries of good and evil—no appeal can be admitted to a higher and morally binding law.

A man imbued with right ideas concerning the State and the authority and power vested therein as the custodian of social order, will never think of offending the majesty of the positive law within the sphere of its natural jurisdiction. But this majesty of human positive law is without appeal only when it conforms—or at least is not contrary—to the absolute order, established by the Creator and put in a new light by the revelation of the Gospel. It cannot subsist except in so far as it respects the foundation on which rests the human person, no less than the State and public power. This is the basic criterion of any sound form of government, including democracy; and by this criterion the moral value of every particular law has to be judged.

It has been Our intention to point out the ways by which a democracy that corresponds to human dignity can, in harmony with natural law and God's designs made manifest through revelation, attain beneficial results. We do feel deeply, indeed, the supreme importance of this problem for the peaceful progress of the human family; but We are at the same time conscious of the high qualities which this form of government exacts from the moral maturity of individual citizens; a moral maturity which it would be vain to try to attain fully and surely if the light of the Stable of Bethlehem did not illuminate the dark path along which the peoples of this stormy present are marching toward a future which they hope will be more fortunate.[†]

Atheistic Dictatorships

A well-known characteristic common to persecutors of all times is that, not content with physically crushing their victims, they want also to make them appear despicable and hateful to their country and to society.

Who does not remember the Roman martyrs immolated under Nero and made to appear as arsonists, abominable criminals, enemies of mankind? Modern persecutors show themselves to be the docile disciples of that inglorious school.

They copy their masters and models, if, indeed, they do not surpass them in cruelty, clever as they are in the art of employing the most recent progress in the technical sciences for the purpose of a domination and enslavement of the people which in the past would not have been conceivable.

The Church of Christ is following the road traced out for her by the divine Redeemer. She feels herself eternal; she knows that she cannot perish, that the most violent storms will not succeed in submerging her. She begs no favors; the threats and disfavor of earthly authorities do not intimidate her. She does not interfere in problems purely economic or political, nor does she occupy herself with debates on the usefulness or banefulness of one form of

† Radio Message to the World (December 24, 1944).

government or another. Always eager, in so far as she is able, to be at peace with all, she renders unto Caesar that which is Caesar's, but she cannot betray or abandon that which belongs to God.

Now, it is well known what the totalitarian and antireligious State requires and expects from the Church as the price for tolerance and its problematical recognition. To amplify, it would desire: a Church who remains silent, when she should speak out; a Church who weakens the law of God, adapting it to the taste of human desires, when she should loudly proclaim and defend it; a Church who detaches herself from the unwavering foundation upon which Christ built her, in order to repose comfortably on the shifting sands of the opinions of the day or to give herself up to the passing current; a Church who does not withstand the suppression of conscience and does not protect the legitimate rights and the just liberties of the people; a Church who with indecorous servility remains enclosed within the four walls of the temple, who forgets the divine mandate received from Christ: Go forth on the crossroads, teach all peoples.

Can the Pope Remain Silent?

The Pope has the divine promises; even in his human weakness, he is invincible and unshakable; messenger of truth and justice, the principle of the unity of the Church, his voice denounces errors, idolatry, superstition, it condemns iniquity, makes charity and virtue loved.

Can the Pope then remain silent when in a nation the churches which are united to the center of Christendom, to Rome, are snatched away through violence or cunning; when all the Greek-Catholic bishops are imprisoned because they refuse to apostatize from their faith; when priests and the faithful are persecuted and arrested because they refuse to leave their true Mother Church?

Can the Pope remain silent, when the right to educate their own children is taken away from parents by a minority regime which wants to alienate them from Christ?

Can the Pope remain silent when a State, surpassing the limits of its authority, arrogates to itself the power to abolish dioceses, to depose Bishops, to overturn the ecclesiastical organization, and to reduce it below the minimum requirements for the effectual cure of souls?

Can the Pope remain silent when things go so far that imprisonment is given as punishment to a priest guilty of refusing to violate the most sacred and inviolable of secrets, that of sacramental confession?

Is all this perhaps illegitimate interference in the political powers of the State? Who could honestly affirm anything of the kind?†

Elections and Voting

It is a right and a duty to draw the attention of the faithful to the extraordinary importance of elections and the moral responsibility which rests on everyone who has the right to vote. Without any doubt, the Church intends to remain outside and above political parties, but how can she remain indifferent to the composition of a Parliament, when the Constitution gives it power to pass laws which so directly affect the highest religious interests and even the condition of life of the Church herself? Then there are also other arduous questions, above all the problems and economic struggles which closely touch the well-being of the people. In so far as they are of a temporal order (though in reality they also affect the moral order) Churchmen leave to others the care of pondering and treating technically with them for the common welfare of the nation.

From all this it follows that:

It is a strict duty for all who have the right, men or women, to take part in the elections. Whoever abstains, especially out of cowardice, commits a grave sin, a mortal fault.

Everyone has to vote according to the dictates of his own conscience. Now, it is evident that the voice of this conscience imposes upon every sincere Catholic the duty of giving his or her vote to those candidates, or those lists of candidates, who really offer sufficient assurances for safeguarding the rights

† Address to the People of Rome (February 2, 1949).

of God and the souls of men, for the real good of individuals, families, and society, according to the law of God and moral Christian doctrine.†

The Class Struggle

A wage which guarantees the existence of the family, making it possible for parents to fulfill their natural duty of rearing a progeny healthily fed and clothed; a dwelling fit for human beings; the possibility of providing children with sufficient instruction and a suitable education, the possibility of planning and making provision for bad times, sickness, and old age—these are social welfare conditions that must be achieved if we do not want society to be shaken in every season by ferments and dangerous quakings, but to grow quietly and advance in the peace and harmony of mutual love.

Conception of the Living Conditions Fit for Man

The Church, guardian and instructor of truth, in her assertion and bold defense of the rights of the working population, on various occasions opposing error, has had to put people on guard against letting themselves be deluded by the mirage of specious and fatuous theories and visions of future well-being or by the deceitful lures and urgings of false teachers of social prosperity who call bad good and good bad and who, claiming to be the friends of the people, do not permit the mutual agreements between capital and labor and between employers and employed that maintain and promote harmony for the progress and benefit of all.

But when have their words ever been answered by facts, or when have hopes smiled upon reality? Deception and disappointment were and are the only rewards of those who believed them and followed them down paths

† Address to the Delegates of the International Conference on Emigration (October 17, 1951).

which, far from improving, only worsen and aggravate the conditions of life and of moral and material advancement. Such false shepherds would have people believe that salvation must proceed with a revolution which would change the social structure and assume a national character.

Social revolution boasts that it can raise the working classes to power: vain words and a mere semblance of impossible reality! The actual fact is that the working population is tied, yoked, and bound to the force of State capitalism, which restrains and subjugates everyone, the family no less than consciences, and transforms workers into a gigantic industrial machine. In a way not differing from other social orderings and systems, which it claims to oppose, it ties up, marshals, and compresses everything into one fearful instrument of war, which exacts not only the blood and health but also the goods and prosperity of the people. And if leaders become proud of this or that advantage or improvement realized in the field of labor, vaunting and boisterously proclaiming it to the four winds, such material profit never represents a worthy return for the sacrifices imposed on each one, which infringe upon personal rights, the liberty to manage one's home and to exercise a profession, upon citizenship and, particularly, upon freedom in the practice of religion and even in the life of the conscience.

No, salvation is not to be found in revolution. To aspire—with only one's own exclusive and material advantage in view, which seems, however, always uncertain to a revolution which is to proceed from injustice and civil insubordination, and to render oneself responsible for shedding the blood of one's fellow countrymen and for the destruction of common wealth, is contrary to the genuine and sincere profession of Christianity. Woe to him who forgets that a genuine national society includes social justice and claims a fair and adequate participation of all in the wealth of the country.

Not in revolution but in harmonious evolution lies salvation and justice. The work of violence has always been to tear down, never to raise up; to inflame the passions, rather than appease them; to create hate and ruin, rather than to make brothers of the contenders; and it has flung men and parties into the bitter necessity of slowly rebuilding, after painful trial, upon the ruins of discord. Only a progressive and cautious evolution, courageous and in harmony with nature, enlightened and guided by the sacred Christian canons of right and justice, can lead to the realization of the honest desires and needs of the working man.

Not destruction, then, but construction and consolidation: not abolition of private ownership, the basis of family stability, but its promotion and spreading as the fruit of the conscientious efforts of every worker, male or female, so as to bring about the gradual reduction of that mass of bold and restless men who, sometimes through gloomy desperation and at other times through blind instincts, let themselves be carried away by every gust of false doctrine or by the subtle arts of agitators destitute of any moral sense. Not the dispersion of private capital, but the promotion of its prudently controlled marshalling as a means and buttress for the achievement and increase of the true material well-being of the whole population. We must not repress or give exclusive preference to industry but secure its harmonious co-ordination with artisanship and agriculture, which makes the national soil render up its multiform and necessary produce. In the exploitation of technical progress, we must not aim solely at the greatest possible profit, but also make use of the fruits which we obtain from it for the improvement of the living conditions of the worker, in order to lighten his labors and strengthen the bonds of his family with the land where he dwells and the work by which he lives. We must not aim at making the life of the individual depend entirely on the will of the State, but rather see to it that the State, whose duty it is to promote the common good, does by means of social institutions such as social security, health insurance, and social welfare integrate, assist, and complement the activity of labor associations, and particularly the endeavors of fathers and mothers who, by their work, secure their own living and that of their children.

Perhaps it will be said that this is but a visionary picture of a too beautiful reality—but how can it be realized and given life among the people? What is needed above all is great integrity of will and perfect loyalty of purpose and action in the conduct and government of public life, on the part of the citizens as much as on the part of the authorities. A spirit of true harmony and brotherhood must animate all, high and low, managers and workers, great and small, in brief, all the ranks of the people.[†]

---

† Address to the Representatives of Italian Workers (January 13, 1943).

Is Religion Opium for the People?

Man is the image of the one and triune God and therefore a person, brother of the God-man Jesus Christ, and with Him and by Him heir to an eternal life: this is his true dignity.

If there is any man in the world who should convince himself evermore of this truth and imbue himself with it, it is the worker. It was affirmed a long time ago, and it is still being affirmed, that religion renders the worker weak and slack in his daily life and in the defense of his public and private interests and that, like opium, it makes him drowsy, pacifying him entirely through the hope of a life to come. A manifest error! If the Church in her social doctrine always insists on the regard due to the innate dignity of man, if she requires in the labor contract a fair wage for the worker, if she claims for him effective assistance in his mental and spiritual needs, what is her reason if not that the worker is a human person, that his working capacity must not be considered and treated as "merchandise," and that his labors always represent a personal service?

It is precisely those reshapers of the world who arrogate to themselves the care of the interests of the workers almost as if it were their monopoly and who declare that theirs is the only truly "social" system, who do not defend the worker's individual dignity but make of his productive capacity a mere object of which the "society" disposes with absolute freedom and entirely at its own discretion.

The Church says that human liberty has its limits in the divine law and in the multiple duties which life brings with it; but at the same time, she strives, and will continue to strive until the end, in order that everyone, in the happiness of the home and in peaceful and decent conditions, may spend his days in harmony with God and men. The Church does not promise that complete equality which others proclaim, because she knows that the human community always and necessarily produces a scale of degrees and differences in physical and intellectual qualities, in inward dispositions and tendencies, in occupations and responsibilities. But at the same time, she does guarantee full equality in human dignity, as also in the heart of Him who summons all those who are weary and burdened, calling on them to take up His yoke, so as to find peace and rest for their souls, because His yoke is sweet and His burden light.

In such manner, in order to safeguard liberty and human dignity and not to sponsor the special interests of this or that group, the Church rejects any kind of State totalitarianism, nor does she weaken with thoughts of a life to come the protection of the rights of the workers on this earth. Rather, those remodelers of the world we have mentioned, while they dazzle the eyes of the people with the mirage of a future of chimerical prosperity and unobtainable riches, sacrifice the dignity of the human person and domestic happiness—by setting up the superstition of technology and organization—to the idols of a misconceived earthly progress.

The Church, experienced educator of the human family and faithful to the mission which the divine Founder has entrusted to her, proclaims the truth of the only perfect bliss which is prepared for us in Heaven. But, precisely for this reason, she puts the faithful firmly, and with a strong footing, on the ground of the present reality. For the Supreme Judge, who awaits us at the end of our earthly life on the threshold of eternity, admonishes everyone, high and low, to make conscientious use of the gifts received from God, to avoid all injustice, and to seize every opportunity for doing works of love and kindness. Such is the only measure of every real progress, because then only is it genuine and not fictitious when it is also advancement toward God and to resemblance to Him. All purely worldly measures of progress are an illusion, We even feel inclined to say a mockery of man in a world which is under the law of original sin and its consequences, and which, therefore, being still imperfect, even with the divine light and grace, without that light and grace would fall into an abyss of wretchedness, injustice, and selfishness.

Moreover, only the religious idea of man can lead to a unified conception of his conditions of life. Where God is not the beginning and the end, where the order of His creation is not for all the guide and yardstick of liberty and action, unity between man and man cannot be achieved. The material conditions of life and work alone can never constitute the foundation of the unity of the working classes on the basis of an asserted uniformity of interests. Such an assumption would indeed do violence to nature and would simply create fresh oppression and division in the human family at a time when every honest worker aspires to a fair and peaceful order in private and public economy and social life as a whole.

Any legitimate power over men can have its origin and existence only from the authority of Him who holds it by His nature in Heaven and on earth, without any limits of time or space: Jesus Christ, who rules over the great ones of the earth, who loves us and has redeemed us from sin with His blood, whose glory and dominion is forever and ever.[†]

Capital and Labor

With benevolence and warm interest, We see come to Us again and again workers and representatives of industrial organizations who, with deeply moving confidence, put their various troubles before Us.

We refer to the troubles of those who take part in industrial production. Erroneous and baneful in its consequences is the prejudice, unfortunately too widespread, which sees in them an irreducible opposition of conflicting interests. The opposition is only apparent. There are, in the economic field, activities and common interests which concern both management and labor. To want to disregard this mutual link and to attempt to break it is the result of the whim of blind and irrational despotism. Management and labor are not irreconcilable adversaries. They are co-operators in a mutual work. They eat, as it were, at the same table since, after all is said and done, they live by the net total profit of the national economy. Both have their own profit, and in this respect their reciprocal relations by no means make one side subject to the other.

Profit

To receive his own profit belongs to the personal dignity of every individual who, in one way or another, as a member of management or labor, contributes to the output of the national economy. In the budget of private industry the figure for wages may appear to be the expense of the employer. But in the

† Address to Fiat Workers (October 31, 1948).

economy of a nation there is only one kind of expenditure, that is, the natural wealth which is utilized for the national output, and which must therefore be continually renewed.

It follows that both sides must undertake to ensure that expenses are proportionate to the yield of the national output. If, therefore, the interest is mutual, why should it not be expressed in a common formula? Why should it not be right to assign the workers a fair share of responsibility in the formation and the development of the national economy?

Our unforgettable predecessor, Pius XI, had proposed a concrete and timely formula for this community of interests and responsibilities in the work of national economy when, in the Encyclical *Quadragesimo Anno*, he recommended "professional organization" in the various branches of production. To triumph over economic liberalism, nothing seemed to him in fact more suitable for the social economy than the adoption of a statute of public law founded on the mutual responsibility of all who are interested in production. This point of the Encyclical caused a great outcry: some saw in it a concession to modern political currents, and others a return to medieval times. It would have been much more reasonable to abandon inveterate and empty prejudices and in good faith to set to work for the realization of the thing itself and its numerous practical applications.

State Ownership

Today, however, this part of the Encyclical seems, unfortunately, to offer us an example of those propitious opportunities that are lost because they were not taken advantage of in time. Too late other forms of public political organization of social economies are devised, among them State ownership and the nationalization of industry, which today are in the foreground of discussion. Considered within just limits, the Church is not opposed to State ownership and holds that certain categories of wealth may legitimately be reserved to the public authorities, that is, possessions endowed with such power that they could not be transferred to individuals without endangering the common good. But to want to make of State ownership the general rule in the public organization of economies would mean subverting the order of things. The task of public rights is to serve, not to absorb, private rights. Economy, and, indeed, any other branch of human activity, is not by its nature a State institution but, on the contrary, the living product of the free enterprise of individuals and freely constituted groups.

It would be equally a mistake to affirm that any individual enterprise is by its nature a partnership where the relations between the partners are determined by the canons of distributive justice and where all, indiscriminately—whether owners or not of the means of production—have a right to their share of the property, or at least of the profits. A conception of this kind presupposes that every enterprise, by its nature, is in the sphere of public rights; but this supposition is incorrect: whether it be constituted in the form of a trust or association of all the workers as joint owners, or whether it be the private property of an individual who stipulates a working contract with all those employed by him, in either case the enterprise falls within the private juridical order of economic life.

The Formation of Capital and the Social Problem

What We have said applies to the juridical character of the enterprise as such, but for its members it may also entail a complex of individual relations and mutual responsibility, which must be taken into account. Whoever owns the means of production—either as an individual or as an association of workers or as a trust—must be the master of his own economic decisions, though always within the limits of the public economic law. It follows that his profit must be greater than that of his collaborators, but at the same time, the individual material well-being of all, which constitutes the object of social economy, must still further impose on him the duty of contributing through his savings to the increase of the national capital. Nor must it be forgotten that, just as it is extremely useful to a sound social economy that this increase of capital should come from the greatest possible number of sources, so is it most desirable that the workers also should contribute with the fruits of their savings to the formation of the national capital.[†]

---

† Address to the International *Union des Associations Patronales Catholiques* (April 27, 1941).

In regard to property and the means of subsistence of mankind, the Encyclical *Rerum Novarum* expresses principles which, with the passage of time, have lost nothing of their original vigor and which today, fifty years later, still preserve their deep and vivifying force.

We Ourselves called the general attention to their basic premise in Our Encyclical *Sertum Laetitiae*, addressed to the Bishops of the United States of America, a basic premise which, as We said, consists in the affirmation of the absolute need for "wealth created by God for all men to flow fairly to all according to the principles of justice and charity."

The Right to the Material Goods of the Earth

Every man, as a being endowed with reason, has from nature the basic right to use the material goods of the earth, it being, however, left to the human will and to the juridical forms of peoples to regulate more particularly its practical achievement. This individual right cannot in any way be suppressed, not even by other sure and unquestioned rights upon material goods. Without doubt, the natural order, derived from God, also requires that there should be private ownership and free reciprocal trading of goods with exchanges and gifts, as also the controlling function of public authority over both these institutions. All this, nevertheless, is subordinated to the natural purpose of material goods and could not make itself independent of the first and fundamental right which grants their use to all; rather, it should serve to make its achievement possible in accordance with its aim. In this way only can and must it be ensured that the ownership and use of material goods will bring to society fruitful peace and stability instead of precarious conditions engendering struggles and jealousy, and leaving society at the mercy of the implacable play between the strong and the weak.

The original right to the use of material goods, being closely connected with the dignity and other rights of the human person, offers him with the above-mentioned forms a sure material foundation of the utmost importance, as it enables him to rise to the fulfillment of his moral duties. The protection of this right will ensure the personal dignity of man and will help him to attend to and carry out freely the sum of those permanent obligations and resolutions for which he is directly responsible to the Creator. Indeed, man has the entirely personal duty of preserving and perfecting his material and spiritual life, in order to secure the religious and moral aim which God has assigned to all men and given them as a supreme law, binding always and in all cases, to be observed before all other duties.

To protect the inviolable sphere of human rights and facilitate the fulfillment of human duties is the essential business of all public authority. Does not, indeed, in this consist the genuine meaning of the common good that the State is called upon to promote? From this ensues that the care for that "common good" does not require so extensive a power over the members of the community that in virtue of it the public authority would be entitled to restrict the development of the individual activity described above, to decide directly on the beginning or (apart from the case of legitimate punishment) on the termination of human life, to determine at will the manner of its physical, spiritual, religious, and moral movement inconsistently with the personal duties and rights of man, and with such intent to abolish or deprive of efficacy the natural right to material goods. To deduce such extensive power from the care for the common good would mean inverting the sense of "common good" and falling into the error of affirming that the goal of man on earth is society, that society is an end in itself, that man has no other life awaiting him but that which ends here below.

So also national economy, as it is the fruit of the activity of men who work united in the community of the State, aims at nothing else but ensuring without interruption the material conditions in which the individual life of the citizens may be able to develop to the full. Where this is durably obtained, a people will in truth be economically rich because the general well-being, and consequently the personal right of all to the use of earthly goods, is in such manner achieved according to the Creator's purpose.

From this it will easily be perceived that the economic wealth of a people does not properly consist in the abundance of goods, measured according to a purely material calculation of their value, but rather in that which such abundance represents and effectively provides, namely, an adequate material foundation for the proper personal development of its members. If such a fair distribution of goods is not realized or is only imperfectly achieved, the genuine aim of national economy has not been reached; since, however great the abundance of available goods, the people not participating in them would not be economically rich, but poor. Instead, let such a fair distribution be actually effected in a durable manner, and you will see a people, even with a smaller quantity of goods at its disposal, become economically healthy.

It seems to Us particularly expedient to bring these fundamental concepts concerning the wealth and poverty of peoples under consideration today, when one is inclined to judge and measure such wealth and poverty with purely quantitative scales and criteria, as they are applied to space and bulk of goods. If, instead, the aim of national economy is rightly considered, it will enlighten the efforts of statesmen and peoples and illuminate them so that they may of their own accord set forth along a road that will not require continuous tributes of goods and blood but will give the fruits of peace and general welfare.

Labor

Connected with the use of material wealth is labor. The Encyclical *Rerum Novarum* teaches us that the properties of human labor are twofold: it is personal and it is necessary. It is personal because it is carried out through the exercise of the personal forces in man; it is necessary because, without it, it is not possible to procure that which is essential to life, the preservation of which is a natural and serious duty of each individual. To the personal duty of labor imposed by nature corresponds as its logical sequence the natural right of each individual to derive from labor the means of providing for his livelihood and that of his children: so highly is the order of nature ordained for the preservation of man.

But note that this duty and the corresponding right to work are imposed on and granted to the individual first and foremost by nature, and not by society, as though man were nothing more than a simple servant or functionary of the community. From this it follows that the duty and the right to organize the work of the people belong first of all to those immediately interested: employers and workers. But if they do not carry out their task or are unable to do so on account of special extraordinary contingencies, then it will be for the State to intervene in the sphere, division, and distribution of work, according to the form and measure required by the common good, properly understood.

In any case, any legitimate and beneficial State intervention in the field of work must be such as to preserve and respect its personal character, both in principle and, within the limits of possibility, as regards execution. And this will happen if the decrees of the State do not abolish or render impossible the exercise of other equally personal rights and duties, such as: the right to the true worship of God; to matrimony; the right of married people, of the father and the mother, to lead a conjugal and domestic life; the right to reasonable liberty in the choice of one's profession and the following of a true calling; this last being, more than any other, a personal right of the spirit of man, and a lofty one when there are added thereto the superior and immutable rights of God and of the Church, as in the choice and exercise of the priestly and religious vocations.

The Family

According to the doctrine of *Rerum Novarum*, nature itself has closely linked private ownership with the existence of human society and with its true civilization and, to an eminent degree, with the existence and development of the family. Such a link is more than openly apparent. Must not private ownership secure for the father of the family the healthy liberty which he needs to be able to fulfill the duties assigned to him by the Creator as regards the physical, spiritual, and religious well being of the family?

In the family, the nation finds the natural and fruitful roots of its greatness and power. If private ownership is to lead to the good of the family, all public regulations, or rather all those of the State which govern the possession of it, must not only render possible and preserve such a function—a function which, in the natural order, is in certain respects superior to any other—but must bring it to ever greater perfection. The boast of civil progress would indeed be unnatural if—either through excessive levies or through too much immediate interference—it should empty private ownership of all meaning, practically depriving the family and its head of the liberty of pursuing the aim assigned by God to the improvement of family life.

Among all the goods which may be the object of private ownership, none conforms more closely to nature, according to the teaching of *Rerum Novarum*, than land, the homestead where the family lives and from whose fruits it derives, in whole or in part, its means of sustenance. And it is in the spirit of *Rerum Novarum* to affirm that, as a rule, only the stability which has its roots in a homestead makes of the family the most perfect and fruitful vital cell of society, marvelously uniting present and future generations through its progressive cohesion.†

The Dignity of Labor

Too long, unfortunately, has the enemy of Christ sown tares among the people, and has not met at all points sufficient resistance from Catholics. Especially among the working class has he done and is still doing much to spread false ideas about man and the world, history, social and economic structures. Not infrequently the Catholic laborer, lacking a solid religious formation, is defenseless when such theories are advanced; he cannot give an answer and sometimes even is infected by the poison of error.

The religious training of Christians, and especially of workers, is one of the main duties of pastoral activity today. Just as the vital interests of the Church and of souls have forced the erection of Catholic schools for Catholic children, so too the well-grounded religious training of adults is of prime necessity...

For these false principles are at work! How many times have We declared and explained the Church's love for the workers! Yet the monstrous lie is still spread about that "the Church is allied with capitalism against labor." She, mother and teacher of all men, is always concerned especially for her children who are in the more difficult circumstances, and in fact has made a great contribution to the equitable progress already obtained by certain categories of workers. We Ourselves said in Our Christmas Message of 1942: "Moved ever by religious motives, the Church condemned the various systems of Marxist socialism, and condemns them today, for it is her abiding duty and right to save men from trends and influences that jeopardize their eternal salvation.

† Encyclical *Rerum Novarum*, Commemorative Broadcast (June 1, 1941).

But the Church cannot be unaware of the fact that the laborer, in his effort to better his condition, strikes against a certain system which, far from being conformed to nature, is opposed to God's order and to the purpose He assigned to the goods of this world. However false, dangerous, and to be condemned are the methods followed, who, and particularly what priest or Christian, could remain deaf to the cry which is rising from the depths, and which, in the world of a just God, appeals to justice and the spirit of brotherhood?"

To enter into the world of social problems with its systems which do not derive from Him, whether they are called "lay humanism" or "socialism stripped of materialism," Jesus Christ does not wait for the door to be opened to Him. His divine kingdom of truth and justice is present even in regions where there is a constant threat of class warfare seizing the advantage. For that reason, the Church does not restrict itself to demanding a social order of greater justice, but sets out its fundamental principles, urging the rulers of nations, legislators, employers, and management to give them practical application.

But this Address is directed especially at the so-called "disillusioned" among Catholics. They are, indeed, not few in number, particularly among the youth, whose intentions remain of the best, but who would have looked for more action among the Catholic force in the public life of the country...

We wish to call once again the attention of these "disillusioned" to the fact that neither new laws nor new institutions are adequate to give to each the security to exist, protected against every misused restriction, and to be able to develop with freedom in society. All will be in vain if the ordinary man lives in fear of coming under arbitrary rule, and does not succeed in freeing himself from the feeling that he is subject to the good and ill will of those who apply the laws, or of those who, as public officials, direct the institutions and organizations; if he perceives that, in daily life, all depends on connections which he—unlike others—perhaps does not have; if he suspects that behind the external show of the State, there is hidden the manipulations of powerful organized groups.

The action of Christian forces in public life, then, certainly means that the promulgation of good laws and building up of institutions suited to the times is fostered; but it means, even more, that there is a setting aside of the rule of empty slogans and deceptive words, and that the ordinary man feels supported and sustained in his legitimate demands and expectations. It is essential to form a public opinion which, without hunting out scandal, points out with frankness and courage, persons and situations which do not conform to just laws and institutions, or which maliciously conceal truth. To give influence to the plain citizen, it is not enough to put the voting card or other similar devices into his hands. If he wants to be associated with the group of leaders, if he intends sometimes—for the common good—to put forward a remedy for the dearth of profitable ideas, and to stem the advance of egoism, he himself must possess the necessary personal energy and the ardent will to contribute to, and to pour into all public arrangements, a healthy morality.

There you have the basis of the hope which We have been expressing over the past ten years, and which We repeat today with redoubled confidence.

Dear working men and women of the whole world—let Us extend to you the tenderness of a father's affection, such as that with which Jesus drew to Himself the multitudes hungering after truth and justice; be assured that in every necessity you will have at your side a guide, a defender, a father.

Yes, beloved workers, the Pope and the Church cannot withdraw from the divine mission of guiding, protecting, and loving especially the suffering, who are all the more dear the more they are in need of defense and help, whether they be workers or other children of the people.

This duty and obligation We, the Vicar of Christ, desire to reaffirm clearly, with the intention that all may recognize the dignity of labor and that this dignity may be a motivation in forming the social order and the laws, founded on the equitable distribution of rights and duties.[†]

To the Labor Unions

THE labor unions and associations of Christian workers tend toward a common goal, which is that of raising the living standard of the worker.

What part will the Christian associations of workers play in the establishment of the new social order?

† Address on the Tenth Anniversary of the Christian Labor Unions of Italy (May 1, 1955).

Socialization

The Christian associations agree to socialization only in those cases where it really seems called for by the common good, that is to say as the only truly efficacious means to remedy an abuse or to avoid the waste of a country's productive forces, and to assure the harnessing of these forces and their direction to the advantage of the economic interests of the nation, so that the national economy, in its regular and peaceful development, will open the way to the material prosperity of all the people, a prosperity such as to constitute at the same time a sound foundation for cultural and religious life, as well. In any case, furthermore, they recognize that socialization implies the obligation of a corresponding indemnity, that is to say, one calculated according to what under the actual circumstances is just and equitable for all the interested parties.

As for the democratization of the economy, it is threatened no less by monopoly, that is by the economic despotism of an anonymous conglomeration of private capital, than by the preponderance of organized masses, ready to use their power to the detriment of justice and the rights of others.

The time has now come to abandon empty phrases and to think, along with the *Quadragesimo Anno*, about a new organization of the productive forces of the people. Rising above the distinction between employers and employees, let all men be able to see and recognize that higher unity which binds to each other all those who collaborate in production. One has to see their bond and their solidarity in the obligations they share to provide together, in stability, for the common good and the needs of the whole community. May this solidarity extend to every branch of production, may it become the foundation of a better economic order, of a healthy and just autonomy, and may it open the way for the laboring classes to acquire honestly their share of responsibility in the conduct of national affairs.

May the Christian associations of workers promote the union and solidarity of men in the whole of economic life! The most efficient agent—indeed, We might say the only efficient agent—for the creation of this sense of solidarity, sure guarantee of rectitude and social peace, lies in the spirit of the Gospel and flows from the heart of the God-Man, Savior of the world.[†]

---

† Address to the Christian Labor Associations of Italy (March 11, 1945).

On the Internationalization of Private Law

CAN anyone who has even briefly leafed through the history of civilization and reflected on the nature of law be surprised at the interest which the Church has unceasingly shown in it?

In a formula whose vigorous incisiveness bears the imprint of his genius, Plato sets down in the following terms the thought underlying the spirit of all antiquity: "In the first place, God is for us the just measure of all things, much more so than any man can be." This same idea is taught by the Church, but in all the fullness and profundity of truth, when, in declaring along with St. Paul that all paternity proceeds from God, it affirms as a consequence that, in order to regulate the reciprocal relations in the midst of the great human family, every law has its roots in God.

This is why the Church, in refuting the extremist juridical positivism which attributes to law a quasi-autonomous "sanctity" of its own, enfolds it in a more sublime and truer sanctity by obligating, in the last analysis, every man who is convinced of the existence and sovereignty of a personal God to be faithful to the law.

Furthermore, since the Church is a great social organism, a supranational community with solid foundations, could she subsist without a determined and precise body of law? Apart from this consideration, the logic of which is incontestable, though of a purely natural order, the Church knows that she was constituted by her divine Founder as a visible society provided with a juridical order; and the basis of this order, of this juridical statute, is none other than divine positive law. The final goal of all the life of the Church, her mission of leading men to God, to promote their union with God, is no doubt to be found in the sphere of the ultraterrestrial, in the supernatural; in short, it is something which takes place immediately and directly between God and man. Yes, but along the road on which this function is exercised and which leads to this end, each believer walks as a member of the ecclesiastical community, guided by the Church, among the particular and concrete conditions of existence. Now, community and the guidance of an authority are synonymous with the power of right and law.

A simple glance at the objective of private international law and at its history suffices to show the difficulty of co-ordinating the various bodies of law.

Could past generations have thought possible, could they have even imagined, the technical progress in communications which in so short a time has brought all men closer together to the extent that the current expression "the world has become too small" is literally exact? The world is becoming so and will become increasingly so.

Furthermore, the Pan-European idea, the Council of Europe, and other movements are a manifestation of the general need to break with, or at least attenuate, the rigidity of the old conceptions of geographical boundaries, and to form large groups of community life and activity among the various countries. These practical considerations may not even be raised; but owing to the inevitable consequences of war and under the pressure of events, the overpopulation of some regions and the unemployment which results bring with them, through emigration and immigration, a real demographic mixture which, in the next half century, will probably greatly surpass in importance the migratory movements toward the two Americas during the course of the last one hundred and fifty years. How useful will the co-ordination of private law be then!

However, will it be possible to extend it to the fullest degree, to specific groups of States as well? Would a radical parity be truly advantageous everywhere? It is not easy to affirm this at the present time. In spite of everything, economic, social, and general cultural conditions could remain so different in some countries that a uniformity involving all countries and the whole body of private law would not fully respond to the needs of the common good.

However that may be, We recommend the following three points: first of all, an increasingly careful and efficient protection of all those who need it most, especially abandoned children and women left without support; toward these persons above all, the legislator should model his conduct on that of a parent. In the second place, a simplification of the juridical regime for all those who, for family motives, are forced to move frequently and periodically from one country to the other. Finally, recognition and direct and indirect application of the innate rights of man which, in so far as they are inherent in human nature, always conform to the common interest, and are furthermore those which must be taken as essential elements of the same common welfare; therefore the State has the duty of protecting them, fostering them, and assuring that in no case will they ever be sacrificed for an alleged reason of State.†

War and Peace

Terror-stricken, the people of the world have had to witness a new, immense improvement of the means and arts of destruction, and, at the same time, be spectators of an inner decay which, through the hardening and aberration of moral sensibility, precipitates the complete suppression of every sentiment of humanity and rushes toward such a darkening of reason and spirit as to verify the words of Wisdom: "All were tied by the same chain of darkness."

Only Christ can drive away the baneful spirits of error and sin, which have yoked humanity to a tyrannical and demeaning slavery, making it subservient to a dominating thought and will set in motion by insatiable greed.

Only Christ, who rescued us from the sad bondage of guilt, can teach, and smooth the way to a noble and orderly freedom resting on, and sustained by, genuine righteousness and genuine moral consciousness.

Only Christ, "on whose shoulders is the government," can, through His succoring omnipotence, elevate mankind, lift it out of the nameless afflictions that torment it in the course of this life, and set it on the road to happiness.

A Christian who is nourished by faith in Christ and lives in Him, in the certainty that He alone is the Way, the Truth, and the Life, takes his share of the sufferings and discomforts of this world to the crib of the Son of God, and in the presence of the newborn Babe finds consolation and support unknown to the world, which gives him the courage and strength to remain unshaken, neither faltering nor succumbing in the most tormenting and gravest ordeals.

It is sad and painful to think that innumerable men, though feeling in their search for a satisfying happiness in this life the bitterness of fallacious illusions and grievous delusions, have closed the way to all hope and, living as

† Address to the First International Congress of Private Law (July 15, 1950).

they do far from the Christian faith, do not know how to find the way again to that consolation which makes the heroes of the faith abound in joy in all their tribulations. They see shattered the edifice of beliefs in which they had humanly placed their faith and their ideal; but they never found that one true faith which would have been able to give them comfort and renew their souls. In this intellectual and moral faltering, they are seized by a depressing uncertainty of spirit and live in a state of inertia which oppresses their soul, and which only he can fully understand and fraternally pity who has the joy of living in the familiar, vivid splendor of a supernatural faith reaching beyond the turmoil of all temporal contingencies to become fixed in the eternal.

Among the host of such embittered and deluded persons it is not difficult to point to those who placed all their faith in the universal expansion of economic life, holding it to be alone fitted to unite all peoples in brotherhood, and awaiting from its grandiose organization, increasingly perfected and increasingly efficient, unique and unsuspected progress in the welfare of the human race.

With how much complacency and pride they contemplated the increase in international trade, the exchange, spanning all continents, of all the goods and all inventions and productions, and the triumphant march of this widespread modern engineering which knows no boundaries of space or time! Today, instead, what are they experiencing in reality? They see by now that this economy with its gigantic world relations and ties and with its intricate division and multiplication of labor has co-operated in a thousand ways to make the crisis of humanity general and more serious since, not corrected by any moral brake and without any ultraterrestrial light to enlighten it, it could not but end in an unworthy and humiliating exploitation of the human person and of nature, in a sad and fearful indigence on one side and in a haughty and provoking opulence on the other, in a tormented and implacable strife between the haves and the have-nots.

Those who awaited the salvation of society from the mechanism of world economy had been so deluded, because they had become not the lords and masters, but the slaves, of material riches which they had served, detaching them from the higher end of man and making them an end in themselves.

The disillusioned of the past thought and acted no differently in pinning their hopes for happiness and well-being exclusively on a certain kind of science and culture, unwilling to recognize the Creator of the universe; those pioneers and followers, not of true science, which is a marvelous reflection of God's light, but of a proud science which, giving no place at all to the work of a personal God subject to no limitations and superior to all that is of the earth, boasted of the ability to explain the happenings of this world through a rigid and deterministic concatenation of iron-clad natural laws.

But such a science cannot give happiness and well-being. Apostasy from the divine Word, by whom all things were made, has led man to apostasy from the spirit, in such manner as to make it hard for him to pursue elevated intellectual and moral ideals and objectives. In this way, science, which had denied the spiritual life, while it vainly thought to have acquired full freedom and autonomy by disowning God, sees itself punished today through the most humiliating bondage, having become the slave and the practically automatic fulfiller of policies and orders that take into no account whatever the rights of truth and of the human person. What to that science seemed to be freedom was a chain of humiliation and ignominy; it will regain its original dignity only through a return to the eternal Word, fount of wisdom so foolishly abandoned and forgotten.[†]

The Spirit of Hatred

No people is immune to the danger of seeing some of its sons succumb to the call of passion and be sacrificed to the demon of hatred. What matters above all is the judgment which the public authority passes on such aberrations and degenerations of the fighting spirit, and the promptness in putting a stop to them.

Hence, it behooves the good name of that authority to see to it that, with the widening of the fields of war beyond their own boundaries, there be no weakening of the dignity of reason which dictates those supreme principles of promoting good and containing evil, which strengthen and lend honor to the dispositions of those in command, and make the subjects more willing and ready to submit their will and action to the common interest. And,

† Broadcast to the World (December 24, 1943).

therefore, the larger grow the territories which the conflict puts under foreign domination, the more urgent becomes the duty of putting the juridical system, which it is proposed to apply there, in harmony with the provisions of international law and, above all, with the requirements of humaneness and equity.[‡]

On Military Occupation

To the occupying powers We say, without lacking in the respect owed to them: May your conscience and your honor guide you in the equitable, humane, and provident treatment of the population of occupied territories. Do not impose burdens upon them which you, in similar cases, have felt, or would feel to be, unjust.

New Weapons and Their Consequences

From the use of still more deadly instruments of strife We entreat belligerents to abstain until the last: every novelty in such means provokes an inevitable counterblow on the part of the adversary, the use of the same new weapon, but often rendered harsher and fiercer.[§]

It is well known to all how some rapid and far-reaching results of human achievements can actually create anxieties and fears in men, putting in grave danger their individual and social life. It is sufficient to consider what has recently taken place in the applications of nuclear energy.

Its use for peaceful purposes is the object of careful and continuous investigation, to which is given Our Blessing. Yet, all are aware that other uses have been sought, and found suitable, for producing, instead, destruction and death. And what a death! Every day is a melancholy step forward on this tragic road, is a hastening on to arrive alone, first, with greater advantage. And the human race almost loses hope of being able to stop this homicidal,

‡ Allocution to the Sacred College, December 24, 1939.

§ Broadcast to the World, April 13, 1941.

this suicidal madness. To increase the alarm and terror, there have come modern radio-guided missiles, capable of traversing enormous distances, to carry thither, by means of atomic weapons, total destruction to men and things.[†]

In any case, there is a duty which is incumbent on all, a duty which tolerates no delay, no postponement, no hesitation, no shuffling: to do everything possible to proscribe and once for all banish a war of aggression as a legitimate solution of international differences and as an instrument of national aspirations. Many attempts have been made in the past toward that end. They have all failed. And they will continue to fail, until the healthier part of mankind demonstrates the firm will power, holily obstinate, as an obligation of conscience, to accomplish the mission which the past had undertaken without sufficient earnestness and determination.

War on War!

If ever a generation had to feel deep down in its conscience the cry "War on war!" it is certainly the present one. Gone, as it has, through an ocean of blood and tears, such as was perhaps never known in the past, it has lived war's unspeakable atrocities so intensely that the recollection of so many horrors cannot but remain impressed in its memory and in the depths of its soul, like the image of a hell upon which anyone who nourishes humane sentiments in his heart can have no more ardent wish than to close the door forever.

Without doubt the progress of human inventions, which was to mark the crystallization of greater welfare for the whole of humanity, has instead been directed to the destruction of what had been built up by the centuries. But this very thing has rendered more and more evident the immorality of wars of aggression. And if now to the recognition of this immorality there will be added the threat of a judicial intervention of the nations and of a punishment inflicted on the aggressor by the United Nations, so that war may always feel itself proscribed, always under the watchful guard of preventive action, then humanity, issuing from the dark night in which it has been submerged for so

† Broadcast to the World (Easter 1956).

great a length of time, will be able to greet the dawn of a new and better era in its history.‡

Nothing Is Lost with Peace

It is with the force of reason, not with that of armaments, that Justice makes its advances. And empires not founded on Justice are not blessed by God. A policy emancipated from morality betrays those themselves who want it so.

Nothing is lost with peace. Everything may be lost with war. Let men come again to understand one another. Negotiating with good will and with respect for their reciprocal rights, they will perceive that honorable success is never precluded to sincere and constructive negotiations.

And they will feel great—with true greatness—if, silencing the voice of passion, both collective and private, and leaving the dominance to reason, they shall have spared the blood of their brothers and spared their country ruins.

May it please the Almighty that the voice of this Father of the Christian family, of this Servant of servants who, unworthily indeed, but really, brings among men the person of Jesus Christ, His word and authority, may find a prompt and willing acceptance in minds and hearts.

Let the strong hear Us, so that they may not become weak in injustice. Let the powerful hear Us if they want their power to be, not destruction, but support for peoples and a safeguard in orderliness and work.

We entreat them through the blood of Christ, whose conquering force in the world was meekness in life and death. And, entreating them, We know and feel that with Us are all the righteous of heart; all those who thirst and hunger for justice; all those who suffer already every pain on account of the afflictions of life. We have with Us the hearts of mothers, which beat in Ours; fathers, who would have to leave their families; the humble, who work and know not; the innocent, over whom hangs a tremendous menace; young men, gallant knights with the purest and noblest ideals. And with Us is all humanity, which awaits justice, bread, freedom, not the sword that kills and destroys. With Us is that Christ who of brotherly love made His Commandment, fundamental,

‡ Broadcast to the World (December 24, 1943).

solemn; the substance of His religion, the promise of salvation for individuals and nations.†

War in Self-Defense

We, as head of the Church, have up to now avoided, just as We did in previous cases, calling Christendom to a crusade. We can, however, call for full understanding of the fact that, where religion is a vital living heritage, men do look upon the struggle unjustly forced on them by their enemy as a crusade.

If unpleasant realities force Us to set forth the terms of the struggle in clear language, no one can properly accuse Us of favoring the stiffening of opposing blocs, and still less of having in some fashion abandoned that mission of peace which flows from Our apostolic office. Rather, if We kept silence We would have to fear the judgment of God. We remain closely allied to the cause of peace, and God alone knows how much We yearn to be able to announce it in full and happy tones with the angels of Christmas.

We are convinced that today, too, in face of an enemy determined to impose on all peoples, in one way or another, a special and intolerable way of life, only the unanimous and courageous behavior of all who love the truth and the good can preserve peace, and will preserve it.

It would be a fatal error to repeat what, in similar circumstances, happened during the years preceding the Second World War, when all the threatened nations, and not merely the smallest, sought their safety at the expense of others, using them as shields, so to speak, and even seeking very questionable economic and political advantages from their neighbors' suffering. In the end all together were overwhelmed in the holocaust.

Hence a definite need of this period—a means of ensuring the whole world's peace and a fruitful share of its goods, a force which embraces, too, the peoples of Asia, Africa, the Near East, Palestine with its Holy Places—is the restoring of European solidarity. But this unity is not assured until all the associated nations realize that the political and economic defeats of one can nowhere, in the long run, result in true gains for the others.

† Broadcast to the World (August 24, 1939).

A good course of action can never be had by mere sentiment; much less can a true political course for today be maintained with the sentiments of yesterday and the day before. Under such influence it would be impossible to judge correctly certain important questions, such as military service, weapons, war.

Present-day conditions, which find no counterparts in the past, should be clear to everyone. There is no longer room for doubt concerning the aims and methods which rely on tanks, when these latter noisily crash over borders, sowing death in order to force civilian peoples into a pattern of life they explicitly detest; when, destroying, as it were, the stages of possible negotiation and mediation, the threat is made of using atomic weapons to gain certain demands, be they justified or not.

It is clear that in the present circumstances a situation may arise in a nation wherein, after every effort to avoid war has been expended in vain, war—for effective self-defense and with the hope of a favorable outcome against unjust attack—could not be considered unlawful.

If, therefore, a body representative of the people and a government—both having been chosen by free elections—in a moment of extreme danger decide, by legitimate instruments of internal and external policy, on defensive precautions, and carry out the plans which they consider necessary, they do not act immorally; so that a Catholic citizen cannot invoke his own conscience in order to refuse to serve and fulfill those duties the law imposes. On this matter We feel that We are in perfect harmony with Our predecessors.

The United Nations

There are, then, occasions and times in the life of nations in which only recourse to higher principles can establish clearly the boundaries between right and wrong, between what is lawful and what is immoral, and bring peace to consciences faced with grave decisions. It is therefore consoling that in some countries, amid today's debates, men are talking about conscience and its demands.

Although the program which is at the foundation of the United Nations aims at the realization of absolute values in the co-existence of peoples, the recent past has shown that a false realism is making headway among not a few of its members, even where it is a question of restoring respect for those values of human society which are openly trampled upon.

The unilateral view, which tends to work in the various circumstances only according to personal interest and power, is succeeding in bringing about accusations of destroying the peace.

No one expects or demands the impossible, not even from the United Nations; but one should have a right to expect that their authority should have had its weight, at least through observers, in the places in which the basic values of man are in extreme danger.

Although the United Nations' condemnation of the grave violations of the rights of men and of entire nations is worthy of recognition, one may nevertheless wish that, in similar cases, the exercise of their rights, as members of this organization, be denied to States which refuse even the admission of observers—thus showing that their concept of State sovereignty threatens the very foundations of the United Nations.

This organization ought also to have the right and the power of forestalling all military intervention of one State in another, whatever the pretext under which it is effected, and also the right and power of assuming, by means of a sufficient police force, the safeguarding of order in the State which is threatened.

If We allude to these defects, it is because We desire to see the authority of the United Nations strengthened, especially for effecting general disarmament, which We have so much at heart. In fact, only in the ambit of an institution like the United Nations can the promise of individual nations to reduce armaments, especially to abandon production and use of certain weapons, be mutually exchanged under the strict obligation of international law.

Control of Armaments

Likewise only the United Nations is at present in a position to exact the observance of this obligation by assuming effective control of the armaments of all nations without exception.

Its exercise of aerial observation will assure certain and effective knowledge of the production and military preparedness for war with relative ease, while avoiding the disadvantages which the presence of foreign troops in a country can give rise to. Indeed, it approaches almost the miraculous, what technical science has been able to attain in this field.

The experiments conducted have given exceptionally important results, permitting one to produce concrete evidence of machines, individual persons, and objects existing on the ground, and, at least indirectly, in subterranean places.

Research thus far has shown how very difficult it would be to camouflage movements of troops or artillery, vast stores of arms, industrial centers important for war production. If these surveys could be permanent and systematic, it would be possible to ascertain the minutest details, and thus give a solid guarantee against eventual surprises.

Acceptance of the control: this is the point crucial for victory, where every nation will show its sincere desire for peace.

The desire for peace: free man's most valuable possession, this life's inestimable treasure, peace is the fruit of men's effort, but also a precious gift of God. The Christian knows it since he has understood it at the cradle of the newborn Son of God; on His truth and on His Commandments, the supreme absolute values, all order is founded and by them guarded and rendered fruitful in works of progress and civilization.[†]

Peace Letter to President Truman

YOUR excellency: We have just received from the hands of your personal representative, Mr. Myron Taylor, Your Excellency's letter of August 6, and We hasten to express Our satisfaction and thanks for this last testimony to the desire and determination of a great and free people to dedicate themselves, with their characteristic confidence and generosity, to the noble task of strengthening the

† Broadcast to the World (December 23, 1956).

foundations of that peace for which all peoples of the earth are longing. As their chosen leader, Your Excellency seeks to enlist and cement the co-operation of every force and power which can help to accomplish this task. No one more than We will hope for its success, and for the happy achievement of the goal We pledge Our resources and earnestly beg God's assistance.

What is proposed is to ensure the foundations of a lasting peace among nations. It were indeed futile to promise long life to any building erected on shifting sands or a cracked and crumbling base. The foundations, We know, of such a peace—the truth finds expression once again in Your Excellency's letter—can be secure only if they rest on bedrock faith in the one, true God, Creator of all men. The task, then, before the friends of peace is clear.

Is Your Excellency oversanguine in hoping to find men throughout the world ready to co-operate in such a worthy enterprise? We think not. Truth has lost none of its power to rally to its cause the most enlightened minds and noblest spirits. Their ardor is fed by the flame of righteous freedom struggling to break through injustice and lying. But those who possess the truth must be conscientious to define it clearly when its foes cleverly distort it, bold to defend it, and generous enough to set the course of their lives, both national and personal, by its dictates. This will require, moreover, correcting not a few aberrations. Social injustices, racial injustices, and religious animosities exist today among men and groups who boast of Christian civilization, and they are a very useful and often effective weapon in the hands of those who are bent on destroying all the good which that civilization has brought to man. It is for all sincere lovers of the great human family to unite in wresting those weapons from hostile hands. With that union will come hope that the enemies of God and free men will not prevail.

Certainly Your Excellency and all the defenders of the rights of the human person will find wholehearted co-operation from God's Church. Faithful custodian of eternal Truth and loving mother of all, from her foundation almost two thousand years ago, she has championed the individual against despotic rule, the laborer against oppression, religion against persecution. Her divinely given mission often brings her into conflict with the powers of evil, whose sole strength is in their physical force and brutalized spirit, and her leaders are sent into exile or cast into prison or die under torture. This is history of today. But the Church is unafraid. She cannot compromise with an avowed enemy of

God. She must continue to teach the first and greatest commandment incumbent on every man: "Thou shalt love the Lord thy God with thy whole heart, with thy whole soul, with thy whole strength," and the second is like unto the first: "Thou shalt love thy neighbor as thyself." It is her changeless message, that man's first duty is to God, then to his fellow man; that that man serves his country best who serves his God most faithfully; that the country that would shackle the word of God given to men through Jesus Christ helps not at all the lasting peace of the world. In striving with all the resources in her power to bring men and nations to a clear realization of their duty to God, the Church will go on, as she has always done, to offer the most effective contribution to the world's peace and man's eternal salvation.

We are pleased that Your Excellency's letter has given Us the opportunity of saying a word of encouragement for all those who are gravely intent on buttressing the fragile structure of peace until its foundation can be more firmly and wisely established. The munificent charity shown by the American people to the suffering and oppressed in every part of the world, truly worthy of the finest Christian traditions, is a fair token of their sincere desire for universal peace and prosperity. The vast majority of the peoples of the world, We feel sure, share that desire, even in countries where free expression is smothered. God grant that their forces may be united toward its realization...

Let Us assure Your Excellency of Our cordial welcome to Mr. Taylor, your personal representative, on his return to Rome; and We are happy to renew the expression of Our good wishes for the people of the United States, for the members of their government, and in particular for its esteemed Chief Executive.†

Atomic Weapons

HUMAN inventiveness, which was destined for quite other purposes, has developed and introduced today instruments of war so powerful as to awaken

† Letter to President Harry S. Truman (August 26, 1947).

horror in the conscience of any person of good will, especially because they do not strike armies alone but often destroy private citizens, children, women, old people, the sick, and, along with them, sacred edifices and the most celebrated artistic monuments! Who is not horrified at the thought that new cemeteries will be added to those already numerous ones of the recent conflict, and that new, smoking ruins of suburbs and cities will pile up new, tragic remains? And who does not tremble at the thought that the destruction of new riches, inevitable consequence of war, may still further aggravate that economic crisis which grips almost all the peoples of the world, especially the more humble classes?

We, who raise Our mind above the tides of human passion and who feel paternally toward the people and nations of all races, desire the safety and tranquil security and daily increase of prosperity; each time We see the clear sky darken with threatening clouds and new dangers of conflict weigh upon humanity, We cannot refrain from raising Our voice to exhort all to put an end to disagreements, to make up differences, and to install that true peace which assures the rights of religion, of peoples, of individual citizens, publicly and sincerely recognized, as is necessary.

However, We know well that human means are inadequate to such a high purpose; what is needed, before all, is a renewal of conscience, a repression of passions, calming of hatreds, truly putting into practice the norms of justice, arriving at a more equitable distribution of wealth, stimulating reciprocal charity, urging all to virtue. To reach such a great objective, unquestionably, nothing can be more helpful than the Christian religion. Its divine doctrine teaches that men are brothers and make up one same family of which God is the Father, Christ is the Redeemer and Vivifier with His celestial grace, and whose immortal homeland is Heaven. If these divine teachings were truly practiced, then most certainly neither wars, discords, disorders, nor violations of civil and religious liberty would make public and private life sorrowful; rather, a tranquil serenity, founded on justice, would flood all hearts and the way would be open to the achievement of an always greater prosperity.

This is arduous, indeed, but necessary. And if it is necessary then there must be no delay and it must be put into practice immediately. And if it is arduous and above human strength, then it is necessary to turn with prayer and supplication to the Celestial Father, as in the course of the centuries, in every sort of difficulty, our ancestors always did, to their profit.†

Let there be punishment on an international scale for every war not called for by absolute necessity. The only constraint to wage war is defense against an injustice of the utmost gravity which strikes the entire community and which cannot be coped with by any other means—for otherwise one would give free course, in international relations, to brutal violence and irresponsibility. Defending oneself against any kind of injustice, however, is not sufficient reason to resort to war. When the losses that it brings are not comparable to those of the "injustice tolerated," one may have the obligation of "submitting to the injustice."

This is particularly applicable to the A.B.C. war (atomic, biological, chemical). It suffices now to ask ourselves if war may become necessary as a defense against an A.B.C. war. The answer will derive from the same principles which are decisive in determining the justification of war in general. In any case, another question poses itself first of all: Is it not possible, through international agreement, to outlaw and efficaciously avoid A.B.C. warfare?

After the horrors of the two world wars, We can only repeat that any kind of glorification of war must be condemned as an aberration of the intellect and the heart. Certainly, courage and devotion carried to point of giving one's life, when duty demands it, are great virtues; but to want to provoke war because it is the school of great virtues and an occasion to practice them, should be considered crime and folly.

What We have said indicates the right direction in which to find the answer to this other question: May the doctor place his science and activity in the service of A.B.C. war? He must never give support to an "injustice," even in the service of his own country; and when this type of war constitutes an injustice, the doctor cannot take part in it.‡

---

† Encyclical *Mirabile Illud* (December 6, 1950).

‡ Address to Military Doctors (October 19, 1953).

Technology and Materialism

Doubtless, technology leads contemporary man toward a peak never before achieved in the domination of the material world. The modern machine makes possible a method of production which substitutes and magnifies the energy of human labor, which frees itself entirely from the contribution of organic forces and assures a maximum of extensive and intensive potential and of precision at the same time…

Technological Thinking

However, it seems undeniable that technology itself, having reached the peak of its splendor and achievement in our century, may, through outward circumstance, become transformed into a grave spiritual peril. To modern man, prone before its altar, it seems to communicate a sense of self-sufficiency and of satisfaction with his aspirations for boundless knowledge and power. With its multiple uses, with the absolute confidence it inspires, with the inexhaustible possibilities it promises, modern technology unfolds before contemporary man a vision so vast as to be confused by many with the infinite itself. As a consequence, one attributes to it an impossible autonomy, which in turn is transformed in the minds of some into an erroneous conception of life and of the world, designated as "technological thinking." But in what, precisely, does this consist? In this: that it is considered the highest value of man and of life to draw the greatest profit and power from the forces and elements of nature; that, in preference to all other human pursuits, one elects as the most coveted objective the development of technical processes for mechanical production, and that in them is seen the perfection of civilization and happiness on earth.

There is, first of all, a fundamental deception in this distorted vision of the world offered by "technological thinking." The panorama, at first sight endless, which technology spreads before the eyes of modern man, however vast it may be, remains nonetheless but a partial projection of life upon reality, expressing only reality's relationship to matter. A fascinating panorama, no doubt, which, however, in the end, encloses the man who too easily believes in the immensity and the omnipotence of technology, in a prison which is vast, it is true, but circumscribed, and therefore in the long run unbearable to man's genuine spirituality. His glance, far from reaching toward infinite reality, which is not material only, will feel mortified by the barriers which are necessarily raised before him. From this springs the hidden anxiety of contemporary man, become blind from having voluntarily surrounded himself with darkness.

Far more serious are the damages caused by "technological thinking," in the man who allows himself to become intoxicated by it, in the sphere of religious truth and in his relations with the supernatural. These, too, are the shadows to which the Evangelist St. John alludes, which the Incarnate Word of God has come to dissipate, and which impede the spiritual understanding of the mysteries of God.

Not that technology in itself, as a logical consequence, requires the renunciation of religious values—on the contrary, as We have said, it leads rather to their discovery—but that "technological thinking" places man in a condition detrimental to the searching, seeing, and accepting of supernatural truths and benefits. The mind which allows itself to be seduced by the conception of life mirrored in "technological thinking" remains insensible, unresponsive, and finally blind before those works of God, by their nature wholly different from technology, such as are the mysteries of the Christian faith. The remedy itself, which would consist in a redoubled effort to extend one's gaze beyond the barrier of darkness and stimulate in the soul the interest for supernatural realities, is rendered inefficacious from the start by the same technological approach, because it deprives man of a critical appraisal of the singular restlessness and superficiality of our times: a defect which even those who truly and sincerely approve technical progress must nonetheless recognize as one of its consequences. Men imbued with the technological spirit hardly ever find the calm, the serenity and interior life needed to be able to see the way which leads to the Son of God, become man.

They will even reach the point of defaming the Creator and His works, declaring human nature to be a defective instrument, if the active capacity of the brain and the other human organs, necessarily limited, impedes the realization of technological calculations and projects. Still less are they able to understand and esteem the lofty mysteries of divine life and economy, as, for example, the mystery of Christmas, in which the union of the Eternal Word with human nature achieves realities and greatness of a very different order from those considered by technology. Their thinking follows other ways and methods under the unilateral suggestion of that "technological thinking" which does not recognize and does not appreciate as reality anything except what can be expressed in figures and calculations. In this way they believe they can break down reality into its elements, but their understanding remains on the surface and moves in only one direction. It is evident that he who adopts the technological method as the sole instrument of research for truth must renounce penetrating, for example, the profound realities of organic life, and still more those of spiritual life, the living realities of the individual and of human society, because these cannot be broken down into quantitative relations. How can one pretend to gain, from a mind so formed, assent and admiration before the imposing reality to which we have been elevated by Jesus Christ, through His incarnation, redemption, revelation, and grace?

Quite apart from the religious blindness which derives from "technological thinking," the man possessed by it becomes handicapped in his reasoning, precisely because he is the image of God. God is infinitely comprehensive intelligence, whereas "technological thinking" does everything possible to restrain in man the free expansion of his intellect. To the technologist, teacher or pupil, who wishes to save himself from this handicap, it is not enough to wish for an informed and profound education of the mind; what he needs, above all, is a religious formation which, contrary to what has been sometimes affirmed, is the most capable of protecting his thinking from unilateral influences. Then the narrowness of his knowledge will be shattered; then creation will appear illuminated to him in all its dimensions. Otherwise, the technological era will perform its monstrous masterpiece of transforming man into a giant of the physical world at the expense of his spirit, reduced to a pygmy of the supernatural and eternal world.

But the influence exerted by technological progress does not stop here, once it has been received in the consciousness as something autonomous and an end to itself. The danger of a "technological concept of life" escapes no one, that is, the danger of considering life exclusively for its technological values, as a technological element and factor. Its influence affects both the manner of living of modern men and their reciprocal relations.

Observe it for a moment, active in the people, among whom it is already spreading, and reflect particularly on how it has altered the human and Christian concept of labor, and what influence it exerts on legislation and administration. The people have received technical progress with favor, and rightly so, because it alleviates the burden of labor and increases productivity. But it must also be confessed that if this feeling is not contained within its just limits, the human and Christian concept of work is necessarily damaged. Equally, from a mistaken technical concept of life, and hence of labor, derives the considering of leisure as an end in itself, rather than regarding and using it as the necessary relief and rest, linked essentially to the rhythm of an ordered life, in which rest and labor alternate in a single texture, and integrate each other in a common harmony.

More visible is the influence of the "technological spirit" applied to labor, when Sunday is deprived of its singular dignity as the day of divine worship and of physical and spiritual rest for individuals and the family, and becomes instead only one of the free days in the course of the week, which can also be different for each member of the family, according to the greater returns that it is hoped to gain from such a technical distribution of material and human energy; or again, when professional labor becomes so conditioned and subjected to the "functioning" of the machine and other instruments, as rapidly to wear out the laborer, as if a year's practice of his profession had exhausted the strength of two or more years of his normal life.

We cannot omit drawing attention to the new form of materialism which the "technological spirit" introduces into life. It is enough to mention that this spirit empties life of its content, since technology is ordered to man and to the complex of material and spiritual values which are part of his nature and his personal dignity. Should the technological spirit reign autonomous, human society would be transformed into a colorless multitude, into something impersonal and mechanical, and therefore contrary to what nature and its Creator have demonstrably willed.

No doubt, a great part of humanity has not been touched yet by this "technological conception of life"; but it is to be feared that wherever technical progress enters without any controls, the danger of the aforementioned deformations will not delay in appearing. And We think with particular anxiety of the danger threatening the family, which in social life is the most solid principle of order, since it knows how to stimulate among its members innumerable personal tasks which are daily renewed, ties them with bonds of affection to house and home, and awakens in each of them love of family tradition in the production and preservation of common goods. On the other hand, where the technological concept of life penetrates, the family loses the personal tie of its unity, loses its warmth and stability.

The "technological concept of life" is therefore nothing else but a particular form of materialism, in that it offers as a final answer to the question of existence a mathematical formula and a utilitarian calculation. For this reason, modern technological development, as if aware of being enveloped by darkness, manifests uncertainties and anxiety, especially noticeable in the measures taken by those who busy themselves in the feverish research for continually more complicated and more risky systems. A world so guided cannot consider itself illumined by that light, nor animated by that life, which the Word, splendor of the glory of God, become man, has come to communicate to all men.

Religion and Life

In the dawning of the history of the Church, during the reign of Trajan, St. Ignatius of Antioch set down a thought fascinating to modern souls as well, as the discovery of a treasure of experience from two thousand years ago: "In times in which it is an object of hate, Christianity is not a matter of persuasive words, but of greatness."

Truly, in the religious crisis of our times—the gravest, perhaps, that humanity has passed through since the origins of Christianity—the reasoned and scientific exposition of the truths of faith, however efficacious it may be and is in reality, is not enough. Nor suffices the often skimpy measure of a Christian life nourished merely from conventional habits. What is necessary today is the greatness of a Christianity lived in its fullness with persevering constancy; what is necessary is the vigorous and valorous host of Christian men and women who, living in the midst of the world, are ready at every instant to fight for their faith, for the law of God, for Christ, their eyes fixed on Him as a model to imitate, as a leader to follow in their apostolic work.

Quite recently, Christianity has been advised (if it intends to maintain a certain importance, and if it wishes to overcome its static period) to adapt itself to modern life and thought, to scientific discoveries, and to the extraordinary power of technological resources in the face of which historical forms and their old dogmas are merely dimming lights of the past on the verge of going out.

What an error this is, and how it lays bare the vain illusions of superficial minds! They seem to want the Church to enter into the narrow forms of purely human organizations. As if the new configuration of the world, as if the present domain of science and technology, occupied the entire field and no longer left any space free for supernatural life, which flows out from every side! Those marvelous discoveries (which the Church favors and promotes) do not suffice to abolish and absorb her; on the contrary, they bring to light, with greater force and effect than before, the "eternal power of God."

But modern thought and life must be led back and won over to Christ again. Christ, His truth, His grace, are no less necessary to the humanity of our times than to that of yesterday and the day before, and of all the centuries past and future. He is the only source of salvation.

The desire to draw a clear line of distinction between religion and life, between the supernatural and the natural, between the Church and the world, as if these had nothing whatsoever to do with each other, as if the rights of God did not have value in all the multiform reality of daily human and social life, is completely alien to Catholic thought, is openly anti-Christian. Therefore, so long as dark powers increase their pressure, so long as they make every attempt to banish the Church and religion from the world and from life, it is all the more necessary on the part of the Church herself to conduct a tenacious and persevering action in order to reconquer and submit all the fields of human life to the gentle reign of Christ, so that His spirit may breathe more fully in it, His law reign more sovereignly, His love triumph more victoriously. This is what must be understood by the Reign of Christ.

This office of the Church is most arduous; but it is only the disillusioned deserters without conscience who, in homage to a misunderstood supernaturalism, would like to reduce the Church to a "purely religious" sphere, as they say, while by doing so they only favor the hand of their adversaries.[†]

† Allocution to the Sacred College (December 24, 1953).

On the Establishment of the Hierarchy in the United States

In Our desire to enrich the crown of your holy joy We cross in spirit the vast spaces of the seas and find Ourselves in your midst as you celebrate the one hundred and fiftieth anniversary of the establishment of the ecclesiastical hierarchy in the United States of America. And this We do with great gladness, because an occasion is thus afforded Us, as gratifying as it is solemn, of giving public testimony of Our esteem and Our affection for the youthfully vigorous and illustrious American people.

When Pope Pius VI gave you your first Bishop in the person of the American, John Carroll, and set him over the See of Baltimore, small and of slight importance was the Catholic population of your land. At that time, too, the condition of the United States was so perilous that its structure and its very political unity were threatened by grave crisis. Because of the long and exhausting war the public treasury was burdened with debt, industry languished, and the citizenry, wearied by misfortunes, was split into contending parties. This ruinous and critical state of affairs was put to rights by George Washington, famed for his courage and keen intelligence. He was a close friend of the Bishop of Baltimore. Thus the Father of His Country and the pioneer pastor of the Church in that land so dear to Us, bound together by the ties of friendship and clasping, so to speak, each the other's hand, form a picture for their descendants, a lesson to all future generations, and a proof that reverence for the Faith of Christ is a holy and established principle of the American people, seeing that it is the foundation of morality and decency, consequently the source of prosperity and progress.

We cannot refrain from a public expression of praise for those missionary enterprises proper to your own nation which devote themselves with zeal and energy to the wider diffusion of the Catholic Faith...

We confess that We feel a special paternal affection, which is certainly inspired by Heaven, for the Negro people dwelling among you; for in the field of religion and education We know they need special care and comfort and are very deserving of it. We therefore invoke an abundance of heavenly blessing, and We pray fruitful success for those whose generous zeal is devoted to their welfare.

You well know where it is necessary that you exercise a more discerning vigilance and what program of action should be marked out for priests and faithful in order that the religion of Christ may overcome the obstacles in its path and be a luminous guide to the minds of men, govern their morals, and, for the sole purpose of salvation, permeate the marrow and the arteries of human society. The progress of exterior and material possessions, even though it is to be considered of no little account, because of the manifold and appreciable utility which it gives to life is nonetheless not enough for man, who is born for higher and brighter destinies...

Social Relations

We desire to touch upon another question of weighty importance, the social question, which, remaining unsolved, has been agitating States for a long time and sowing among the classes the seeds of hatred and mutual hostility. You know full well what aspect it assumes in America, what acrimonies, what disorders it produces. It is not necessary therefore that We dwell on these points. The fundamental point of the social question is this, that the goods created by God for all men should in the same way reach all, justice guiding and charity helping. The history of every age teaches that there were always rich and poor; that it will always be so we may gather from the unchanging tenor of human destinies. Worthy of honor are the poor who fear God because theirs is the Kingdom of Heaven and because they readily abound in spiritual graces. But the rich, if they are upright and honest, are God's dispensers and providers of this world's goods; as ministers of divine Providence they assist the indigent through whom they often receive gifts for the soul and whose hand—so they may hope—will lead them into the eternal tabernacles.

God, who provides for all with counsels of supreme bounty, has ordained that for the exercise of virtues and for the testing of one's worth there be in the world rich and poor; but He does not wish that some have exaggerated riches while others are in such straits that they lack the bare necessities of life.

Now if the rich and the prosperous are obliged out of ordinary motives of pity to act generously toward the poor their obligation is all the greater to do them justice. The salaries of the workers, as is just, are to be such that they are sufficient to maintain them and their families. Solemn are the words of Our predecessor, Pius XI, on this question: "Every effort must therefore be made that fathers of families receive a wage sufficient to meet adequately normal domestic needs. If under present circumstances this is not always feasible, social justice demands that reforms be introduced without delay which will guarantee such a wage to every adult workingman. In this connection We praise those who have most prudently and usefully attempted various methods by which an increased wage is paid in view of increased family burdens and special provision made for special needs" (Encyclical *Quadragesimo Anno*).

Because a social relation is one of man's natural requirements and since it is legitimate to promote by common effort decent livelihood, it is not possible without injustice to deny or to limit either to the producers or to the laboring and farming classes the free faculty of uniting in associations by means of which they may defend their proper rights and secure the betterment of the goods of soul and of body, as well as the honest comforts of life.

But let the unions in question draw their vital force from principles of wholesome liberty; let them take their form from the lofty rules of justice and of honesty, and, conforming themselves to those norms, let them act in such a manner that in their care for the interests of their class they violate no one's rights; let them continue to strive for harmony and respect the common weal of civil society.

What a proud vaunt it will be for the American people, by nature inclined to grandiose undertakings and to liberality, if they untie the knotty and difficult social question by following the sure paths illuminated by the light of the Gospel and thus lay the basis of a happier age![†]

To the Christians in Russia

When the last terrible conflict broke out, We did everything within Our possibilities, by word, exhortation, and action, to contribute toward the end

† Encyclical *Sertum Laetitiae* (Feast of All Saints, 1939).

of dissensions with an equitable and just peace, and that all peoples, regardless of differences of race, might unite in friendship and brotherly love and collaborate with one another to reach greater prosperity. Never, in those times, did We utter one word that might seem unjust or harsh to any group among the belligerents. We did, of course, as is Our duty, censure any iniquity and any violation of law; but We did this in such a way as to avoid scrupulously anything that would add to the afflictions of the oppressed peoples. And when from some sides pressure was brought to bear upon Us to induce Us to approve, in any way, by voice or in writing, the war waged against Russia in 1941, We never consented to do this, as We stated openly on February 25, 1946, in the allocution addressed to the Sacred College and all diplomatic representatives to the Holy See.

When there is question of defending the cause of religion, truth, justice, and Christian civilization, We certainly cannot be silent; but Our thoughts and Our intentions have always this aim in view: that not by force of arms, but by the majesty of law, should all peoples be governed; and that each of them, in possession of civil and religious freedom within the boundaries of their own country, should be led toward concord and peace... Our words and Our exhortations did and do concern all the nations, and therefore you too, who are always present in Our heart, and whose pressing needs and calamities We desire to alleviate as much as is within Our power. Those who love truth and not falsehood know that throughout the course of the recent conflict We showed Ourselves impartial toward all the belligerents, and We often gave proof of this with words and deeds; and in Our ardent charity We have embraced all nations, even those whose rulers profess to be enemies of the Apostolic See, and those, too, in which the enemies of God are fiercely opposed to Christianity or divinity, and seek to blot it out from the minds of the citizens. For by Christ's mandate, which entrusted the whole flock of Christian people to St. Peter, the Prince of Apostles—whose unworthy successor We are—We love all peoples intensely and desire to procure for all of them prosperity on earth, and eternal salvation. All of them, therefore, whether in armed warfare with one another or separated by grave dissensions, are considered by Us as so many beloved children; and We desire nothing else, We pray to God for nothing else for them, than mutual concord, just and real peace, and ever greater prosperity.

What is more, if some of them, led astray by lies and calumnies, openly declare their hostility to Us, We feel for them a greater commiseration and a more ardent affection.

We have, it is true, condemned and rejected, as the duty of Our office demands, the errors that the upholders of atheistic Communism teach and try to spread, to the great detriment of nations; but, far from rejecting the erring, We want them to return to truth and to be led back on the right road. We have also unmasked and condemned those lies that were often presented in the false guise of truth, precisely because We cherish paternal affection for you and seek your welfare. For We are firmly convinced that nothing but great harm will come to you from these errors, and that they not only deprive your souls of that supernatural light and those supreme comforts that piety and worship of God bestow, but also strip you of human dignity and of that just freedom which is every citizen's birthright.

We are aware that many of you cling to the Christian faith in the sanctuary of your conscience, that in no way do you allow yourselves to be induced to favor the enemies of religion, but that, on the contrary, it is your ardent desire to profess the precepts of Christianity, the only sure foundation of civil life, not only in private but, if it were possible, as it should be for all free people, also openly. And We know, too—and this gives Us hope and great comfort—that you love and honor with eager affection the Virgin Mary, Mother of God, and that you venerate Her sacred images. We know that in the Kremlin itself a temple was built—today, unfortunately, no longer used for divine worship—dedicated to the Most Holy Mary assumed into Heaven; and this is evident proof of the love your ancestors and you bear the Great Mother of God.

Russia and the Mother of God

Now, We know that where people turn with sincere and ardent piety toward the Most Holy Mother of God, there is always hope of salvation. In fact, though men, however impious and powerful, seek to uproot from the hearts of the citizens holy religion and Christian virtue, though Satan himself strive to foster with every means this sacrilegious struggle, in accordance with the saying of the Apostle of the peoples: "For our wrestling is not against flesh and blood, but against the principalities and the powers, against the world rulers of this darkness, against the spiritual forces of wickedness on high...," yet, if Mary intervenes with her support, the gates of Hell will not prevail. For She is the benign and powerful Mother of God and of all of us, and never has it happened in the world that anyone has turned to Her in supplication without experiencing Her all-powerful intercession. Go on, then, as is your wont, venerating Her with fervent piety, loving Her ardently, and invoking Her with these words, which are familiar to you: "To thee alone it has been granted, most holy and pure Mother of God, never to be refused."

We, too, together with you raise to Her Our supplicant invocations, that the Christian truth, the adornment and support of human society, may flourish and gain vigor among the peoples of Russia, and that all the deceptions of the enemies of religion, all their errors and deceitful tricks, may be rejected by you; that public and private conduct may once more conform to evangelical standards; that those especially among you who profess the Catholic faith, although deprived of their shepherds, may intrepidly resist the assaults of impiety, if it is necessary, even unto death, so that just freedom which is the heritage of the human being, of citizens and of Christians, may be restored to all, as is their due, and in the first place to the Church, who has the divine mandate of bringing up mankind in religious truths and in virtue; and, last of all, that true peace may shine upon the whole of humanity, and that this peace, founded on justice and fed on charity, may successfully guide all the nations toward that general prosperity of citizens and peoples which springs from mutual concord.

May our loving Mother deign to look with benign eyes also at those who are organizing the forces of militant atheists and encouraging their initiatives in every way. May She illuminate their minds with the light that comes from above, and direct with divine grace their hearts to salvation.

And We humbly beg the most merciful Mother to assist each one of you in the present calamities, and to obtain from Her divine Son that light that comes from Heaven for your minds, and to stamp upon your souls that virtue and that strength which will enable you, supported by divine grace, victoriously to overcome impiety and error.[†]

† Apostolic Letter *Sacro Vergente Anno* (July 7, 1952).

The Church Suffering Persecution in Central and Eastern Europe

WHILE with heavy heart We consider the grave trials the Catholic Church is suffering in many lands at the hands of atheistic materialism in control there, Our thoughts turn to the situation prevailing in Central Europe five centuries ago, which occasioned the Apostolic Letter *Cum his superioribus annis* of Our predecessor of immortal memory, Callistus III, on June 29, 1456.

A grave danger threatened, where it had not already befallen, the Christian peoples dwelling in the fruitful regions washed by the Danube River, and the surrounding lands, a danger to their lives, their property, their very faith. This was especially the case of Hungary and the lands today called Albania, Bulgaria, Czechoslovakia, Yugoslavia, Rumania; threatened, too, were those who lived in more distant regions, especially the Germans and Poles. Taking account of that crisis, the tireless Pontiff Callistus III saw it as his duty to exhort paternally the Catholic shepherds and flocks to repent and expiate their own sins, to reform their customs in accord with Christian moral principles, to invoke God's powerful aid through fervent prayer. Moreover, the Pontiff labored with tireless energy to remove by every possible means the danger threatening the Church's children; he attributed to divine help the victory finally won by those who—under the inspiration of St. John Capistrano and the military leadership of John Hunyady—so strenuously defended the fortress of Belgrade. To commemorate this event in the Liturgy, and to give due thanks to God, the feast of the Transfiguration of our Lord Jesus Christ was instituted, to be celebrated throughout the world on August 6th.[†]

Today, also, alas, you who dwell in those countries We have mentioned suffer grievous conditions, along with many other Catholics of the Eastern as well as of the Latin rite, whose boundaries are east of your own, or north, along the Baltic coast. More than ten years have passed, as you know by experience, since Christ's Church was stripped of her rights, though not in the same way everywhere. Pious associations and religious groups were dissolved and scattered, and shepherds, either hindered from exercising their office or forced from their sees, have been sent into exile, or jailed. The Catholic

† Cf. Apostolic Letter, *Inter divinae dispositionis* (August 6, 1457).

dioceses of the Eastern Rite also have been recklessly suppressed, and their clergy and faithful urged by every ruse to schism. We know, moreover, that many have been bitterly persecuted for their fearless, sincere, and courageous efforts to profess and defend their faith. Our greatest grief springs from the realization that the minds of children and youth are being steeped in false and perverse doctrines, so they may be separated from God and His divine precepts to their great loss here below and to the danger of their eternal salvation.

We, who by divine Providence sit upon the throne of Peter, contemplate this sad, sad vision, which We have already commented on in previous Apostolic Letters; and We cannot in conscience remain silent today. For We must obey that grave, yet sweet, command Christ our Lord gave to the Prince of the Apostles and to his successors: "Strengthen thy brethren" (Luke 22:32). We, too, must be faithful in fulfilling it; hence again and again do We wish to strengthen your holy determination and show you Our affection, you who, in your loyalty to and love for Christ, bear so many sorrows and trials, and such anguish.

Our eyes and heart turn to Our Venerable Brothers in the episcopacy, who are distinguished for their active fidelity to the Apostolic See; to the priests also, both secular, as they say, and religious, and to the phalanx of all those men and women consecrated to the divine service, and finally to all the other beloved sons and daughters who under so many and such great difficulties are defending and advancing as far as they can the peaceful and peace-bringing Kingdom of Jesus Christ. In Our solicitude for you who have for the cause of Christ endured suffering, sacrifice, and loss, We offer daily prayer and supplication to Almighty God that in His merciful kindness He will sustain and strengthen your faith, that He will alleviate your sorrow, that He will console you with heavenly blessings, that He will heal perfectly the afflicted and ailing members of the mystical body of Christ, and that finally, when this present storm has passed, He will command to shine forth among you, among all peoples, a true and serene peace which will be fostered by truth, justice, and charity.

Never, as you know so well, does our Redeemer forget His Church. Never does He abandon it. Rather the more the Bark of Peter is tossed by the raging waves, the more the Divine Pilot is vigilant, although at times He seems to sleep (cf. Matt. 8:24; Luke 8:23). Meditate daily on His promise which pours certain hope and solace into the souls of Christians when they are especially harassed: "I am with you all days even unto the consummation of the world" (Matt. 28:20); and, "if God is for us who is against us?" (Rom. 8:31). Christ, therefore, is with you. He will never deny His help to you if you ask it. And yet He demands from all that they obey diligently and perfectly the precepts of the Catholic Church, and that they preserve with magnanimous heart their faith. You know what is at stake: it is your eternal salvation and the salvation of your children and neighbors, which today, owing to the ever growing course of atheism, is placed in the gravest peril.

But in this spiritual struggle if each and every one shows strength and loyalty in the fight—as We trust they will—they may be glorious victims but never conquered. Thus from unjust persecution and the sufferings of martyrs will be born new triumphs of the Church, to be inscribed in her annals in letters of gold. And far from us the thought that the disciples of Jesus Christ are leaving the field of battle broken in spirit, that they are concealing or belittling the profession of their faith, that they have thrown away their arms, cowards, or are asleep while the enemy is striving to overthrow the Kingdom of God. Even if this were partly the case—which God forbid—irreparable harm and calamity would befall not only the deserters but also the Christian world.

We realize—and it is consoling to Us—that there are very many among you who with noble determination are ready to sacrifice all, even liberty and life, rather than jeopardize the integrity of the Catholic religion. We also realize that not a few of Christ's shepherds have already given to others in this an example of unconquerable fortitude. You especially, beloved Sons, Cardinals of the Holy Roman Church, have been made a spectacle to the world, to angels, and to men (cf. 1 Cor. 4:9). However, We also realize with regret that human frailty and uncertainty totters especially when these sufferings and persecutions last for a long time. For then some lose heart and their courage slackens. And, what is worse, they think that the doctrine of Christ must be mitigated and adapted, as they say, to the times and circumstances of things and places. They say it is necessary to mitigate and change the principles of the Catholic religion so that there may be a certain false union between it and the errors of the advancing age.

If some there are who, weak and bewildered, cause others to be likewise, let the pastors of the Church remind them of that solemn promise of the divine Redeemer: "Heaven and earth will pass but My words will never pass" (Matt. 24:35). Likewise it is their duty to encourage them to put their trust and confidence in Him whose Providence does not err in act and who will not deprive of His assistance those whom He has confirmed in His love (cf. *Missale Romanum*).

Never will He permit the faithful and brave children of His Church to be lacking divine grace and fortitude, and thus miserably yield to the enemy in this struggle for salvation, be unhappily drawn from the side of Christ, and helpless, contemplate the spiritual and pitiful ruin of their people.

You, however, beloved Sons, priest and lay, be always united to those whom the Holy Spirit has chosen to rule the Church of God; even though these are at the present time restrained and cannot strengthen you by their word, still religiously and faithfully reflect in mind and soul upon the exhortations which they gave you in the past. Still, though the greatest difficulties impede you, may you, compelled by apostolic zeal, generously and industriously perform all your religious duties, and above all preserve the faith intact. What is more, in so far as it lies within your power, strive earnestly that the light of Christ shall illumine all others, and above all do this through the example of constancy in your Christian life after the manner of Christians of old when the wave of persecutions broke upon the Church.

Let those who are slipping, who waver, who are weak, learn from you to fortify their spirit, to profess the faith candidly and openly, to attend to their religious duties, and to dedicate themselves entirely to Christ. The upright and vigorous forces of your soul and effective Christian piety, of which illustrious testimony has often been reported to Us, affords Us no little solace and bids Us hope that you may be able to transmit intact to future generations the most precious treasure of Christian faith and of your loyalty to the Church and the Apostolic See and establish it as a sacred heritage.

Be convinced that the entire Christian family looks with reverential awe at what you bear so long in silence, in tribulation, and in all dire straits; and turn your supplications to the most merciful God that you succumb not to the sharp blows of impiety nor to the insidious fallacies of error, but that with the strenuous fortitude of the holy martyrs you give testimony before all of your faith so that even your persecutors—the command of Christian charity extends also to them—may obtain pardon from Him who expects to embrace lovingly all His prodigal sons.[†]

The Eastern Churches

All the Eastern Churches—as history teaches—have always been loved with the tenderest affection by the Roman Pontiffs, and therefore they, hardly able to bear the separation of the East from the original fold, and driven, not indeed by human interest, but only by divine charity and by the desire for common salvation, by repeated entreaties invited these separated brothers to return as early as possible to that unity from which they had so unhappily broken away. Indeed, the same Supreme Pontiffs know well from experience the fruitful abundance which will derive from this happily reintegrated union for all Christian society, and in particular for the Eastern Churches themselves. In fact, from the full and perfect unity of all Christians there cannot but come a great increase to the mystical body of Jesus Christ and to all its individual members.

No Abandonment of Rites and Usages

In this connection it must be noted that the Eastern Churches need have no fear of being constrained, upon their return to unity of faith and government, to abandon their legitimate rites and usages; this fact Our predecessors declared openly more than once. "There is no reason to doubt, therefore, that We or Our successors will take away anything from your law, your patriarchal privileges, or from the rituals in use in each of your churches."

And although the happy day has not yet arrived in which it will be given to Us to embrace with paternal affection all the peoples of the East, once

† Apostolic Letter to the Archbishops and Bishops of Central and Eastern Europe (June 29, 1956).

more returned to the true fold, nevertheless We note with joy that not a few children of these regions, who have recognized the Chair of the Blessed Peter as the bulwark of Catholic unity, persevere tenaciously in the defense and strengthening of this unity.‡

The Eastern Churches, in more recent times, and also in Our own, have always been the particular object of Our solicitude, as everyone knows. In fact, as soon as We were elevated, without any personal merit of Ours, by the mysterious design of God, to the Chair of the Prince of Apostles, We turned Our mind and Our heart to those who "are outside the Catholic Church" and whom We ardently wish to see return as soon as possible to the fold of Our common Father, home of their ancestors. We have given other proofs of Our paternal benevolence during the course of Our Pontificate. But at present, unfortunately, additional considerations call for Our care and Our solicitude. In fact, in many regions where the Eastern rite is in general use, a new tempest has been unleashed which seeks to upset, devastate, and utterly destroy flourishing Christian communities. If, in the past centuries, some particular dogma of Catholic doctrine was attacked, today they rashly go far beyond; and they seek to eradicate from civilized society, from the family, from universities, schools, and from the life of the people everything divine or pertaining to divinity, as if these were absurd or nefarious things, and they trample upon rights, institutions, and sacred laws. We know that there are many Christians of the Eastern rite who weep bitterly at seeing their Bishops murdered or banished, or so hindered as not to be able to talk freely to their flocks or to exercise over them, as it should be, their proper authority; at seeing many of their temples put to profane uses or left in a state of the most squalid neglect; at knowing that now those who pray can no longer raise to Heaven from these temples their voices, beautifully intoned according to your liturgy, to call down the dew of heavenly grace for the elevation of minds, the consolation of hearts, and the remedy of such a great burden of afflictions.

We know that many are relegated to prisons or concentration camps, or, if they live in their own homes, they cannot exercise those sacrosanct rights which are theirs: that is, not only the right to profess their faith in the sanctuary of their conscience, but also to be able to teach it openly, to defend it and

‡ Encyclical *Orientales omnes Ecclesias* (December 23, 1945).

propagate it in the family circle, for the necessary education of the children, and in school for the upright formation of the pupil's character.

We know also, however, that the sons of the Eastern Churches, united in brotherhood with the faithful of the Latin rite, together endure with fortitude the bereavements of these persecutions, and both participate equally in the martyrdom, the triumph, and the glory which derive from it. In fact, they persevere in their faith with heroic spirit; resist the enemies of Christianity with the same indomitable strength with which their forefathers once resisted; raise their supplications to Heaven, if not publicly, at least in private; remain faithfully attached to the Roman Pontiff and to their pastors; and also venerate especially the Blessed Virgin Mary, most loving and most powerful Queen of Heaven and earth, to whose Immaculate Heart We have consecrated them all. All this is without doubt a pledge of certain victory in the future—of that victory, however, which does not spring from the blood of men in conflict with one another, which is not nourished by an unbridled desire for earthly power, but which is based upon proper and legitimate freedom; upon justice, not practiced with words alone, but also with deeds, toward citizens, peoples, and nations; upon peace and Christian charity which unite all in the bonds of friendship; upon religion, above all, which regulates conduct according to what is right, tempers private ambitions, placing them in the service of the public welfare, raises the minds to Heaven, and, finally, safeguards civilized society and concord among all.

Slander and Persecution

This constitutes the object of Our fondest hopes. Meanwhile, however, the news which comes to Us is such as to deepen the bitterness of Our grief. Day and night, with paternal solcitude, We turn Our mind and heart to those who had been entrusted to Us by divine mandate and whom We know to be treated, in some places, in such an unseemly manner as to be made the objects of slander because of their firm attachment to the Catholic faith, and to be deprived of their legitimate rights, sometimes not excluding even those so innate in human nature that, if they are violated by force, fear, or any other means, the very dignity of man is degraded.

All this is such a bitter cause of grief to Us that We cannot withhold Our tears when We pray to the most merciful God and Father of compassion that He may benevolently enlighten those responsible for so sad a situation and put an end to these many evils.

But, in the midst of so many and such great calamities which sadden Our soul and yours, We can find some reason for comfort in the news which has come to Us. In fact, it is known to Us that those who are in such deplorable and desperate circumstances remain firm in their faith with such intrepid constancy as to awaken Our admiration and that of all decent people. To all of them, therefore, goes Our paternal praise; may their strength increase, may they be firmly convinced that We, as a common Father whom the care for all the Churches moves and "the charity of Christ presses," raise fervent prayers every day that the Kingdom of Jesus Christ, herald of peace for individual souls, peoples, and nations, may triumph everywhere.

Before the unhappy spectacle of such evils, which have struck not only Our sons among the laity but above all those invested with sacerdotal dignity, precisely so that what is written in the Sacred Scripture: "They will smite the shepherd and the sheep of the flock shall be scattered," may come to pass, We cannot fail to call the attention of all to the fact that, in the course of centuries, not only among civilized peoples but also among barbarians, priests, as intermediaries between God and man, have always been regarded with proper veneration. And when the divine Redeemer, having dispelled the darkness of error, taught us the heavenly truths, and out of His great benevolence wished to make us sharers in His eternal priesthood, this veneration increased even more so that Bishops and priests were considered as most loving fathers, desirous of nothing else but the common welfare of the flock entrusted to their care.

Nevertheless the divine Redeemer Himself had said: "No disciple is above his teacher"; "If they have persecuted Me, they will persecute you also"; "Blessed are you when men reproach you and persecute you and, speaking falsely, say all manner of evil against you for My sake. Rejoice and exult, for your reward is great in Heaven."

There is, therefore, no reason to wonder if in our day, and perhaps more than in past centuries, the Church of Jesus Christ and especially His ministers are stricken with persecutions, falsehoods, calumnies, and all sorts of affliction; but rather let us place our trust in Him Who, if He predicted future calamities, also admonished us with these words: "In the world you will have affliction. But take courage, for I have overcome the world."

If, for those innumerable legions of people who, in those regions, suffer infirmities, grief, and anguish, or are in prison, We cannot put into practice the words of Jesus: "[I was] sick, and you visited Me, I was in prison, and you came to Me," we can at least do something for them; with our prayers and works of penance we can implore our most merciful Lord to send His consoling angels to these our suffering brothers and sons, and shower upon them ample heavenly gifts which will console and strengthen their spirits, and lift them up to heavenly things.

And We wish especially that all priests, who can offer up the Holy Eucharist every day, shall remember those Bishops and priests who, far from their churches and their faithful, do not have the opportunity of approaching the altar to celebrate the divine Sacrifice and nourish themselves and their faithful with that divine Food from which our souls draw a sweetness which surpasses all desire and receive that strength which leads to victory. Drawn together in close brotherly union, let the faithful also do this, as they participate in the same offering and in the same sacrifice: to the end that in every part of the earth and in all rites which constitute the ornament of the Church, there will go up to God and to His heavenly Mother the unanimous voices of those who pray to obtain divine mercy in behalf of these afflicted communities of Christians.[†]

The Task of the Christian Press

THE press must be undeviatingly loyal to the truth, lest its tremendous influence be exercised amiss. The truth of which We speak is the truth in vision, whereby you see events really as they happen, and the truth in presentation, whereby you report faithfully events as you have seen them, and interpret them by no other standards than those of justice and of charity.

---

† Encyclical *Orientales Ecclesias* (December 15, 1952).

Now truth is dispassionate, not partisan; factual, not fanciful. Truth is not venal; it does not fear to be known, but it asks only to be presented in the clear, white light of objectivity, not in any spectral tint of prejudice or conjecture. Truth, too, is discreet and knows that reality must at times be circumscribed by reserve, that evil is not to be garnished while the good is slurred over. Truth is modest and aware that death may enter the soul through the windows of the eyes. Alas, does not experience teach that incalculable harm may come to domestic and civil society through an unethical press that would lose sight of the demands of truth?‡

The Catholic Journalist

Modern man likes to appear free and independent. But very often this is only a façade, behind which hide paltry, empty beings, without the spiritual strength to unmask falsehood, without the energy to resist the violence of those who are capable of putting into effect all the discoveries of modern technology, all the refined arts of persuasion, to deprive them of freedom of thought and reduce them to the state of "reeds shaken by the wind."

Could one affirm, without hesitancy, that the majority of men are capable of judging and understanding facts and currents at their true value, in a way that shows that their opinion is guided by reason?...

Numerous are those whose vision does not transcend their own limited specialization or purely technical capacity. The education of public opinion in everyday life certainly cannot be expected from such men, nor firmness on their part in the face of clever propaganda which unduly claims the privilege of molding opinion just as it wishes. In this respect, men of Christian spirit, straightforward, upright, and clear, even though often without much formal education, are far superior.

Thus the men to whom the task of enlightening and guiding public opinion should be entrusted are often found to be in a highly unfavorable condition freely and successfully to carry out their task, some because of ill will or incapacity, others because they are being obstructed and impeded. This

‡ Address to U.S.A. Press Representatives (April 27, 1946) [in English].

unfavorable situation damages above all the Catholic press in its action at the service of public opinion.

In this situation, the evils most to be feared for the Catholic journalist are faintheartedness and discouragement. Look at the Church: for almost two thousand years, through the most varied tribulations, contradictions, lack of understanding, and persecutions, both hidden and open, she has never been dejected and has never allowed herself to become disheartened. Take her as your example. Consider, in the deplorable shortcomings We have pointed out, the double picture of what should not be and what should be the Catholic press.

In every aspect of its being and its activity it should oppose an insurmountable obstacle to the growing retrogression and disappearance of the basic conditions for a healthy public opinion, and consolidate and reinforce that which still survives. Let it renounce with pleasure the fleeting advantages of vulgar interests or cheap popularity; let it know how to resist with energetic and proud dignity all direct and indirect attempts at corruption. Let it have the courage—even at the cost of pecuniary sacrifices—to banish from its columns every advertisement or publicity item which is offensive to faith or morals. By so doing, it will gain in intrinsic value and succeed in winning esteem, then confidence; it will justify the oft-repeated injunction: "A Catholic newspaper in every Catholic home."

Educating the Public

But, even under the best internal and external conditions in which to develop and propagate, public opinion is not infallible or always absolutely spontaneous. The complexity or the novelty of events and situations can exercise a notable influence on its formation, without taking into account that it cannot easily free itself from preconceived judgments and prevailing currents in the field of ideas, even when the reaction is objectively justifiable or frankly imposes itself. It is in this case that the press has an outstanding job to do in forming opinion, not by dominating or governing it, but by serving it usefully.

This delicate mission presupposes, in those who concern themselves with the Catholic press, competence, general culture, above all philosophical and theological, writing talent, and psychological tact. But the foremost prerequisite is character. That is to say, a profound love and unalterable respect for the divine order which embraces and pervades every aspect of life: a love and respect which the Catholic journalist should not feel and nourish only in the intimacy of his own heart, but should cultivate in the hearts of his readers. Sometimes the flame burning in this way is enough to relight or revive the almost extinguished spark of conviction and feeling stifled in the depths of conscience. In other cases, broadness of viewpoint and judgment may open their eyes, too timidly fixed upon time-worn prejudices.

We believe that this Catholic conception of public opinion, of its function and the service rendered it by the press, is both adapted to and necessary for pointing out to mankind, according to your ideal, the path of truth, justice, and peace.

This Catholic conception of public opinion and of the service rendered to it by the press is also a solid guarantee of peace. Peace is served by a true freedom of thought and by man's right to his own judgment, always, that is, in the light of divine law.

Where public opinion ceases to express itself freely, peace is in danger.

We wish to add yet another word concerning public opinion within the sphere of the Church herself, regarding those questions open to free discussion. This will astonish only those who do not know the Church or who have a wrong impression of her. Since she is a living body, something would be lacking in her life if she were deficient in public opinion and if this lack were attributable to her pastors and faithful. But here, also, the Catholic press can perform a very useful service. However, it is extremely important that in this service the journalist must possess, above all, the character of which We have spoken, consisting of an unalterable respect and a profound love for the divine order, that is, in the present case, for the Church who not only forms part of the eternal designs but also of the earthly life here below, in space and in time; divine, yes, but formed of human members and organs.

If he possesses this character, the Catholic journalist will know how to guard himself against mute servility as well as uncontrolled criticism. He will join, with acute discernment, in the formation of a Catholic opinion within the Church, especially in a situation such as exists today in which this opinion wavers between the equally dangerous poles of an unreal and illusory spiritualism and a defeatist and materialistic realism. Keeping equally distant from these two extremes, the Catholic press should exercise its influence on public opinion within the Church, in the midst of the faithful. Only thus can be avoided false ideas on the mission and possibilities of the Church in temporal matters, and, especially today, on the social question and the problem of peace.[†]

The European Union

WHEN, after the last war, the leaders of several nations decided to bring international institutions into being which would be charged with the task of organizing peace, the cruel experience of the past half century weighed upon their debates and continually reminded them that to obtain a chance of success a generous idea is not enough. In particular, the practical realization of a European Union, the urgency of which was felt by everybody, and toward which everybody almost instinctively oriented himself, encountered two principal obstacles: one inherent in the structure of the State, the other psychological and moral. The first involves a series of economic, social, military, and political problems. The nations desirous of forming an association find themselves on different planes, from the viewpoint of natural resources and industrial development and of social progress. They cannot proceed to a life in common without first providing for the means necessary to maintain a general equilibrium. But much more important appears the need for the so-called European spirit, the consciousness of internal unity, founded not upon the satisfaction of economic necessity but rather on the perception of common spiritual values, a perception so clear as to justify and keep alive the steadfast will to live united.

It is easy to recognize that of all the backers of a united Europe serious concessions are required. The transfer of industries, re-adaptation of labor, local fluctuations and difficulties in certain sectors of production—here are some of the matters which governments and peoples will have to face. They

† Address to the International Congress of the Catholic Press (February 1, 1950).

may be temporary difficulties, but also of long duration, which will surely not always be compensated for by short-term economic advantages, as within a single nation when the poorer regions get to enjoy an equal standard of life only by virtue of the contribution of the richer regions. It is necessary, therefore, to cause public opinion in each nation to accept sacrifices, perhaps of a permanent nature, to explain their necessity and inspire the desire to remain, notwithstanding these sacrifices, united with the other nations and to continue to help them.

It is easy to imagine the natural reaction of the egoisms, almost instinctively ready to shut themselves off from the others, a dangerous weapon in the hands of the opponents and of all those whose discreditable purpose is to profit by the sufferings of others. It is necessary, then, right from the beginning, to realize that a prospect of material advantages will not be enough to foster the will for sacrifices indispensable to final success. Sooner or later these advantages will be seen to be illusory or fallacious. The interests of common defense will also be offered as a reason; without doubt fear easily awakens a violent reaction, but usually very brief and without constructive force, incapable of directing and co-ordinating the various energies toward a common goal.

If solid guarantees are sought for co-operation among peoples, as indeed in every form of human co-operation, in the private or public sphere, in circumscribed sectors as well as on an international plane, only values of a spiritual order turn out to be effective. They alone bring about a triumph over the vicissitudes which fortuitous circumstances or, more often, human wickedness are not slow in provoking. Both among nations and among individuals nothing lasts without a true friendship.‡

Our grave apprehensions with regard to Europe are motivated by the incessant disillusionments which for many years have wrecked the sincere desire for peace and relaxation of tension cherished by the European peoples, largely because of a materialistic approach to the problem of peace. We are thinking especially of those who consider the question of peace as being of a technical nature and view the life of individuals and of nations under a combined technical-economic aspect. This materialistic concept of life threatens to become the rule of conduct of the busy agents of peace and the recipe of their pacifist

‡ Address to the Representatives of the "European College" (1953).

policy. They believe that the secret of the solution would be to give material prosperity to all peoples through constant increase in the productivity of labor and the standard of living, just as, a hundred years ago, another similar formula won the absolute confidence of statesmen: Free trade means eternal peace.

But no sort of materialism has ever been a satisfactory means for the establishment of peace, since peace is above all an attitude of the spirit and only on a secondary level is it a harmonious equilibrium of external forces. It is, then, an error in principle to entrust peace to modern materialism, which corrupts man at the roots and suffocates his personal and spiritual life. Besides, experience leads to the same state of mistrust in that it demonstrates that, even in our time, when the costly potential of technical and economic forces is distributed more or less equally between both sides, it imposes a reciprocal fear. The resultant peace therefore would be one based solely on fear, not the peace which means certainty of the future. It is necessary to repeat this untiringly and to persuade those among the people who allow themselves to be easily deceived by the mirage that peace consists in an abundance of wealth, whereas a stable peace is above all a problem of spiritual unity and moral inclinations.[†]

The Church and History

ALTHOUGH history is an ancient science, it was only during the last few centuries and with the development of historical criticism that it reached its present perfection. Thanks to the scrupulousness of its methods and the indefatigable zeal of its specialists, historians can congratulate themselves on being able to know the past in greater detail and to judge it more accurately than any of their predecessors.

History is one of the sciences which have a close relationship to the Catholic Church. The Catholic Church is herself a historical fact; like a mighty

† Allocution to the Sacred College (December 24, 1953).

range of mountains, she is present throughout the history of the last two thousand years; whatever the attitude taken toward her, it is, therefore, impossible to avoid her. The judgments passed on her are extremely varied; they range from total acceptance to the most determined rejection. But whatever the final verdict of the historian may be, whose task it is to see and to expound—as far as possible just as they happened—facts, events, and circumstances, the Church expects him in any case to be aware of the historical consciousness she has of herself, that is, of the way in which she considers herself as a historical fact and in which she considers her relationship to human history.

We should like to say a word about this consciousness the Church has of herself, mentioning facts, circumstances, and conceptions which seem to Us to take on a more fundamental significance.

God as Lord of History

To begin with, We should like to refute an objection which arises, as it were, at once. Christianity, it used to be and still is said, necessarily takes up a hostile position in relation to history because it sees in it a manifestation of evil and sin; Catholicism and historicism are antithetical concepts. Let us first of all notice that the objection thus formulated considers history and historicism as equivalent concepts. In this, it is wrong. The term "historicism" designates a philosophical system, one which sees in all spiritual reality, in knowledge of the truth, in religion, morality, and law, nothing but change and evolution, and consequently rejects all that is permanent, eternally valid, and absolute. Such a system is certainly irreconcilable with the Catholic conception of the world and, in general, with any religion which recognizes a personal God.

The Catholic Church knows that all events occur according to the will or the permission of divine Providence and that God reaches His objectives in history. As the great St. Augustine said with classical brevity: what God intends "*hoc fit, hoc agitur; etsi paulatim peragitur, indesinenter agitur*—that happens, that is done; and though it is done only step by step, it still is being done incessantly." God is really the Lord of history.

This statement in itself already answers the objections mentioned. Between Christianity and history there is no opposition in the sense that history is only an emanation or manifestation of evil. The Catholic Church has never taught such a doctrine. From the days of the early Christians, from the Patristic period, but especially at the time of the spiritual conflict with Protestantism and Jansenism, she has always ranged herself on the side of nature; she says of the latter that it has not been corrupted by sin, that it has remained inwardly intact, even in fallen man, that pre-Christian man and the non-Christian could and can perform good, virtuous actions, not to mention the fact that the whole of humanity, including pre-Christian humanity, is under the influence of Christ's grace.

The Church readily recognizes the good and the great in the pre-Christian era as well as outside Christianity...

The Church as Historical Fact

Let Us now speak about the Church herself as a historical fact: at the same time as she fully affirms her divine origin and her supernatural character, the Church is conscious of having entered humanity as a historical fact. Her divine Founder, Jesus Christ, is a historical personality. His life, death, and resurrection are historical facts. It sometimes happens that even those who deny Christ's divinity admit His resurrection, because it is, in their opinion, too well vouched for historically; anybody wanting to deny it would have to annul the whole of ancient history, for none of its facts is better proved than that of the resurrection of Christ. The mission and the development of the Church are historical facts.

The Excavations under St. Peter's Basilica

Here in Rome, St. Peter and St. Paul can be cited: Paul belongs, even from a purely historical point of view, to the most remarkable figures in humanity. As for the Apostle Peter and his position in the Church of Christ, although proof of his stay and death in Rome is not of essential importance for the Catholic faith, We nevertheless caused the well-known excavations to be carried out under the Basilica. The method is approved by critics; the result—the discovery of Peter's tomb under the dome, exactly under the present papal altar—was recognized by the great majority of critics, and even the most extreme skeptics were impressed by what the excavations revealed.

The Mission of the Church

The origins of Christianity and of the Catholic Church are historical facts, proved and determined in time and place. Of that the Church is quite conscious. She knows, too, that her mission, although belonging by its nature and aims to the religious and moral domain, situated in the beyond and in eternity, nevertheless penetrates right into the heart of human history. Always and everywhere, constantly adapting herself to the circumstances of time and place, she tries to form, according to Christ's law, persons, the single individual and, as far as possible, all individuals, thus reaching, also, the moral foundations of life in society. The aim of the Church is the naturally good man, penetrated, ennobled, and strengthened by truth and Christ's grace.

The Church wants to make men "firm in their inviolate integrity as images of God; men proud of their personal dignity and wholesome liberty; men rightly jealous of equality with their fellow men in all that concerns the very heart of human dignity; men solidly attached to their country and their traditions." That is the intention of the Church as We formulated it in Our address of February 20, 1946, on the occasion of the investment of the new Cardinals. We add: in the present century as in that which has passed, in which the problems of the family, society, the State, and the social order have acquired an ever-increasing and even capital importance, the Church has done everything possible to contribute to the solution of these questions and, let Us hope, with some success. The Church is convinced, however, that she cannot work more efficaciously than by continuing to form men in the way We have described.

To attain these aims, the Church does not act only as an ideological system. No doubt she is also defined as such, when the expression "Catholicism" is used, which is a term not fully adequate. She is much more than a mere ideological system; she is a reality, like visible nature, like the people, or the State. She is a living organism with her own finality and vital principle. Unchangeable in the constitution and structure which the divine Founder Himself gave to her, she has accepted and accepts the elements which she needs or considers useful for her development and her action: men and human institutions, philosophical and cultural inspirations, political forces and social ideas or institutions, principles and activities. Therefore, the Church, spreading throughout the whole world, underwent various changes in the course of the centuries; in her essence, however, she always remained identical, because the multitude of elements she received from the beginning were subjected to the same basic faith. The Church could be astoundingly broad and at the same time inflexibly severe. If we consider the whole of her history, we see that she was both, with an unfailing instinct as to what suited different peoples and the whole of humanity. Hence she has rejected all movements which are too naturalistic, contaminated to some extent by the spirit of moral license, but also gnostic tendencies, falsely spiritualistic and puritan. The history of canon law, up to the code which is now in force, gives a large number of significant proofs. Take, for example, the ecclesiastical legislation on marriage and the recent pontifical declarations about questions of conjugal partnership and the family in all their aspects: you will find there an example, among many others, of the way in which the Church thinks and works.

Church and State

By virtue of a similar principle, she has regularly intervened in the field of public life, to guarantee a fair balance between duty and obligation on the one hand, and right and freedom on the other. Political authority has never disposed of a more trustworthy advocate than the Catholic Church; for the Church founds the authority of the State on the will of the Creator, on God's commandment. Certainly, because she attributes a religious value to public authority, the Church has opposed arbitrariness in the State, and tyranny in all its forms.

And now We come to two problems which deserve special attention: the relations between Church and State, between Church and culture.

In the pre-Christian period, the public authority, the State, was competent both in profane matters and in the field of religion. The Catholic Church is conscious that her divine Founder transmitted to her the field of religion, the religious and moral guidance of men in its entirety, independently of the power of the State. Since then, there exists a history of relations between the Church and the State, and this history has greatly interested inquirers.

Leo XIII has summed up, as it were, in a formula, the very nature of these relations, in the luminous presentation of his Encyclicals *Diuturnum illud, Immortale Dei* (1881) and *Sapientiae christianae* (1890): the two powers, Church as well as State, are both sovereign. Their nature, like the ends they pursue, fixes the limits within which they rule "*iure proprio*—in their own right." Like the State, the Church, too, possesses sovereign rights over everything she needs to achieve her aim, even over material means. "*Quidquid igitur est in rebus humanis quoquo modo sacrum, quidquid ad salutem animarum cultumve Dei pertinet, sive tale illud sit natura sua, sive rursus tale intelligatur propter causam ad quam refertur, id est omne in potestate arbitrioque Ecclesiae*—Everything, therefore, which in human things is in any way sacred, anything pertaining to the salvation of souls and the worship of God, be it such by its nature or be it understood as such for the connection with its end—all this falls within the power and authority of the Church." The State and the Church are independent powers, but they must not therefore ignore each other, still less combat each other; it conforms far more with nature and the divine will that they should collaborate in mutual understanding, since their activity is applied to the same subject—the Catholic citizen. Of course, cases of conflict are possible: when State laws attack divine law, the Church is morally obliged to oppose them.

It can be said that, with the exception of a very few centuries—for the first millennium as well as for the last four centuries—the formula of Leo XIII reflects more or less explicitly the consciousness of the Church; and even during the intermediate period, there were representatives of the doctrine of the Church, perhaps even a majority, who shared the same opinion.

If Church and State knew hours or years of struggle, there were, from Constantine the Great up to contemporary and even recent times, periods of quiet, often long ones, during which the two powers collaborated in complete harmony in the education of men. The Church does not hide the fact that on principle she considers this collaboration as normal, and that she takes as her ideal the unity of the people in the true religion and unanimity of action between herself and the State. But it is known, too, that for some time now events have been moving rather in the opposite direction, that is, toward multiplicity of religious denominations and conceptions of life within the same national community—in which Catholics make up a more or less strong minority. It may be interesting and even surprising for the historian to meet in the United States of America an example, among others, of the way in which the Church succeeds in taking root and flourishing in the most disparate situations.

In the history of relations between Church and State, the Concordats play, as is known, an important part. What We said in this connection in a discourse on December 6, 1953, holds true for historical appreciation. In the Concordats, We said, the Church seeks juridical security and the independence necessary for her mission. "It is possible," We added, "that Church and State may proclaim in a Concordat their common religious conviction; but it can also happen that the Concordat has the aim, among others, of preventing quarrels about questions of principle, and of eliminating, from the outset, possible occasions for conflict. When the Church has put her signature to a Concordat, it is valid in all its contents. But the underlying meaning may involve fine distinctions of which both contracting parties are aware; it may signify express approval, but it may mean also mere tolerance, according to principles which serve as standards for the coexistence of the Church and her faithful with powers and men of another faith."

The Church and culture: the Catholic Church has exercised a powerful, even decisive, influence on the cultural development of the last two thousand years. But she is convinced that the source of this influence lies in the spiritual element which characterizes herself, her religious and moral life, to the extent that if she were to weaken, her cultural sway, too, for example in the field of order and social peace, would suffer.

The Church and the Western World

Several historians, or perhaps more exactly, historical philosophers, maintain that the place of Christianity, and therefore of the Catholic Church, is in the Western world... The Church is conscious of having received her mission and task for all time to come and for all men, and consequently of being tied to no determined culture. St. Augustine, in the past, was deeply moved when the conquest of Rome by Alaric shook the Roman Empire with the first blow that presaged its ruin; but he had not thought that it would last forever. In the *City of God* he drew a clear distinction between the existence of the Church and the destiny of the Roman Empire. In this his thought was Catholic.

What is called the West or the Western world has undergone profound modifications since the Middle Ages: the religious schism of the sixteenth century, rationalism and liberalism leading to the nineteenth-century State, to its policy of force and its secularized civilization. It was, therefore, inevitable that the relations of the Catholic Church with the West should undergo a change. But the culture of the Middle Ages itself cannot be characterized as Catholic culture; it, too, although intimately linked to the Church, drew its elements from different sources. Even the religious unity characteristic of the Middle Ages is not specific to it; it was already a typical note of Christian antiquity in the Eastern and Western Roman Empire, from Constantine the Great to Charlemagne.

The Catholic Church does not identify herself with any culture; her essence prevents this. She is, however, ready to maintain contacts with all cultures. She recognizes and leaves untouched what, in them, is not contrary to nature. But into each of them, she introduces the truth and grace of Jesus Christ and thus confers a deep similarity to them all. This, in fact, is her most efficacious contribution to universal peace.

The whole world today is still undergoing the action of another element, which it is predicted will cause the history of humanity (in its profane aspect) considerable upheaval: modern science and technology, which Europe, or, rather, the Western countries, have created during these last centuries; however, people who assimilate them must also consent to the dangers they entail "*für das Menschsein*—for human existence," as the philosopher Jaspers says. In fact, science and technology are in process of becoming the common good of humanity. What causes anxiety are not only the dangers with which they threaten the human way of life, but the realization that they prove incapable of damming the spiritual alienation which separates races and continents; in fact, the latter seems to be increasing. If we desire to avoid catastrophe, it will, therefore, be necessary to set up, at the same time, on a higher plane, powerful religious and moral forces of unification and thus ensure the common welfare of humanity. The Catholic Church is conscious of possessing these forces and believes she is no longer obliged to provide historical proof. Moreover, she does not take up a position of hostility toward modern science and technology, but acts rather as a counterweight and a factor of equilibrium. Therefore, in a period in which science and technology are triumphant, she will be able to fulfill her task just as well as she did during the past centuries.[†]

† Address to the International Congress of Historical Sciences (September 7, 1955).

GLOSSARY

AGNOSTICISM. *Philosophical doctrine that considers the existence and the nature of God as unknowable.*

ALLOCUTION. *Solemn address delivered by the Pope, dealing with matters of faith or grave immediate problems.*

CHARISMATIC GIFTS. *Supernatural gifts, as, for instance, the healing of the sick.*

ENCYCLICAL. *Circular letter issued by the Pope.*

EUGENICS. *Science dealing with methods for influencing hereditary strains.*

ELECTRON. *A particle of the atom spinning around the nucleus of the atom.*

GENETICS. *The study of the biological development of living organisms, with special emphasis on hereditary factors.*

HEDONISM. *Philosophical teaching which considers pleasure the foremost goal of man.*

HIERARCHY. *The authority given by Christ to the Apostles for governing the Church; also, the organized body of the clergy in its successive orders and grades.*

JANSENISM. *A theological system laid down by Bishop Cornelius Jansen* (1585–1638) *and involving the doctrine of grace. Jansen's teachings were repudiated by the Church.*

MACROCOSM AND MICROCOSM. *Macrocosm designates the great world as universe; microcosm designates man as "the small world" which reflects the large world.*

MANICHAEISM. *Heresy named for its founder, the Persian Mani; he envisaged two conflicting worlds as the origin of things, one of light and one of darkness, from the mingling of which the creation of the world originated.*

MONISM. *Derived from the Greek,* monos, "*single, unique,*" *monism is the name for those theories that deny any principle of duality, as, for instance, body and soul, spirit and matter, etc.*

NEUTRON. *A particle of the atom of nearly the same mass as the proton, but not electrically charged.*

PALEONTOLOGY. *The study of extinct animals and plants known to us through fossilized specimens.*

PHYLOGENESIS. *The evolution of a race or of a related group of organisms as contrasted to the development of individual organisms.*

POSITIVISM. *A system of philosophy that admits only positive facts and phenomena observable by the senses.*

PROTON. *A unit particle of matter belonging to the atom.*

RATIONALISM. *A system of philosophy that sets intellect and reason above feeling and will.*

Designed by Fiona Cecile Clarke, the CLUNY MEDIA *logo depicts a monk at work in the scriptorium, with a cat sitting at his feet.*

The monk represents our mission to emulate the invaluable contributions of the monks of Cluny in preserving the libraries of the West, our strivings to know and love the truth.

The cat at the monk's feet is Pangur Bán, from the eponymous Irish poem of the 9th century. The anonymous poet compares his scholarly pursuit of truth with the cat's happy hunting of mice. The depiction of Pangur Bán is an homage to the work of the monks of Irish monasteries and a sign of the joy we at Cluny take in our trade.

"Messe ocus Pangur Bán,
cechtar nathar fria saindan:
bíth a menmasam fri seilgg,
mu memna céin im saincheirdd."

Made in the USA
Middletown, DE
09 February 2025

70579154R00205